UNIVERSITY OF NORTH CAROLINA AT CHAPEL HILL
DEPARTMENT OF ROMANCE LANGUAGES

NORTH CAROLINA STUDIES
IN THE ROMANCE LANGUAGES AND LITERATURES

Founder: URBAN TIGNER HOLMES
Editor: MARÍA A. SALGADO

Distributed by:

UNIVERSITY OF NORTH CAROLINA PRESS

CHAPEL HILL
North Carolina 27515-2288
U.S.A.

NORTH CAROLINA STUDIES IN THE
ROMANCE LANGUAGES AND LITERATURES
Number 243

DISCOVERING THE COMIC
IN *DON QUIXOTE*

DISCOVERING THE COMIC IN *DON QUIXOTE*

BY
LAURA J. GORFKLE

CHAPEL HILL

NORTH CAROLINA STUDIES IN THE ROMANCE
LANGUAGES AND LITERATURES
U.N.C. DEPARTMENT OF ROMANCE LANGUAGES

1 9 9 3

Library of Congress Cataloging-in-Publication Data

Gorfkle, Laura J., 1952-
  Discovering the comic in Don Quixote / by Laura J. Gorfkle.
  p. – cm. – (North Carolina studies in the Romance languages and literatures; no. 243)
  Includes bibliographical references and index.
  ISBN 0-8078-9247-5 (pbk.)
  1. Cervantes Saavedra, Miguel de, 1547-1616. Don Quixote. 2. Cervantes Saavedra, Miguel de, 1547-1616 – Humor. 3. Comic, The, in literature. I. Title. II. Series.
  PQ6353.G595   1993   92-80591
  863'.3–dc20   CIP

© 1993. Department of Romance Languages. The University of North Carolina at Chapel Hill.

ISBN 0-8078-9247-5

DEPÓSITO LEGAL: V. 1.009 - 1993   I.S.B.N. 84-599-3310-5

ARTES GRÁFICAS SOLER, S. A. - LA OLIVERETA, 28 - 46018 VALENCIA - 1993

CONTENTS

	Page
Preface	9
1 The Comic: A Two-faced Janus	15
2 The Making of the Comic Hero	31
3 The Hero Divided	60
4 Word Play	100
5 Comic Argumentation	125
6 The Speaker-Listener Relationship	169
Epilogue	202
Works Cited	217
Index	225

PREFACE

The interpretation of *Don Quixote* as a comic work has not received much support among Cervantine scholars. Romantic and post-romantic critics have impugned those endorsing the burlesque, satiric, and parodic intentions of the book, labelling them as "hard" and "idiosyncratic." The legitimacy of the status of *Don Quixote* as a great work seems to be at stake in the matter. The comic was perceived by the Romantics as an inferior genre, incompatible with the serious, dignified or noble emotions they wished to confer on the hero (Close, *The Romantic Approach*; Russell, *Cervantes* 94-96). Even intellectually the comic had its limitations since the comic, according to the Romantics, requires a mechanical, physical response, which does not lend itself well to scrutiny.

Since the beginning of the nineteenth century, *Don Quixote* has no longer been perceived as a comic work as it was in the time of Cervantes. The madman is now perceived as a heroic defender of noble ideas which all others compromise in favor of the more mundane practicalities of life. Don Quixote's insanity is tragic, but it is one capable of insights denied those possessing "reason." In *Our Lord Don Quixote*, published in 1905, Miguel de Unamuno portrays Don Quixote as a Christian saint and condemns Cervantes for putting the knight's highest illusions into ridicule. Unamuno thus carries to a limit the type of post-romantic idealist criticism that has dominated Cervantine scholarship up to the present.

Closer to our own time, Vladimir Nabokov has heatedly raised objections to the humor of the work in his lectures to his Harvard students, published posthumously in 1983. In order to support his beliefs that "tragedy wears better than comedy" and that "the guffaw is dispelled in space and time," he affirms that Sancho's cracks and proverbs are "not mirth provoking either in themselves or in their repetitive accumulation," and that the horseplay "does not really convulse the modern diaphragms" (13). His analysis of the practical jokes causes him to confirm that there is a "hideous cruelty which riddles the whole book and befouls its humour" (52). He concludes that we are fortunate that the hero has finally separated from his book:

> Don Quixote is greater today than he was in Cervantes's womb. He has ridden for three hundred and fifty years through the jungles and tundras of human thought – and he has gained in vitality and stature. We do not laugh at him any longer. His blazon is pity, his banner is beauty. He stands for everything that is gentle, forlorn, pure, unselfish, and gallant. The parody has become a paragon. (112)

Ernst Gombrich's discussion of the role of the critic and his relation to a "great work" offers a perspective on artistic values that contrasts radically with the subjectivity of the Romantics. He insists that artistic values obey objective standards. In opposition to Romantic relativism, he believes that the arts "send their roots deep down into the common ground of universally human response" (159). Before condemning *a priori* a great work, he suggests that one be more critical with one's own reactions. If a work is indeed preserved, it is because somehow it transcends its own culture and communicates the human condition from which it emerged:

> However much art is invariably rooted in the life and value system of its age and society, it will transcend these situations when, as we say, it 'stands the test of time'. Not, to be sure, by making us forget the human condition from which it grew, but precisely by making accessible to our imaginative response experiences which no longer form part of our practical lives. (162)

The role of the critic should be, then, to participate in the process of communication, in the transmittance of the aesthetics of the artist. It is not the critic's role to put the great work to a test; rather, it is the great work that puts him or her to a test. In acceptance of that challenge, I wish to explore in Cervantes' great work his aesthetics of impiety and violence, inextricably bound up with the comic. An examination of the comic leads us to the very core of the author's ideological inquiries, always irreverently polemicized in the text: the validity of chivalric ideals (justice, heroism, and the ideal of human love), humanist ethics (the quest for knowledge and truth as dictated by Antiquity) and finally the validity of the literary theory of the time as a model from which to create a truthful image of reality in the text (mimesis, verisimilitude and decorum).

The discovery of the comic in *Don Quixote* is a twofold process. It must necessarily begin with the analysis of the sources and mechanisms of humor found in the text. Yet as these mechanisms uncover the fallacies in the discovery process within thought and language, that is, in our manner of perceiving and understanding ourselves and others, the discovery process itself becomes imbricated in the analysis. By means of the comic in *Don Quixote*, knowledge becomes an object of representation and inquiry. As the reader identifies with the hero's values and becomes increasingly conscious of their comic representation in the text, his or her own position as "target" of the author's humor becomes increasingly evident. While this impiety may not at times produce a guffaw, it does show the reader that the comic can be pretty serious business. An understanding of it will serve, at the very least, to restore the hero once again to the text, away from which no understanding of the hero and his epistemology can be achieved.

In Chapter 1 I trace the descent of the comic from the primitive fertility rites described by Frazer, and show its link to Roman decorative art, the ancient satyr plays, the graffitti on the walls at Pompeii, the Kerch collection of the *Sileni*, and the parodies of ancient Greece and Rome. An analysis of Mikhail Bakhtin's works on the comic and the grotesque in literature allows for the recognition of comic structures in the narrative, and provides a description for them at varying levels of the narrative (character, plot and language). The contrasting views of other theoreticians on the comic, comedy, and caricature, as well as of critics of Bakhtin's work, will illuminate some of the ambiguities of the comic not always made clear in Bakhtin's work. The dialectical tension between the two myths contained in the comic, embodied in a dramatic struggle between the old and the new, destruction and regeneration, can thus be restored.

In Chapter 2, entitled "The Making of a Hero," I show how the chivalric hero is comically represented by means of Don Quixote's disguise. The knight's destruction of his own bodily image, and by extrapolation, of the heroic model he wishes to emulate, is explained by René Girard's concept of mimetic violence. In a world without God, man comes to worship a false god, another human being. The subject views the model ambivalently, as a god to immortalize and a rival to destroy. The *hidalgo* attempts to reconstruct the figure of the hero by gathering his arms and steed, elements which are essential to the eventual fulfillment of the heroic identity. Yet his selection of the knightly trappings as well as his employment of them in his adventures lead him to revile and travesty the characters he imitates. The ineffectiveness of the knight's trappings results in the inversion of the image of the virtuous and triumphant hero and exposure of his other faces: the criminal, the carnival fool, the scapegoat victim, and the Lenten figure of death.

In Chapter 3, "The Hero Divided," I examine how the chivalric hero is comically transformed by means of the device of "splitting." I explore the comic figure of the "double" in order to interpret the character of Sancho Panza and his relationship with his master. As the knight consistently fails to protect his squire or to reward him for his services, the squire becomes disillusioned and turns against his master. The aggressive acts carried out by Sancho align him with the figure of the primitive *eiron*, the mock-modest "Ironical Man" and the "trickster," a figure that descended from the fertility rites described by Frazer and Cornford. In the fertility rite the mock-king or *alazon* represents the "old king" who is crowned but who must also be ritually killed so that the community can be regenerated. Sometimes the unpleasant duties of the *alazon* were assumed by the *eiron*, a secondary figure, a double of the *alazon*, often an outcast or fool. The squire imitates his master, but as he does so, he lays bare the underlying fraudulence in his master's words and actions and the ideals they transmit, and he is ultimately punished for doing so. His verbal abuse, traps and deceits give rise to the reversal of roles, the culmination of the action of carnival by means of which the squire comes to control the action the knight will undertake. Yet the introduction of other characters who function as secondary *eiron* figures implement the comic law of just retribution and "trick" the trickster.

I begin Chapter 4 entitled "Word Play" with a review of Bakhtin's notion of "dialogic discourse." I examine the techniques by which multiple meanings or "voices" are made to emerge in the text. I then describe the various types of word play. One of the major types discussed is the homonym, by means of which a word is reproduced in a manner that new meanings are brought out, often in conflict with the intended one. Rhetorical and poetic devices such as word and phrase repetition, play with suffixes and prefixes, and the repetition of like-sounding words, conventionally employed to embellish discourse, are employed in the text in contexts and situations that cause the unheroic and often sordid action and conduct of the knight to be underscored. Finally, the speaker's intentional or inadvertent use of a word belonging to romance for another of like sound or spelling gives rise to word error or misuse, word substitution and word invention.

The comic use of the rhetorical argument is studied in Chapter 5 of this study, entitled "Comic Argumentation." A description of classical rhetorical theory within the neo-aristotelian humanist tradition shows the ways that learned writers of the period posited language as the bearer of "truth." Jacques Derrida's theories on rhetoric and writing in his essay on Plato in *Of Grammatology* are discussed in order to make explicit the metaphorical, rhetorical or artificial nature of truth in Western thought, and consequently its underlying metaphysical limitations. I then explore how the characters and narrators in the text reproduce classical rhetoric in contexts that underscore these limitations. Some of the devices to be analyzed are the false syllogism, the *non sequitur*, the technique of retortion, comic comparisons, antitheses, metaphors and the comic use of arguments of authority, derived from codes, laws, customs, precedents, poetry, and *exempla*. While underscoring the fallibility of classical reason, these arguments simultaneously function to undermine the truths the knight espouses: the worthiness of his profession, the beauty of his lady, and the existence of the world of chivalry.

In Chapter 6 I analyze one of the central aspects of rhetoric, that of the speaker-listener relationship. According to classical theories on rhetoric, prescriptive norms governing the speaker-listener relationship should insure the successful communication of the truth to the listener. A review of Bakhtin's concept of the "double-voiced" word, Jacques Derrida's disclosure of the ambiguities of "signature" and finally an extensive analysis of the speeches of a variety of speakers in the text discover the impossibility of controlling context in order to transmit "truth."

In the second part of the chapter, I explore the speaker-listener relationship established betweeen the narrator and the reader and the narrator and other fictional authors. Analysis of the extended dialogue that develops between them reveals that the speaker-listener relationship functions as a critical exploration of the laws of the literary text, and as an inquiry into how such laws cause the tale to be perceived as "truthful" by the reader.

In the Epilogue I will construct a theory of the comic based on the analysis of the text of *Don Quixote* and on the theories used. I will also compare and contrast the comic elements in episodes examined in the previous chapters with those in episodes conventionally perceived as emblematic of the "serious" and therefore more "important" sections of the novel, in order to determine the extent to which Cervantes' work can be considered comic.

This book would not have been possible without the generous support of a number of institutions and individuals. My discovery of the comic in *Don Quixote* evolved out of my dissertation at the University of Wisconsin. I would like to thank Benito Brancaforte, my thesis advisor, and David Hildner for their close reading and critical commentary of that manuscript. I gratefully acknowledge the financial support and thinking space I was provided as Mellon Teaching Fellow at the University of Rochester (1988-1989). I am particularly indebted to Robert ter Horst, whose faith and guidance during that year gave me the stimulus to bring the present work to fruition. Thanks also to my friend and colleague, Beth Jorgensen, for her support. I should further like to thank the Department of Foreign Languages and Literatures and the College of Arts and Sciences at Virginia Tech, where I am presently employed, for generously defraying the cost of the manuscript. I owe much to my current colleague, Lloyd Bishop, for his critical comments in the final stages of writing. Thanks also to Susan Farquahar for her insights on some of the thornier theoretical issues this study tries to elucidate. Finally, I would like to thank my husband, Antonio, and sons, Eduardo and Sean Michael, who have shared with me an appreciation for the comic vision of life – with all of its ambivalences – and untold delight in Cervantes' masterpiece. This book is dedicated to the memory of my father, Aaron Gorfkle, with love.

CHAPTER 1

THE COMIC: A TWO-FACED JANUS

Theory has become such an overriding preoccupation with many scholars that Josué Harari in the preface to his edition of collected critical writings, *Textual Strategies*, was compelled to remark that "critics need to be reminded that theory is most useful insofar as it serves the criticism of specific works" (9). The manner in which a theory on the comic can serve this purpose can be better shown by placing it in the context of post-structuralist theories on the narrative.

The trend of recent literary criticism is to provide a description of the transformative structures of the narrative as well as to account for the production of meaning. Post-structuralist criticism begins where structuralism left off. The work of art is no longer perceived as a finished product but as a "methodological field" in which systems of knowledge, latent in the text, meet and interact with linguistic ones, and yet somehow escape the domain of language. Barthes explains this concept of the text:

> Writing . . . is always rooted in something beyond language, it develops like a seed, not like a line, it manifests an essence and holds the threat of a secret; it is an anticommunication, it is intimidating. All writing will therefore contain the ambiguity of an object which is both language and coercion: there exists fundamentally in writing a "circumstance" foreign to language, there is, as it were, the weight of a gaze conveying an intention which is no longer linguistic. (*Writing Degree Zero* 20)

According to this perspective of the text, no one structure underlies the literary work. The text is seen instead as an intersection of an infinite number of "languages" that fill in the void left by the signifiers.

The application of theories pertaining to such fields as psychoanalysis, sociology, history and the science of language (semiology and semiotics) to literature causes the translinguistic systems of a work to be made explicit, triggering the production of meaning. A study of the comic, an aesthetic representation linked to primitive ritual, can also generate this kind of activity.

While several important works have been written linking the structures of comedy to ancient myth, Mikhail Bakhtin is the first to signal the mythic origins of prose fiction. His works, available in English only since the late sixties, have been of seminal importance to the study of the comic and its relation to the rise of the novel. In his work *Rabelais and His World*, Bakhtin offers a detailed account of the ceremony of carnival as it was experienced in the Middle Ages and Renaissance in Europe, and of how this and other ceremonies akin to it are assimilated in the discourse of the novel. In order to better understand the transformation of primitive ceremony in the Middle Ages and the Renaissance, it will be useful to review Frazer's description of the pagan rites.

According to Frazer's account in *The Golden Bough*, an ancient custom existed in different parts of the world of periodically sacrificing the priest-king of the community (273-328, 609-22). It was believed that because the reigning figure was invested with the divine power of the gods, his authority represented a threat to their power. He was to be slain in order to placate the potential wrath of these deities, who at the slightest provocation could bring on drought, famine and death to the group.

As society evolved, the ritual act of murder was replaced by a dramatic representation. The ceremony typically involved an "agon" or contest, in the form of dialogue, between a mock king or "Impostor" identified with the dying year and a young king identified with the new one. The contest was followed by the expulsion and simulated sacrifice of the former. The reincarnation of the dead king, whose powers were miraculously resurrected and transferred to the triumphant youth, was consecrated by a feast and a marriage, symbols of the victory of life over death. During the contest the protagonist and antagonist disguised themselves as their gods. They wore costumes made of leaves, vines, or animal skins and masks of animals such as the horse, the bear, the bull, the goat, etc. These animals and plants were associated with gods of the underworld, either those reigning over death or those whose powers could bring fertility and eternal salvation.

The ceremony between the old and the young kings was duplicated during the agrarian rites. Within the main ceremony itself, the mock king often escaped the unpleasant side of his office, his punishment falling onto a substitute scapegoat figure known as "The King of Years" (Sypher 36-44). This figure was an abusive jester who mocked the old king and the group in general. Disguised as a demonic figure, he embodied the evils of the group which had to be expelled. His face was painted black or white and he wore a leaf dress or animal skin and dragged behind him a calf's or donkey's tail. Along with the King of Years, other smaller scapegoat figures, disguised in similar fashion, also mocked and were mocked by the collectivity. These disguises and transformations, at varying levels of the fertility rite, symbolically reinforced the drama of death and regeneration that was mimetically represented.

Archaic ceremonials continued to thrive during the classical period. Renowned are the Roman *Saturnalias*, which like the former agrarian ceremonies they descended from, celebrated the closing of the year with a period of general license, Frazer tells us, when

> the customary restraints of law and morality are thrown aside, when the whole population give themselves up to extravagant mirth and jollity, and when the darker passions find a vent which would never be allowed them in the more staid and sober course of ordinary life. (641)

During this time the ceremonies lost their original religious motivation. It was at this point in the evolution of comic representation that theorists of the postclassic period began to identify the ugly masks and costumes with the term "grotesque."[1] This was a technical term first used to describe a Roman decorative style of the Augustan Era that was brought to light during the excavations of Titus' baths in the late fifteenth century. The ancient drawings cov-

---

[1] Frazer did not link these rites to the concept of the grotesque. Theorists of this century have turned to Frazer's work in order to explain the presence of primitive ritual in the literary work, and have used the term "grotesque" to describe these rites. See Cornford.

ering the walls of the caverns or "grottas" from which they take their name impressed art theorists for their fanciful treatment of plant, animal and human forms.[2]

Bakhtin uses the term "grotesque realism" to describe the folk ceremonials of the Middle Ages and the Renaissance. Medieval carnival inherited a three part structure from the primitive ceremonies: the conflict between the old and the new, the ensuing expulsion of a scapegoat figure, and the consequent renewal of the community. The main action of carnival, like that of the primitive rites, begins by negating an anterior structure, figure or object that prevents renewal:

> The essence of the grotesque is precisely to present a contradictory and double-faced fullness of life. Negation and destruction (death of the old) are included as an essential phase, inseparable from affirmation, from the birth of something new and better. (*Rabelais* 67)

Bakhtin then removes this dramatic conflict from the framework of pagan ritual provided by Frazer. He detaches it as well from a Christian one, to which carnival is generally linked, as its festivities mark the last days before Lent. He views the drama of death and renewal instead as a socio-political struggle. For Bakhtin, who grew up in the period of the Russian Revolution [1917], myth gains in explanatory power when it expresses social conflict. The conflict between the old and the new is represented as a conflict between the ruling classes and the oppressed. The second world of carnival presents an occasion, albeit of short duration, for the liberation of the lower classes:

> Medieval laughter is not a subjective, individual and biological consciousness of the uninterrupted flow of time. It is the social consciousness of all the people. Man experiences this flow of time in the festive marketplace, in the carnival crowd, as he comes into contact with other bodies of varying ages and social castes. He is aware of being a member of a continually growing and renewed people. This is why festive folk laughter presents an element of victory, not only over supernatural awe, over the sa-

---

[2] A semantic study of the grotesque as well as its historical development in the plastic arts has been thoroughly documented by Barasch.

cred, over death; it also means the defeat of power, of earthly kings, of the earthly upper classes, of all that oppresses and restricts. (92)

The ceremonies and rituals of carnival have a marked social frame of reference. Most of the medieval feasts are parodies of official ceremonies of the church and state. These folk ceremonies involve the election of a mock bishop, priest or king, chosen from among the lower classes. Once elected, the clown-king is allowed to reign for a short period of time over the crowd at the marketplace, after which time he is "uncrowned":

> The clown was first disguised as a king but once his reign had come to an end his costume was changed, "travestied," to turn him once more into a clown. The abuse and thrashing are equivalent to a change of costume, to a metamorphosis. Abuse reveals the other, true face of the abused, it tears off his disguise and mask. It is the king's uncrowning. (197)

The king's uncrowning is portrayed by Bakhtin as a revelation or discovery of the false gods, those values and so-called "truths" that the king embodies. This movement toward renewal creates what Bakhtin calls the "festive spirit" of carnival. While the Dance of Death represents the action of human defeat and the folly of man's earthly ambitions, the ceremonies of carnival season are a time for rejoicing, for if man cannot prevent death from approaching, he can at least assist in the killing of Winter, or of the malignant social forces within the group so that the Golden Age of Saturn can reign anew. This is the meaning attached to such festivals as the Feast of Fools and the Feast of the Ass, so popular throughout the Middle Ages and the Renaissance.

The main character of these feasts, the clown-king, resembles the primitive King of Years. His calf's skin, soot-covered or whitened face, and wild leaps and antics reveal his descent from the old sacrificial victim. He too represents the misfortunes of the social group and serves as its instrument of renewal by means of his self-sacrifice. He is an ambivalent figure. Disguised as king or priest, his buffoonish movements and gestures, as well as the indecent curses he directs to the crowd aim at unmasking the falsity of official truths. He laughs at and hurls insults to the crowd, superior to them for his short-lived period of rule. His madness frees him from social restraints and allows him to blot out official reason. His actions are not gratuitous, however. While destroying official ranks, he establishes new ones patterned after those he overturns. He now sets himself at the top. He puts on the king's crown in order to conceal his lowly rank. His goal is not only to purge the crowd at the marketplace of social ills, but to gain power as well.

The crownings and uncrownings are repeated throughout the marketplace, where every act becomes ritual. Women disguise themselves as men and men as women, each reflecting a different aspect of the clown's disguise. The woman, like the buffoon, rebels against her subordinate role in society; her male counterpart willingly relinquishes his power and allows himself to be "uncrowned." In doing so, he, like the clown-king, undermines his own desires. In similar fashion, the servant exchanges roles with his master. He sits at his master's table, drinks his wine and insults him without fear of reproof while his master waits on him.

The final aspects of the popular comic tradition that Bakhtin discusses in his work on Rabelais are his most important contribution: scatological imagery and the grotesque speech of carnival. The scatological image complements the grotesque situation described above: the struggle between life and death and between the old and the new. Bakhtin calls this aspect of folk humor the "material bodily principle" of grotesque realism. The grotesque body, like the movements and actions of the clown, represents the renewing life of the people at the marketplace. That is why "all that is bodily is portrayed as grandiose, exaggerated" (19). The body's openings and convexities, such as the lolling tongue, the gaping mouth, the big nose and ears, the oversized phallus and buttocks, and the potbelly are emphasized. In these areas the body reaches out to blend with the world, materialize it, and grow at its expense. In what Bakhtin calls the "lower body stratum," which encompasses the area of the womb, the genital organs and the reproductive tract, the struggle between life and death is symbolically portrayed. The womb is the earth that swallows up but also gives forth new life. Bakhtin underscores the positive nature of the grotesque image:

> The unfinished and open body (dying, bringing forth and being born), is not separated from the world by clearly defined boundaries; it is blended with the world, with animals, with objects. It

is cosmic, it represents the entire material bodily world in all its elements. It is an incarnation of this world at the absolute lower stratum, as the swallowing up and generating principle, as the bodily grave and bosom, as a field which has been sown and in which new shoots are preparing to sprout. (26-27)

Powerfully portrayed by Rabelais, this concept of the body, with all of its symbolic and allegorical implications, can also be found in art forms of the Middle Ages, such as the frescoes and bas-reliefs which adorned the cathedrals and village churches. Its elements are present in Renaissance painting. Noteworthy examples include the paintings of Hieronymus Bosch whose sources of inspiration were the grotesque figures found in Gothic church art, the medieval bestiaries, texts of the mystics of the Middle Ages, popular narrations and the popular festivals discussed by Bakhtin. Bosch in turn exercised a profound influence over the paintings of the elder Brueghel.

The language of carnival is subject to the same kind of transformations and reversals previously observed within the ceremonies, characters and imagery of carnival. The use of oaths, curses, and abusive language serves as a means by which official speech is subverted. Bakhtin links the tradition of verbal abuse to ancient comic cults, in which the deities were mocked and insulted. Like the beatings and laughter that unmask the clown-king, oral abuse humiliates and debases, but at the same time has the power to revive, for it breaks down distinctions between social groups creating more sincere relations among the people at the marketplace.

The bulk of Bakhtin's study of Rabelais is devoted to the construction of a descriptive model. In another work, *The Poetics of Dostoevsky,* Bakhtin places more emphasis on a formal analysis of grotesque realism.[3] In this study, Bakhtin underscores the idea that the interplay between the old and the new does not occur only within the individual parts that make up the narrative, but in the very writing process itself. The work of art is like a "continuing dialogue" that takes place between human beings. The bridge of communication is not built exclusively by means of a common linguistic system, but by a cultural tradition as well, which the dialogue absorbs, recreates and extends.

---

[3] See also Bakhtin, "The Problem of the Text (An Essay in Philosophical Analysis)." For a detailed discussion of these works, see Kristeva, "Word, Dialogue and Novel."

What the author creates or recreates does not belong to him alone, nor is it limited to his own experience. Myth exists as something continuously latent in the order of words, independent of direct influence. The task of the critic is to produce meaning by recognizing the translinguistic language expressed by means of the dialogue. Bakhtin affirms that writers use such myths to inform their works in times of change, in periods which interrupt, like carnival, the apparently smooth, continuous rhythm of events. This occurs at the closing of one historical period and at the birth of a new one. At these moments, social, political and cultural forces confront and "dialogue" with one another (19-37).

Fundamental to Bakhtin's formal approach to the problem of folk humor and its relation to the novel is his concept of intertextuality.[4] He employs various terms to explain this notion, not always easily distinguishable: "polyphony," "heteroglossia," "parody," "dialogue" and "indirect discourse." In his essay "From the Prehistory of Novelistic Discourse," Bakhtin defines indirect discourse as the appropriation and representation of another's word. This discourse was already known in most ancient times:

> During its germination and early development, the novelistic word reflected a primordial struggle between tribes, peoples, cults, and languages. It is still full of echoes of this ancient struggle. In essence . . . this discourse always developed on the boundary line between cultures and languages. (*The Dialogic Imagination* 50)

One widespread ancient form of representation by quotation was the parody, "after the song." The most ancient form of "polyglossia" was nothing more than the mimicking or ridiculing of another's language. The interanimation of languages associated with it elevated these forms to a new artistic and ideological level which made possible the genre of the novel (50-51). The importance of the parodic, travestying forms in world literature is enormous. There never was in Antiquity a single, strictly straightforward genre that did not have its own parodying and travestying double. The satyr play was the comic counterpart of the tragedy, showing the

---

[4] For a review of Bakhtin's notion of intertextuality, see Todorov, especially Ch. 5, "Intertextuality," 60-74.

tragic myth in a different aspect. A popular figure of the satyr play was the comic Odysseus, found in ancient doric farce and pre-Aristophanic comedy. The comic Hercules was popular both in Greece and Rome.

The accompaniment of every tragic or serious work with a comic, parodying counterpart in literature found its reflection in art as well, in the so-called "consular diptychs" and in the mural paintings in Pompeii. The representation of the most primitive mime corresponds to this parodic imitation of another's word. He had to possess the ability to imitate the voices of animals, but also the speech of a slave, a peasant, a procurer, a pedant, etc. (53-57).

These comic mediums constituted an "intergeneric" world, offering laughter as a corrective to the ideologies and values of all existing, serious genres, embedded within their words – a laughter that was by its very definition impious:

> ... this world was unified, first of all, by a common purpose: to provide the corrective of laughter and criticism to all existing straightforward genres, languages, styles, voices; to force men to experience beneath these categories a different and contradictory reality that is otherwise not captured in them. Such laughter paved the way for the impiety of the novelistic form. (59)

These parodic-travestying forms were decisive in the creation of a new discourse that the novel was to appropriate, a discourse which was capable of distancing the object from the language that named and defined it, that freed the consciousness of the reader or spectator from the power of the direct word and its power to evoke and impose unilateral truths:

> Linguistic consciousness – parodying the direct word, direct style, exploring its limits, its absurd sides, the face specific to an era – constituted itself outside this direct word and outside all its graphic and expressive means of representation. A new mode developed for working creatively with language: the creating artist began to look at language from the outside, with another's eyes, from the point of view of a potentially different language and style. (60)

Intertextuality is thus seen as a process by means of which two linguistic consciousnesses and the ideological perspectives they represent meet and come into conflict with each other. The parodying consciousness penetrates into the interior of the parodied one, and with its stylistic accents, its expressions, and its contexts, creates for it what Bakhtin calls a "dialogizing background," the only means by which understanding of self and other is possible.

Bakhtin's formal theory probes more deeply the ambivalence of the comic, not always clearly defined in his description of carnival. In *Rabelais*, Bakhtin provides a description only for those narrative acts which have absorbed archaic or folkloric ritual in their most pristine forms. Yet beyond them lies a wide range of narrative acts which have absorbed myth in ways that somehow defy such clearcut identification and analysis. As Barthes affirms in *Mythologies*, the signifier in myth is always double: it contains its historical "meaning" and its "form." The meaning is there to present the form and the form is there to "outdistance" the meaning. To focus on the mythical signifier as on an inextricable whole made of meaning and form, is to become receptive to an ambiguous signification, to finally respond to the "constituting mechanism of myth, to its own dynamics" (120-27).

An examination of recent theories of myth and their relation to the grotesque and other comic forms will illuminate the doublefaced, double-textured nature of the comic. These theories are useful inasmuch as they show that it is precisely its mythic content that makes the comic an appropriate vehicle for such diverse and contradictory modes of expression and accounts for the perdurability of its imagery.

Northrop Frye affirms that myth is an imitation of the actions of the gods at the conceivable limit of desire. Its content is the conflict between desire and reality. In the pure form of myth or "undisplaced" myth, desire is fulfilled. This form of myth can most commonly be found in such literary forms as romance, legends and folk and fairy tales, in which characters are either supernatural figures such as satyrs, dwarfs, giants and centaurs, or human beings that are physically or morally superior to normal human beings.

Myth, however, is not always resolved by the fulfillment of desire. Frye asserts that "the fact that myth operates at the top level of human desire does not mean that it necessarily presents its world as attained or attainable by human beings" ("Theory of Myths" 136). The contrast between the actions of the gods, resulting in perfection, and those of men, resulting in frustration and failure, is brought into sharper focus in realistic modes of fiction. In ironic or what Frye calls the "low mimetic" forms of fiction, men are portrayed not only as being inferior to the gods, but as being inferior even to other human beings, a condition that Aristotle had defined as one of the distinguishing characteristics of comedy.

The possible unrecognizability of myth in these modes is due to its inherent incompatibility with the incapacity of human beings and the representation of human experience. Myth becomes "displaced" or adapted to circumstances of daily life and common experience. In the process, the ritual content often becomes blurred, disguised, and in many cases subject to transformation and reversals. The critic causes the mythic or folkloric structures to emerge only after carrying out a comparative study of the story type. A comparison of the ritual content of the grotesque realism found in the folk comic tradition with that found in comedy and caricature will permit Bakhtin's descriptive model to be expanded so that narrative acts which have absorbed ritual in more adulterated forms might be included.

The ritual patterns of comedy are consistent with those found in the folk comic tradition described by Bakhtin as well as those found in the primitive rites described by Frazer and Cornford. In Greek New Comedy, transmitted by Plautus and Terence, the pattern consists of a conflict between the young hero who desires a young woman and an authority figure, usually paternal, who obstructs his desires. The plot device that brings the hero to the achievement of his goal causes a new society to crystallize around him. This new society is signalled by a wedding or some festive ritual indicating that the resolution of the action has occurred (Frye 163-86). The same elements found in carnival are present: the struggle between the powerful and the weak, the old and the young, and fear and desire. The obstacle of desire forms the action of comedy, and the overcoming of it the comic resolution.

The comic pattern, marked by the removal or expulsion of a threatening figure, or at the least, the undermining of his power, is the one described by Aristotle in his *Poetics*. In contrast to tragedy, which starts off calmly but moves toward conflict and finally towards death, comedy begins immediately with conflict and dangers. These dangers are eventually overcome, however, and, Aristotle insists, in a way that is innocuous both to the characters and the spectators. On this point Frye attempts to go beyond Aristotle.

In a standard comic pattern, one on which classical theory is based, attention is focused on the moment of "recognition" or *anagnorisis* of the new hero. Such a focus neutralizes the more painful moments produced by the expulsion of a scapegoat figure. Frye points out that a deviation from this pattern occurs in comedies where attention is focused on the scapegoat ritual. The emphasis on ridicule and physical violence upsets the comic balance, creating a sense of pathos and even tragedy. The emphasis on blocking characters is the general tendency of works containing comic irony and comic satire. Abuse, especially if it is directed towards our "entertainer," that is, he who has created the comic atmosphere throughout, produces one of the most terrible ironies. Comic irony moves us away from myth on the one hand, but at the same time, paradoxically, moves us again towards it, towards its other spectrum, that of bondage and death. Frye explains:

> In ironic Comedy we begin to see that art has also a lower limit in actual life. This is the condition of savagery in the world in which Comedy consists of inflicting pain on a helpless victim. Ironic Comedy brings us to the figure of the scapegoat ritual and the nightmare dream, the human symbol that concentrates our fears and hates. ("Theory of Modes" 45)

Another deviation from the comic pattern described by classical theory is the contrived comic ending. For Aristotle, comedy differed from tragedy not so much in the action, which in both was often filled with dangers and violence, as in the working out of these dangers. While comedy is distinguished by its "happy ending," in some comedies the victorious comic resolution is unconvincing, either due to the shift in focus described above, the inferior moral conduct of the young hero, or simply because we do not witness the transition towards an improved or altered state that culminates in *anagnorisis*. In comedies that reflect this kind of deviation, the work often ends before the altered state is even defined or represented. These comedies reflect an arbitrary victory of plot over consistency of character.

While some dramatists may not have enough artistry to bring about a comic ending in a convincing manner, the action of the play resulting in a series of rapid and illogical reversals that are necessary for bringing about the comic resolution, an experienced dramatist may take advantage of the priority of plot over character. Drawing on the audience's expectations of the final comic triumph, he or she can weave within the structure of the comic pattern a whole series of events that undermine a movement towards renewal or alteration. The potential pain and anxiety that such events might create are disguised rather than exposed. In his article on the Shakespearean comedy *A Midsummer's Night Dream*, René Girard points out that if an event occurs within the action of the play, explicitly neturalizing the comic movement towards a desired alteration, it will never be acknowledged by the spectator, due to the tacit agreement between dramatist and spectator on the priority of plot over character:

> As long as the standard plot is vaguely outlined, even in the crudest and least believable fashion, the author can subvert his own myths and state the truth at every turn with no consequence whatsoever. The audience will instinctively rally around the old clichés so completely blind and deaf to everything which may contradict them that the presence of this truth will not even be noticed. . . . (T)he most worn out myth will always triumph over the most explicit demythification. ("Myth and Ritual in Shakespeare" 194-95)

The structure of comedy can also subvert the movement towards the achievement of a desired state. In the primitive rites, in medieval carnival, and in comedy, there is a pattern of multiplication. In the rites, the king is split into two halves, the mock king and the King of Years. The latter is in turn split into several parts, the smaller scapegoat figures. In carnival, the clown acts as double for the king. His role as victim is further split into other sacrificial victims. Duplication and repetition also occur in comedy, as the young hero's conflict is reproduced. A second conflict takes place between the hero's slave or servant and the antagonist's, who both compete for the attention of the same servant girl.

The multiplication of events produces an apparent sense of regeneration. The dramatist intends to include as many people as possible in the new society. Comedies often end in double or triple weddings. In some comedies even the scapegoat figure is eventually included. In the final scenes of the play an atmosphere of festive triumph is attained. However the multiplication of characters and situations can function as an obstacle to the attainment of desire. The buffoon, slave or servant often frustrates his master's desires, either inadvertently by means of his natural ineptness, or by intentional maliciousness. The master's final victory can be neutralized by the servant's constant ridiculing of his master's actions and the sardonic asides he whispers to the audience behind his master's back. Finally, in comedy, primitive ceremonies, and carnival, punishment for the hero's misconduct or bad fortune usually falls on the double. These double figures bring us closer to the world of demonic imagery, the scapegoat ritual and expulsion, which in ironic comedy is never far away, Frye tells us. The tricky slave is always at the point of being flogged or having his head dipped in tar and then feathered ("Theory of Myths" 16).

The analysis of caricature will further underscore the potential ambiguity of the popular comic tradition. In his study on caricature, Ernst Kris tells us that the term caricature was invented at the end of the sixteenth century from the Italian *caricare*, meaning to exaggerate or overcharge (190-205). Since then, caricature has often been closely identified with the grotesque. Quite often they have been used alternately to describe the same concepts.[5]

Like the comic modes discussed above, caricature is based on a logic of reversals. The artist attempts to alter an undesirable state produced by the threat of an authority figure. This figure is represented so as to make him appear powerless. The threat he represents is consequently diminished or removed. The techniques used to recreate the threatening figure are the same ones employed in the grotesque imagery of carnival. His shape as well as his individual features are reproduced only to be broken apart and remolded along new lines, now violently exaggerated and distorted. The purpose of such distortion is to unmask him and show his true face. Caricature has a tendentious nature which conditions its mechanisms. It seeks to discover a likeness in deformity.

The practice of the art of caricature is linked to primitive magical rites, specifically to effigy magic. In a primitive stage of witchcraft, the threatening figure was reproduced in order to render true harm to him, when "to pierce the wax dummy meant to destroy the enemy" (Kris 203). As society gradually evolved, the

---

[5] Wright, writing on the grotesque at the end of the nineteenth century, relates caricature to the grotesque, often using the terms interchangeably in his work.

hostile action came to consist merely in the alteration of the figure's pictorial likeness. Pain was replaced by laughter, and the savage act was reduced to play.

According to Kris, the aggression that the artist expresses is rooted in infantile fears and desires. The pent-up instincts that must be released are turned against an authority figure. The caricature brings out the frightening, threatening aspects of the authoritative figure to the childlike part of us. At the same time, the "ego defense mechanism" that is, our adult rational consciousness, takes action against the threat by means of the comic measures which produce degradation, such as exaggeration and deformation. The true source of fear is disguised and aggression is finally allowed to be released. If the comic techniques of caricature are successful and the defenses are complete, all anxiety will be eliminated and pleasure will be gained. Yet often the threatening material in caricature may be distorted in the direction of harmlessness unsuccessfully. Anxiety is retained or even increased in these cases.

Failure to eliminate anxiety is often brought about by the extreme to which the aggressive tendencies are carried out. Comic devices such as exaggeration and distortion can cause the object of the caricature to become somehow subhuman or diabolical. The employment of extreme measures in the expression of the comic creates so much anxiety that no defense mechanism is strong enough to disguise it. In psychological terms it could be said that too much libidinal energy is at work, making it impossible to eliminate the anxiety-producing situation. Since the comic balance is lost, the artist and spectator alike suffer the exposure of fears and ultimately displeasure.[6] Kris thus puts Aristotle's faith in the cathartic capacity of the comic into doubt, that is, its power to release unconscious tension and "purge" the soul.[7]

Critics are finally beginning to expand Bakhtin's theory of carnival in order to account for a wider spectrum of aesthetic expression. In a recent article, "Towards a Mechanics of Mode: Beyond Bakhtin," David Hayman attempts to account for the contradictory

---

[6] Steig applies intrapsychic ego psychology to the grotesque, departing from Kris' study on caricature. He arrives at similar conclusions on the grotesque, namely, that while the grotesque is an attempt on the part of the artist to overcome his or her fears and limitations, the goal is not necessarily achieved.

[7] Modern theorists on the comic that challenge the belief in the liberating power of the comic are heavily indebted to Bergson. For the extent of Bergson's influence on theorists on the comic of this century, see Charney, especially the Preface.

aspects of carnival (death-life) by contrasting Bakhtin's joyous view of carnival, symbolized by the drive for renewal and the motif "death into birth," with the Romantic use of grotesque imagery, described by Wolfgang Kayser, with its "fear of life" (105-06).[8] Julia Kristeva recalls the destructive aspects of carnival: "There is a tendency to blot out carnival's dramatic (murderous, cynical and revolutionary dialectical transformation) aspects...." ("Word, Dialogue and Novel" 80).[9] In his study "When the Carnival Turns Bitter," Michael André Bernstein confesses his anxiety-ridden response to the carnivalesque conflict portrayed in Rabelais' work:

> I think it only just to confess that there are moments when Rabelais' glee in depicting the various torments inflicted upon the novels' villains leaves me considerably more nervous than Bakhtin's account would suggest possible. Indeed, my sense of the energy released by Rabelais' laughter depends in no small measure upon both the nervousness he elicits and his skill in assuaging it. (128)

Finally, René Girard's *Violence and the Sacred* offers a perspective of carnival in radical contrast to Bakhtin's. He does not see ritual as a joyous festival with a tragic background. For Girard, the "dark event" (the killing of the scapegoat victim) is at the center of myth (118-42).

In my analysis of the comic in *Don Quixote*, Bakhtin's works will be used as a main model. Other theories reviewed have been considered initially because they provide a historical background for Bakhtin's concept of grotesque realism as well as a critical vantage point to his theory. They also bring out the versatility of the comic, revealing the possibility it offers of being interpreted from the standpoint of a number of disciplines, such as anthropology, the social and political sciences, psychology, and of course, the arts. These approaches will be incorporated in this study along with Bakhtin's inasmuch as they can aid in evaluating the manner in which philosophical and literary ideals (chivalric heroism, platonic love, humanist ethics and Renaissance literary theory) are posited and polemicized in the text, both in the embodiment of the characters and their conflicts and in the writing and reading processes.

---

[8] See also Kayser's classic work on the Romantic grotesque.
[9] For an opposing point of view on Bakhtin's theory of the grotesque, see Gump Stewart, 14-16.

CHAPTER 2

THE MAKING OF THE COMIC HERO

> Pues sabed, hermana mía, que caballero aventurero es una cosa que en dos palabras se ve apaleado y emperador.
>
> Don Quixote, I, 16

The reenactment of the heroic myth forms an essential part of the action of *Don Quixote*. Yet the conflicting points of view projected by the varying characters and narrative voices as well as the contradictions between words and deeds, and between one event and another combine to create an ambivalence in the text that makes it difficult to determine if the protagonist embodies any ideal at all. Some readers find themselves identifying with the character, viewing him as a victimized hero and rebel whom society has turned against. Others view him as a fool and a madman.[1]

The action of the hero, conventionalized by legend, folk tale, and myth, and later incorporated into romance and epic, is a successful quest. As a completed form, it occurs in three main stages:

---

[1] Di Battista, for example, perceives Don Quixote as a hero placed in a world where the heroic milieu is missing, his quest doomed to failure. This concept of the hero is rooted in romantic criticism of the text which, as Close has chronicled, has had a pervasive influence on Cervantine critics. According to the romantic perspective, the hero represents the world of spirit and beauty, and when society confronts this hero and attempts to assimilate his world, the hero becomes degraded. See *The Romantic Approach to "Don Quixote": A Critical History of the Romantic Tradition in "Quixote" Criticism*. In current criticism on *Don Quixote*, however, the main character is increasingly viewed as a comic one, and the world that surrounds him as a humorous society. See for example Auerbach, 334-58, Eisenberg, "Cervantes 'Don Quijote' Once Again: An Answer to J. J. Allen" and *A Study of Don Quixote*, 109-56, Riquer, "Cervantes and the Romances of Chivalry," Russell, "*Don Quixote* as a Funny Book, and *Cervantes*.

the perilous journey and preliminary minor adventures, the crucial struggle, usually some kind of battle in which either hero or enemy must die, and the final exaltation of the hero.[2] In Cervantes' work, as W. H. Auden has shown, the main character is lacking the heroic *areté* of youth and destiny (76).

The purpose of the prehistory of the knight is to make the mediocrity of the hero evident to the reader before the action of the novel actually begins. The narrator's use of stable irony is instrumental in this process. The narrator uses this rhetorical device in order to alert the reader to a covert but intended communication he wishes to make to him or her, at variance with what he seems to be saying, and invites the reader to share in his attitudes (Booth 1-31). In chivalric romance the narrator creates an aura of mystique around the hero by keeping his place of birth secret. In Cervantes' work, the narrator seems to imitate his predecessor, remaining silent about the name of the hero's village, but he then reveals that the unnamed village is in the region of La Mancha, an agricultural region that can lay no claim to nobility. The destiny of the hero of romance is sealed by the prophetic description of the knight's birth and childhood. Such detail sets the future hero apart from others and signals the fulfillment of his destiny. In Cervantes' work, the life of the hero begins when he is at the end of his life, and no longer able to go through the long and laborious growth process necessary for the formation of the heroic identity. In his portrayal of the hero, the narrator includes only those elements that blend him with an entire social group. He introduces the hero as a "type," ". . . un hidalgo de los de lanza en astillero . . ." (I, 1: 69). Our hero is like *any* hidalgo living at the time of Cervantes.[3]

The subject's lack (of heroic singularity) leads him to the desire to possess, and his desire leads him to imitate the heroic models he reads about as a means of obtaining the desired heroic identity. When the gentleman adopts the disguise of knight errant, the first important incident in the novel, he annihilates his own personality in order to give birth to a new one. As Bakhtin explains, the partici-

---

[2] As Frye explains in his description of the quest, these stages can be described in Greek terms: first, the *agon* or conflict, secondly the *pathos* or death struggle, and finally the *anagnorisis* or the recognition of the hero, 187; see also Campbell, 317-29.

[3] On the comic presentation of Don Quixote, see Rosenblat and Mancing, 9-12.

pant of carnival expresses his desire to regress to a state of liberty, but in order to do so, he must transgress the limits of his own personality, too limited and restricted by daily life and family obligations. He takes on the disguise of an ideal "other" and gives himself up to a world of wish fulfillment and fantasy (Durán 79). Discovering what that "other" is and how it is represented will be the object of my inquiry.

The hero's imitation of the knight errant is rooted in the most archaic principle of education. Roleplay is important, for identity is anchored in the individual's ability to "play" his role well. Indeed, the role player's ultimate knowledge of self will depend on his or her ability to take on an identity.[4] Obedience to the authority of the written word, even that contained in romance, accords the *hidalgo* the sensation of self knowledge and knowledge of the world by providing him with models, values, and codes of behavior with which he can identify.

For Marthe Robert, the imitator is like a child or a believer. Becoming deeply entrenched in the ideals of the model, his or her devotion evolves into a more mature need to violate the limits prescribed by the model. The imitator's feelings become more ambivalent. The ideal, "no longer sheltered by absolute faith, becomes vulnerable to the profanation of scrutiny and criticism." Finally, harmony with the loved object gives way to an irrepressible hostility (31-35).[5]

René Girard's studies on the mimetic process within scapegoating rituals increase the possibilities for the analysis of mimesis within the literary work. Girard provides a non-conscious motivation for the ambivalence the imitator experiences towards his model: metaphysical desire.[6] Girard starts from Lukacs' premise that the

---

[4] See Cascardi, 55-60 and Welsh, 167-78. In contrast to the conclusions I will be postulating, Cascardi contends that through role play, the knight gains personal identity. Welsh, quite interestingly, registers in the knight's altering models of imitations the instability of role playing and indeed, of identity itself. He concludes that the modernity of this novel lies in its expression of the crisis of the personality and of the self.

[5] The comparison of Don Quixote's fantasy and role playing to that of a child's has been elucidated by critics apparently distrustful of psychological explanations for the knight's behavior. See for example Serrano-Plaja and Torrente Ballester. Huizinga has pointed out the essentially mimetic nature of chivalric behavior. See also Riley, "Don Quixote and the Imitation of Models."

[6] Culler provides a helpful although brief analysis of Girard's theory and its place within post-structuralism, 25-30; see also Lacoue-Labarthe.

novel represents man in a world without God. Self-knowledge no longer issues from the subject's ability to discover the relation or resemblances between events and objects in this world and the divine order as in the period of medieval idealism. Nor can the knowledge of self always be obtained by rational methods, by empirical observation and imitation, because knowledge cannot always be grasped by conscious, mental faculties.

Girard contends that since human beings live in a world without God, they will turn to an idol, another human being to imitate and in whom to seek knowledge. From the deviation of the transcendental to the immanent emerges metaphysical desire. The subject becomes fascinated by the false idol. The objects the subject comes to desire are no longer desirable in themselves. Nor are they henceforth directly observable. They are re-presented through the model, that is, by means of mediated desire. The closer the subject comes to imitating the model, the more he or she comes to perceive the model ambivalently, as god, but also as rival. The subject's love is constantly subject to transmutation into hatred. Thus, desire is inextricably bonded with violence.

Girard's hypothesis is enticing. He invites the reader to seek an explanation for the subject's desire within the framework of mimetic violence, a violence which impinges on all human beings. In *Don Quixote*, the ambivalence of the hero is expressed when the author instills in him a desire to share Amadís' desire and then creates contexts that progressively distort the model's desire and erodes the image of the chivalric rival. As the subject comes to embody his rival, the latter becomes subject to a violent victimization. He is ultimately transformed into surrogate victim, not in his own person since he is, as Girard has shown, the external mediator of Don Quixote, but in his carnival double, in the figure of Don Quixote.

The aim of my analysis of the construction of the character of the hero as a comic figure will be twofold: First, I will identify the objects and images associated with the romance hero and show how they are replaced in the text by objects and images pertaining to the world of the comic and of carnival. Secondly, I will show how these objects and images, when propelled in the plot action, deviate the standard plot sequence of romance from a movement towards the transcendence of the romance hero to one towards immanence, resulting in the unveiling of the false idols of romance. The Manchegan knight's inability to attain the desired heroic identity reflects on his own shortcomings. Yet in the heteroglossic, double-directed discourse of Cervantes' work, his inability to re-construct and/or acquire and possess the mediated objects of his desire is instrumental in the deconstruction of the hero and his quest, and the absolute values they embody.

The movement from the knight's desire for alteration, stimulated by his obsessive reading of chivalric romance to the decision to carry out tasks to implement change opens up the possibility for the gentleman to fulfill his desires. Before he can transform himself into knight, however, he must acquire armor, arms, and a steed. These elements will intervene as means believed capable of insuring the successful achievement of his task, namely, of becoming an acclaimed hero. Comic situations arise as the knight carries out the task of the acquisition of these object-means backwards and acquires object-means appropriate to obtain a result opposing his end.

The knight's armor, arms, and steed are linked to the heroic identity. The arms must be worthy of the hero, hence the importance of their forging and testing, for they in turn are destined to test and acclaim the superior strength and capacity for self-defense of the knight who wields them. The knight's arms often have a mysterious or supernatural origin. The custom of passing arms from father to son was common, and for this reason the arms embody not only the identity of the hero, but the fame and glory of an entire lineage. As a member of a lineage that descends from the gods, the knight is conscious of the importance of maintaining its glory and realizing the potential of its origin (Bowra 149).

Although not of royal or divine lineage, Don Quixote attempts to imitate the action of the noble hero in obtaining arms. He takes the arms of his great-grandfather that have been out of use for ages, laid aside to collect mildew and rust: "Y lo primero que hizo fue limpiar unas armas que habían sido de sus bisabuelos, que, tomadas de orín y llenas de moho, luengos siglos había que estaban puestas y olvidadas en un rincón" (I, 1: 75). By means of the knight's imitation, the high object is transformed into its opposite, negating the object imitated. The object is mutilated, disfigured, its "other side" left bare. Bakhtin describes this process:

> Negation reconstructs the image of the object and first of all modifies the topographical position in space of the object as well

> as of its parts. It transfers the object to the Underworld, replaces the top by the bottom, or the front by the back, sharply exaggerating some traits at the expense of others. Negation and destruction of the objects are their displacement and reconstruction in space, the nonbeing of an object is its other face, its inside out. (*Rabelais* 410)

The comic image negates the exalted object by replacing it with pieces of junk, rags, garbage, or useless, worn-out items. These objects suggest the obsolete character and the ridiculous pomposity of the heroic world they represent. A careful analysis of the specific elements of the knight's trappings (the armor, the arms, and the horse) as well as of the features constituting his physical constitution will reveal the adverse effect of the trappings on the knight's physical well-being and on the development and outcome of his "heroic" adventures.

The narrator begins his description of the knight's preparation for departure with the object of the helmet. The attempt to construct, obtain, or maintain control over the helmet forms a major complex sequence of action in Part I of *Don Quixote*. The narrator explains that it was a simple head-piece, the visor missing. In order to remedy this, the gentleman fabricates a visor out of cardboard: "... mas a esto suplió su industria, porque de cartones hizo un modo de media celada, que, encajada con el morrión, hacían una apariencia de celada entera" (75).

The comic mask is constructed when the knight replaces the noble object with one built with false parts. The pseudo-being reveals the lack of substance and the intrinsically fraudulent nature of the figure imitated. The narrator underscores the fraudulence of the object by refering to it as "una apariencia." This initial reproduction of the heroic object results in its immediate destruction. In imitation of his heroes, the knight tests out the strength of the object with a swordblow, and it falls apart. The knight rebuilds the object for a second time, securing the cardboard visor with iron bars. The knight ventures on the road without testing it, and almost at once the object prevents the realization of his task.

On the evening of the first day, the knight rests at an inn he imagines to be a castle. The two whores standing at the door of the inn help the knight remove his armor. He does not consent to the removal of the helmet, however, since in order to do so, he would have to cut the green ribbons tied onto it. The color green is one identified with the carnival victim. Green ribbons are tied on the clown's hat when he is crowned "king" (*Rabelais* 202). Here, the result of the knight's prohibition is his conversion into victim. With the helmet on and the visor raised, the knight is unable to have his meal, an act that will replenish his strength and insure his success in battle. The knight admits this fact as the poor meal is offered to him: ". . . sea lo que fuere, venga luego, que el trabajo y peso de las armas no se puede llevar sin el gobierno de las tripas" (I, 2: 86-87).[7] The rich feast held in honor of the knight in the palaces of kings is parodied here as the maidens/whores stretch their services to inconceivable limits, not simply waiting on him but spoon-feeding him, revealing the knight's total helplessness.

In the first adventure of the following day, the episode of the Merchants from Toledo, the helmet not only fails to protect the knight in battle, but is once again destroyed. The knight enters into battle with the travelers in defense of the unsurpassed beauty of his lady. The knight takes a fall before arriving at his enemy and a muleteer who is present gives him a beating that "a despecho y pesar de sus armas, le molió como cíbera" (I, 4: 101). Pedro Alonso chances by and lifts up the cardboard visor in order to look at the face underneath. On doing so, the piece of armor falls apart. The sally ends as the neighbor carries the battered knight back to his village.

At the onset of his second sally, in the battle with the Basque, the knight attempts to defend a lady-in-distress when his newly built helmet and the part of the body it is to protect are once again threatened. The knight erroneously believes that he has rescued the lady in question from evil enchanters. While Don Quixote is requesting of the lady that she go to Dulcinea to advise her of his feat, a Basque gentleman who is present orders the knight to leave the carriage. In the ensuing duel, Don Quixote deals the triumphant blow on his opponent, putting an end to the duel. Yet before his defeat the Basque discharges a blow on the knight that destroys a good part of his armor, including the helmet, and with it, the knight's ear. In spite of his victory, the knight is left in a more precarious state than before, exposed to danger and possible defeat in

---

[7] Depriving the victim of food forms part of the persecuting ceremonies of carnival.

future battles. The knight is well aware of this fact, for when he later discovers that his helmet has been destroyed in the battle, it causes him almost to "perder el juicio" (I, 10: 150).

The knight sorely needs to salvage his badly damaged self-esteem, dependent on the opinion of others. He thus takes a vow to live outside of villages and not to eat on tablecloths until he can win another helmet in battle. He will perform this action in imitation of Sacripante, who, according to the knight, won his helmet in battle with the noble Moor, Mambrino. Unfortunately, a series of misfortunes befall the knight and squire before he is able to do so: the adventure with the Yanguesan mares, the blanket tossing of Sancho, the misadventures at the inn with the muleteer from Arévalo and Maritornes, and finally the blows and falls suffered in the battle with the warring armies of sheep. Sancho attributes these misfortunes to his master's inability to comply with his vow:

> –Paréceme, Señor mío, que todas estas desventuras que estos días nos han sucedido, sin duda alguna han sido pena del pecado cometido por vuestra merced contra la orden de su caballería, no habiendo cumplido el juramento que hizo de no comer pan a manteles ni con la reina folgar . . . hasta quitar aquel almete de Malandrido . . . (I, 19: 228)

Faced with such an accusation, the knight quickly seizes the occasion to acquire the helmet when he sees a man riding towards him on a mule, wearing something on his head that is shining like gold. The knight informs his squire that the man before them is a knight wearing a golden helmet. The narrator intervenes to inform the reader that the approaching figure is really a barber riding to a neighboring village. In order to prevent his hat from getting wet in the rain, he had put his basin on his head.[8]

In folk humor, the exalted object is debased by replacing it with domestic, household tools or tools of trade, such as the barber's basin (*Rabelais* 411). These objects were commonly used in battle

---

[8] A literal reading of the episodes narrating the adventure of Mambrino's helmet have provided proof for a number of critics of the author's belief in the notion of "perspectivism." Castro and Spitzer initiated perspectivist criticism on *Don Quixote*, explaining the presence of the multiple perspectives offered in the text as an aesthetic expression of the philosophy of skepticism and of the notion of the relativity of truth.

scenes in comic satire, bedroom farces, and the comic visual arts of the fifteenth and sixteenth centuries. In his study on caricature and the grotesque, Thomas Wright offers an example of an engraving from this period in which a kitchen lad is holding a knight's helmet tucked under his arm and is wearing on his head a bellows, an instrument employed to keep the fire going. The portrait exemplifies a typical satire on the aristocratic order of the knight, who is distinguished from the rest by his helmet and armor (411).

The barber's basin is linked to another household instrument, the "bacín" or chamberpot. Murillo explains that in the time of Cervantes, the barber's basin came to have this usage, a fact that is supported by Don Quixote's angry reaction in the galley slave episode when the sergeant tells the knight to straighten his "bacín" (I, 22: 274, note 35). In the comic perspective of the world, reversal is topographical. The head and the face, as well as the objects worn over them, are perceived as the other side of the ass. Don Quixote triumphantly retrieves this inverted object from the ground where the barber had inadvertently left it in his flight from the knight's attack. The knight must prove his capacity of prowess in battle with this object, and he must also maintain the spoils of battle in his power if his "victory," such as it is, is to earn him the esteem of others.

The liberation of the galley slaves follows immediately after the flight of the barber. It is the first and only adventure in which the knight uses his new helmet in battle. The absolute ideal of freedom is questioned as the knight puts himself on the side of the dangerous criminals, and frees them after they have openly admitted their guilt. The criminals, somewhat less than enthusiastic about the knight's demand that they go to his lady to advise her of his feat, begin to shower stones on both knight and squire. Don Quixote falls to the ground, and almost immediately one of the galley slaves approaches, removes the helmet from the knight's head, strikes him with it and then throws it against the ground several times: ". . . y apenas hubo caído, cuando fue sobre él el estudiante, y le quitó la bacía de la cabeza, y diole con ella tres o cuatro golpes en las espaldas y otros tantos en la tierra, con que la hizo pedazos" (276).

The use of the object-means for self-defense and protection not only proves to be a failure, but is even given a reversed function, that of aggression. Already debased by a transformation into barber's basin/chamberpot, the object is finally turned into a piece of junk in this scene, for we discover later that the helmet is completely dented. Sancho finally eliminates the heroic significance of the helmet completely, and along with it the legitimacy of his master's heroic achievement of having won it, by transmuting the object back into barber's basin. He advises his master that he is going to fix the dented basin in order to use it at home to shave his beard: "La bacía yo la llevo en el costal, toda abollada, y llévola para aderezarla en mi casa y hacerme la barba en ella . . ." (I, 25: 306).

In the closing chapters of Part I, the helmet once again becomes engaged in the main action. Strife begins anew when the barber enters the inn after having recognized his pack saddles in the stable. The barber comes to reclaim the "spoils" of battle, both the pack saddle and the basin. The pseudo-assistance the priest and the barber lend to the knight is completed as they pay the barber the eight royal crowns the new basin was originally worth so that the knight can keep it in his power. The barber reclaims the spoils lost in battle and Don Quixote is left with a piece of junk which he is able to maintain only by means of an act of deception. In the culmination of this plot sequence, the ameliorated condition that should have resulted is shown to have been falsely achieved.

The arms of the knight have a function similar to that of the armor, that of reversing heroic action. When inserted in the comic work, the heroic arms are replaced by prosaic objects, such as domestic utensils. This substitution is linked to the ascending and descending movement that animates all carnival images and forms. All that is sacred and exalted is debased, thrown to the earth. The epic duel is incorporated into the action of carnival and imitated, but the sword and the lance are replaced by beatings, blows and stonings, that "bury" their victim. When the noble arms do appear, they are portrayed as useless items.

In the battle with the Basque, the use of the arms has an instrumental role in debasing the epic duel and its contestants. In the epic, the narrator exalts the courage and worth of the victorious hero in battle by exalting the strength and courage of the enemy. The greater and more fearful the enemy, the more worthy is the act of defeating him. The Basque is a worthy opponent for the knight, but the narrator's comments on this figure reveal his unheroic nature, precisely with regard to the nature and use of his arms.[9]

---

[9] On other comic aspects of this character, see Percas de Ponseti, *Cervantes y su concepto del arte*, 1: 76-84.

As the battle begins, Don Quixote draws his sword to attack. The Basque has no shield with which to defend himself, but the narrator explains that he was lucky enough to be near the coach and seize from it something he could use as a means of protection. What he seizes is a cushion, an unlikely substitute for a shield, for it is easily penetrable. The Basque becomes the butt of the narrator's irony. He is described as "aforrado con su almohada," and "bien cubierto de su almohada" (I, 8: 137). The narrator thus signals the uselessness of the cushion as a means of protection and the true explanation for the knight's victory:

> ... se alzó de nuevo en los estribos y, apretando más la espada en las dos manos, con tal furia descargó sobre el vizcaíno, acertándole de lleno sobre la almohada y sobre la cabeza, *que, sin ser parte tan buena defensa,* como si cayera sobre él una montaña, comenzó a echar sangre por las narices y por la boca, y por los oídos, y a dar muestras de caer de la mula abajo.... (I, 9: 145, emphasis added)

The knight is still euphoric over his "victory" when he encounters the Yanguesans. These herders defend their drove of Galician mares against the amorous attack of Rocinante by giving the hack a sound beating. Sancho informs his master that the Yanguesans outnumber them but the still arrogant knight charges while declaring, "Yo valgo por ciento" (I, 15: 191). The Yanguesans begin to shower blows on both knight and squire with their pack staves, and the narrator comments on the powerlessness of the knight's noble weapons and character against their prosaic tools of trade and the heroic ire with which they wield them:

> Los gallegos, que se vieron maltratar de aquellos dos hombres solos, siendo ellos tantos, acudieron a sus estacas y cogiendo a los dos en medio, comenzaron a menudear sobre ellos con grande ahínco y vehemencia. Verdad es que al segundo toque dieron con Sancho en el suelo, y lo mesmo le avino a don Quijote, *sin que le valiese su destreza y buen ánimo* ... donde se echa de ver la furia con que machacan estacas puestas en manos rústicas y enojadas. (191-192, emphasis added)

Don Quixote's attempt to exalt himself occupies the final part of the episode. In order to justify his defeat, he tells Sancho that he is not affronted because the arms employed by the carriers are not those specified by the chivalric code: ". . . quiero hacerte sabidor, Sancho, que no afrentan las heridas que se dan con los instrumentos que acaso se hallan en las manos; y esto está en la ley de duelo . . ." (195). The rhetoric of the knight is counteracted by his actions. From the time he initiates his task the knight employs objects and materials he finds at hand, such as the cardboard visor and the rusted arms. In his misadventure with the windmills, the knight replaces his broken lance with a branch, again in imitation of a chivalric hero. We never hear of the knight using this lance in battle. He replaces it when he finds a real lance while departing from the inn after the taking of the balm of Fierabrás. Sancho finally questions his master's claim for honor as he confronts the knight's elusive ideal with his own bodily pain:

> –No me dieron a mí lugar –respondió Sancho– a que mirase en tanto; porque apenas puse mano a mi tizona, cuando me santiguaron los hombros con sus pinos, de manera que me quitaron la vista de los ojos y la fuerza de los pies, dando conmigo adonde ahora yago, y adonde no me da pena alguna el pensar si fue afrenta, o no lo de los estacazos, como me la da el dolor de los golpes, que me han de quedar tan impresos en la memoria como en las espaldas. (195)

The replacement of the hero's armor by domestic costume forms the bulk of the parody of the "crucial struggle" of romance in the rescue of the Princess Micomicona. The knight's battle with the wineskins reveals the other side of the hero's quest. The battlefield is transformed into a bedroom. The knight, in his enthusiastic anticipation of the forthcoming encounter with the giant Malambruno, acts out the duel in his sleep. With his eyes shut, he wields his sword against the innkeeper's wine skins hanging on the wall. The romance hero's shining armor is replaced by the knight's greasy night shirt that exposes the knight's dirty thighs and skinny weakness. Indeed, the nightshirt exposes so much flesh in the rear that the modesty of the "Princess" forces her to take leave of the room, preventing her from witnessing her own "salvation."[10] The helmet is

---

[10] In his article, "The Beheading of the Giant," Herrero examines the erotic imagery linked to the innkeeper's winebags. On the knight's supposed killing of the giant and completion of the "crucial struggle" in this episode, see Dudley.

replaced by a greasy red nightcap and the shining shield by a blanket, wound about his left arm.

The replacement of heroic arms by prosaic or domestic ones is further illustrated in the last chapter of Part I. The chapter is divided into two episodes, the encounter with the goatherd Eugenio and the confrontation with the penitents. The episodes share similar themes and imagery. In each, the knight wishes to rescue a damsel in distress. In the first encounter, Eugenio shares his table with Don Quixote and the other members of his party while he tells the story of how Leandra had "betrayed" him and the other men of his village by fleeing with the poet Vicente. The knight offers to come to the goatherd's aid and "rescue" his damsel from the monastery where her father had sent her upon discovering that she had been abandoned by Vicente. The goatherd is surprised by the knight's speech and begins to mock him. The knight's desire to rescue the damsel results in a fight with a bread loaf, which happens to be still lying on the table. A typically farcical fist fight ensues, as plates, cups, and tablecloth are upturned.[11] The narrator likens the "heroic" struggle to the amusement of a dogfight: "Reventaban de risa el Canónigo y el Cura, saltaban los cuadrilleros de gozo, zuzaban los unos y los otros, como hacen a los perros cuando en pendencia están trabados . . ." (I, 52: 597). The hero, singled out by the gods to carry out heroic feats, is transformed into the carnivalesque image of the dog, a symbol of evil, traditionally employed in folk festivities as the victim of beatings, tossings and persecutions.[12]

The struggle between the goatherd and the knight is brought to a standstill by the sound of trumpets, announcing the approach of a procession of penitents carrying a figure of the Virgin to a nearby hermitage. Don Quixote, "defender" of the Catholic faith, mistakes the penitents for evildoers and the figure of the Virgin for a kidnapped damsel. He attacks the penitents with his sword in order to "rescue" the damsel while the penitents defend themselves with

---

[11] For an excellent description of the action of farce and a discussion of its similarities to the action of carnival, see Bentley and Asensio. Charney's discussion of this genre is also of interest, 95-105.

[12] The response of the so-called respectable bystanders seems to affect our modern sensitivity. This is evidenced by several critics' inclination to interpret this scene as a social satire against a society that expresses negative social values. See Efron, 98. Such a hypothesis underlies the modern reader's loss of contact with the idiom of carnival. See Moreno Báez 33 and Russell, "*Don Quixote* as a Funny Book."

what they have at hand. One of the bearers of the litter seizes a pronged stick used to support the litter. In the "duel," the knight deals the penitent a sword blow that cuts his pole into three parts. With the third part still in his hand, the penitent manages to return the blow. The narrator informs us that the knight's shield was "powerless" as a means of protection against such an attack:

> ... con el último tercio, que le quedó en la mano, dio tal golpe a don Quijote encima de un hombro, por el mismo lado de la espada, *que no pudo cubrir el adarga contra villana fuerza*, que el pobre don Quijote vino al suelo muy mal parado. (600, emphasis added)

The heroic vision of war is reversed as the narrator continues to comment on the scene. He compares the other bearers of the litter gathered around the figure of the virgin to a squadron of soldiers. The penitents turned soldiers are prepared to defend their inanimate damsel as well as their fellow penitent with the only weapons that have at hand, their scourges and candlesticks, the tools and objects used for their procession. They wield these instruments as they wait for the other members of the knight's party to approach. The gripping outcome is that no bellicose action is undertaken. The priests of the respective parties recognize one another. The unravelling of the action of epic and romance, involving the near death and resurrection of the hero, is parodied as Sancho renders a eulogy over his master's fallen body. He debases the heroic image by replacing the image of the heroic sword blow with that of the cudgelling of the candlestick, as he describes his master's actions: "¡Oh flor de la caballería, que con solo un garrotazo acabaste la carrera de tus bien gastados años!" (601).

The "pedrea" or stone fight forms a particularly rich tradition within carnival activities as a means of offering a new perspective on the medieval duel, waged with exalted weapons (Caro Baroja 47-63). The stonings have as their target, as do all of the tendentious activities of carnival, those that prevent the regeneration of the collectivity. The stone fights can occur between individuals in single battle or between larger groups, such as towns or nations.

The Wagon of Death episode illustrates the manner in which the individual stone fight replaces the epic battle. After the disappointing discovery of the "enchantment" of Dulcinea, the knight and squire leave El Toboso. As they continue a distance, they encounter a wagon full of strangely dressed individuals. They stop to inquire the reason for such strange dress, and the driver explains that they are a wandering theatrical company. It is Corpus Christi Day, and they have just given a performance in one village and are traveling to a nearby village to perform again. Since they are in a hurry, they have kept their costumes on. The illusive, festive impression that the scene offers is thus given a realistic explanation.

Bakhtin explains that the company of itinerant actors of the Middle Ages and the Renaissance is not merely a tiny professional world. It stands in contrast to all the well-ordered and established world. Its members live outside the sphere of conventions and rules and enjoy certain license enjoyed by all during the time of carnival, for "the actor's bandwagon spreads the festive carnival atmosphere that pervades the life and manners of the performers themselves" (*Rabelais* 106). Don Quixote no longer needs to transform reality to correspond to his illusions. Other characters enter his sphere of action and carry out these transformations for him.

The motley group begins to exercise its carnival license when the actor disguised as a clown approaches the knight. The clown frightens the knight's hack by beating the ground with his stick, to which are tied three ox bladders. Finally, fencing and jumping, he causes the bells about him to jangle loudly. The frightened Rocinante flees, throwing his master.

Bakhtin explains that the image of the bells, usually the cow bell, appears in even the most ancient carnivals as an indispensable accessory. Figures representing the Devil, such as the carnival clown, jump and writhe their bodies as they chase the crowd, and the loud bells on their costumes can be heard jangling. In fact, Caro Baroja explains that any kind of artifact that could produce loud, abominable noises was used: pots and pans, mule bells, bull roarers, and tin cans (60-62). These figures of evil generally carried weapons with which to flagellate the crowd, such as animal bladders bound in leather or stones.

Still on the ground, the knight hurls insults at the players riding away. The performers return and collect stones in preparation for a stone fight. The narrator describes the aggression of the bellicose encounter in military terms, mixing the high with the low in a single image:

> ... todos se cargaron de piedras y se pusieron en ala esperando recebir a don Quijote en las puntas de sus guijarros. Don Quijote, que los vio puestos en tan gallardo escuadrón, los brazos levantados con ademán de despedir poderosamente las piedras, detuvo las riendas a Rocinante y púsose a pensar de qué modo los acometería con menos peligro de su persona. (II, 11: 119)

No battle takes place, however. Sancho is able to dissuade Don Quixote from entering into battle, and one of the reasons the squire gives to his master reveals the ineffectiveness of the knight's arms against his opponents: "... considere vuesa merced, señor mío, que para sopa de arroyo y tente bonete, no hay arma defensiva en el mundo..." (119).

The stone fight between collective groups is well illustrated in the braying adventure, in which a new context for the heroic vision of war is projected. The story of the two aldermen who take to the mountains and bray together in order to attract a missing donkey forms the nucleus of the story. Their exaggerating praise of each other's ability to bray ("de vos a un asno, compadre no hay alguna diferencia en cuanto toca al rebuznar..." [II, 25: 231-32]) eventually turns into joking abuse when it passes outside the radius of the aldermen's village into nearby towns, causing the members of these towns to bray upon seeing the villagers from the aldermen's town. The joke goes so far that the town is eventually prepared to go to war with one of these villages.

The image of the braying ass is a central one in the festivals of laughter. Bakhtin tells us that one of the expressions of the Feast of Fools is the Feast of the Ass, a popular celebration commemorating Mary's flight into Egypt (*Rabelais* 78). The central protagonist is the ass. The priest gives his service, but at the end of the mass, the priest's blessing is replaced by braying. The image of the ass and his braying materializes church ritual. It is one of the most ancient and lasting symbols of the carnavalesque abuse of officialdom. Caro Baroja explains that during carnival, in battles between nearby villages, aggressive activities included simply braying at the inhabitants of the other town, or putting up figures of asses in their villages (91-100).

The braying forms part of the intersubjective language of praise and abuse of the language of the marketplace. In marketplace speech, in an atmosphere of familiarity and community spirit, abusive words, especially indecent ones, are used in an affectionate and complimentary way. This is the context of praise that is first presented to the reader in the initial scene in which members of the aldermen's village praise the aldermen for their talent in braying.

The topsy-turvy action of the comic is set into motion when the news reaches the ears of the villagers in towns nearby. The abuse meant as praise is turned back into abuse. The shift from order and communal harmony to disorder is again reproduced when Don Quixote and Sancho begin to take part in the confrontation. Upon leaving the inn, knight and squire encounter the squadron formed by members of the aldermen's village, waiting for their opponents to appear. The knight delivers a speech to them on the noble ideals for which one ought to engage in battle and cautions them not to debase these ideals by entering into battle for foolish reasons. When he stops to take a breath, Sancho intervenes and breaks up the harmony that his master's speech seems to produce.

Using a technique similar to that used by the neighboring villagers, Sancho praises in a way that abuses. He compliments his master's speech and agrees with him that it is folly to fly into a rage over hearing one bray. He goes on to explain that as a lad he brayed all the time, and no one had ever taken notice of it. Indeed, he was quite talented at it. To prove his ability he begins to bray before the group. Sancho's braying is suddenly converted into an act of aggression directed simultaneously towards his master and the villagers. He overturns his master's eloquence by provoking the reaction of offense and humiliation that his master's speech aims to mitigate. Yet his braying is not left unanswered. In the activities of carnival, an act of just retribution, in which the aggressor is transformed into victim, is the usual outcome. The villagers set aside their halberts and lances, pick up stones and begin to attack Don Quixote and Sancho. The knight is able to flee on Rocinante but the culprit is caught in the middle of the attack. Don Quixote observes from a distance, but he is not left unscathed. The noble ideals of war he had so recently defended are lost among the shower of stones, his heroic task thus reversed.

The replacement of the heroic figure at war by a figure from the animal world forms an essential part of comic imagery. This type of substitution is widely represented in Cervantes' text in the final component of Don Quixote's trappings: his horse. In romance and epic, the origin and character of the horse are a reflection of the character and destiny of his master. He is represented as being larger than life and superior in strength, intelligence, and speed to the ordinary horse. He has human understanding, a heroic spirit, and even the ability to fly (Potter 17). The knight tries to integrate this ideal image of the steed of the hero into his disguise of knight errant, after having prepared his arms and reconstructed his helmet for the second time. The narrator counteracts this attempt as he makes comparisons that invert the knight's ideal image:

> Fue luego a ver su rocín, y aunque tenía más cuartos que un real y más tachas que el caballo de Gonela, que *tantum pellis et ossa fuit*, le pareció que ni el Bucéfalo de Alejandro ni Babieca el del Cid con él se igualaban. (I, 1: 75-76)

The heroic horse is stripped of his mask of superior strength and revealed in all of his thinness. The bony anatomy and bald spots suggest death and decay. The portrait of hunger puts into action the process of destruction of the being and gives rise to a body in retreat. The skeletal anatomy denotes an exhausted, pathetic horse with a spirit lacking in inventiveness, adventure and insight.

In the knight's encounter with the galleyslaves, Rocinante begins to give proof of his death-like spirit. The knight spurs Rocinante on in order to escape from the stoning, but the narrator explains that "no hacía más caso de la espuela que si fuera hecho de bronce" (I, 22: 276). In the knight's attack on the procession of penitents, he digs his heels into Rocinante and manages to persuade the horse to go at a canter, a feat that is unusual, the narrator informs us, since "carrera tirada no se lee en toda esta verdadera historia que jamás la diese Rocinante" (I, 52: 599). The weak horse does not even need to be brought to a halt. As the knight reaches the procession, Rocinante "ya llevaba deseo de quietarse un poco" (599). The image of the tired horse is exemplified at the end of the first day's journey. The knight arrives at the inn and approaches the door, for he notices that his horse is in a hurry to retreat to the stables in order to rest. Upon leaving the inn the following day, the knight comes upon a road opening up in four directions. Imitating the knights of romance, he lets his horse decide which road to take. The domesticated horse can think of taking no other than the one that leads to his stable.

The horse's bony anatomy and his naturally skittish nature reverse the myth of the flying horse, in which the hero's ascending destiny towards heroism is fulfilled. Resonances of folk humor are found in the descending movements of the knight's hack. As Knud Togeby states, Rocinante is "símbolo del tropiezo" (74). When the knight attacks the merchants from Toledo, Rocinante falls and throws his master to the ground. In the Wagon of Death episode, Rocinante, frightened by the clown's bells, flees and finally throws his master. The knight's glorious entrance to a big city is parodied as the knight enters Barcelona in the company of Don Antonio. Some young boys tie furze on Rocinante's tail, causing the horse such discomfort that he jumps and finally throws his master to the ground.

The conditions that invert the image of the flying horse are shared by other horses in the text. These conditions have an important impact on the outcome of the battles in which the knight becomes engaged. Indeed, in the knight's duels with the Basque and the knight of the Mirrors, his victories are due more to the defects of his opponents' steeds than to the knight's meritorious action. In the duel with the Basque, the narrator explains that the Basque would have liked to dismount because the hired mule he was riding could not be trusted. The Basque braces himself for the knight's approach, unable to charge because the mule will not move in any direction, "que ya, de puro cansada y no hecha a semejantes niñerías, no podía dar un paso" (I, 8: 137). In spite of this count against him the Basque is able to deal the first blow. The knight returns the attack with a blow that ends the battle. Yet stunned as he is, the Basque manages to stay on his mule for a bit. Only when the terrified beast begins to run about does the Basque lose control, to be finally thrown and defeated.

In the episode of the knight's duel with the Knight of the Mirrors, the narrator's stable irony systematically precludes the reader's possible acceptance of Don Quixote's alleged victory over his opponent. The narrator first intrudes to call attention to Sansón's horse. He compares it to Rocinante, claiming that "no era más ligero ni de mejor parecer que Rocinante" (II, 14: 142). He informs the reader that when Sansón halts in the middle of his charge to watch Sancho's ascent into a tree, his horse is most grateful, "a causa que ya no podía moverse" (142). The narrator finally emphasizes the role that luck plays in the knight's victory when he explains that in addition to Sansón's problem with his steed, Rocinante perversely deviates from his naturally tranquil conduct and manages to ride at a gallop as a one-time response to his master's spurring:

> Don Quijote, que le pareció que ya su enemigo venía volando, arrimó reciamente las espuelas a las trasijadas ijadas de Rocinante, y le hizo aguijar de manera, que cuenta la historia que esta sola vez se conoció haber corrido algo; porque todas las demás siempre fueron trotes declarados. . . . (142)[13]

The knight is thus able to attack and defeat his opponent who at the time is at a complete standstill, entangled with his horse and lance. The narrator's final comments exaggerate Sansón's obstacles, in a manner that eliminates the merit of the knight's victory:

> En esta buena sazón y coyuntura halló don Quijote a su contrario, embarazado con su caballo y ocupado con su lanza, que nunca o no acertó, o no tuvo lugar de ponerla en ristre. Don Quijote, que no miraba en estos inconvenientes, *a salvamano y sin peligro alguno* encontró al de los Espejos, con tanta fuerza, que mal de su grado le hizo venir al suelo por las ancas del caballo, dando tal caída, que sin mover pie ni mano, dio señales de que estaba muerto. (143, emphasis added)

The duel waged in defense of the beauty of the knight's damsel is a constituent part of the knight's task. As portrayed in chivalric romance, the knight's duties as defender of the idealization of love might include the protection of a damsel in distress, or perhaps the display of a conduct that causes beautiful women to admire and fall in love with him, such as courage or extraordinary valor.[14] Rocinante is instrumental in parodying the ideal of human love, as he threatens this part of the knight's task.

The narrative sequence which includes the adventure with the Yanguesan muleteers and the knight's second meeting with Maritornes at the loft or attic of the inn illustrates Rocinante's aggression against his master. In both scenes, the hack reveals his capacity for

---

[13] Luck and coincidental acts appear as conventions in the comic work of art, employed to undermine the epic concept of heroic destiny. Predmore explores these conventions in his study on *Don Quixote* and reaches the conclusion that the adventures of the knight are governed by a doctrine of error.

[14] On the conventions of the romances of chivalry and the characteristics and functions of the characters, see Eisenberg, *A Study of "Don Quixote,"* 109-56.

movement and vitality in precisely those circumstances where his habitual dormant nature would have protected his master against failing in his task. In the meeting with the Yanguesans, Rocinante's sexual desire for the Yanguesan mares is set against the noble Grisóstomo's idealized love for Marcela, narrated in the preceding chapter. In her speech at Grisóstomo's funeral, Marcela had defended her innocence with regard to the desperate passion that had driven the young man to suicide. The freedom of the heart's will granted her the right not to have reciprocated his desires. Grisóstomo's love and implicitly Don Quixote's love for Dulcinea are refracted through the figure and actions of Rocinante, who in the following scene is taken with the desire to "refocilarse con las señoras facas, y saliendo, así como las olió, de su natural paso y costumbre, sin pedir licencia a su dueño, tomó un trotico algo picadillo y se fue a comunicar su necesidad con ellas" (I, 15: 191).

Rocinante's lustful advances are a comic imitation of Grisóstomo's insistent demands for Marcela's love. The aggression of the mares, who reply to Rocinante's advances with teeth and hooves, imitates Marcela's fatal indifference in a manner that causes the reader to question the ideal of free will that her conduct is to uphold. Her cruelty acts as a first step that alienates the reader from this or any doctrine she espouses and prepares the reader to beware of any possible identification with her. Her philosophy of free will ("yo nací libre") is then thrown incongruously against Rocinante's creature instincts, where it is suddenly seen as an ideal that cannot hold up to reality. In her escape into the country, Marcela had attempted to recreate a world based on art, that of the pastoral novel, a world excluding all physical needs, attractions or desires, and denying physical matter in support of the ideal of spiritual purity. Rocinante's movement takes us back out of art and into reality and reminds us that human beings are subject to animal instincts, and only with much difficulty can they ever be free of them.

The comic reversal of heroic action occurs when the knight finds that he is obliged to come to the defense of his hack. The knight carries out his task backwards, defending the seducer against the "lady" who is attacked. The outcome is that the knight himself is rendered defenseless and receives the same treatment as Rocinante for his error when, with one blow of the muleteers' pack staff, he is beaten and thrown to the earth.

The romance sequence of the rescue of the damsel in distress is carried over and completed in the following episode. The knight is resting on his make-shift bed in the loft alongside the rich muleteer from Arévalo, who is waiting for the servant girl Maritornes to come to his bed. When the young Maritornes tiptoes in to join the muleteer, the knight erroneously believes that the daughter of the warden of the "castle" is coming to visit him. The physical portrait of Maritornes and the description of her actions materialize the female ideal the knight defends and at the same time undermine the ideal heroic conduct he wishes to imitate. Her agreement to "fool around" ("refocilarse") with the muleteer aligns her conduct with that of Rocinante, who was also described as wanting to "refocilarse" with the mares. The link between the animal lust of Rocinante and that of Maritornes is further underscored as the narrator likens the coarseness of her hair to that of a horse's mane. In the "starry" loft, a resting place more appropriate for animals than for human beings, the figure of the horse and its creatural desire is superimposed on the figure of Maritornes.

Don Quixote's heroic conduct is in turn reversed when he seizes the servant girl's wrist tightly. As he feels her shift and draws her close to him, forcing her to sit on his bed while she struggles to free herself, the knight acts against the very codes of chivalry that he had defended on behalf of Marcela (the defense of the security of the lady and of the freedom of the heart's will). Don Quixote carries out his quest backwards as he places himself in the role of Rocinante, the seducer. Inversely, the carrier acts as "knight." Seeing his "damsel" struggling, he enters into a duel to rescue her from the seducer just as the Yanguesan muleteers had come to the defense of their "lady" mares.

Rocinante plays an instrumental role in undermining his master's task of knight errantry as he is again thrown together with Maritornes in Chapter 43 of Part I. The priest and barber have retrieved the knight from the Sierra Morena, and they are resting at the inn for the night while they plan how to take their friend back to the village. That evening Don Quixote decides to stand watch over the "castle," in imitation of his chivalric heroes. Mounted on his hack, he begins to lament over Dulcinea, but is suddenly interrupted by the voices of two ladies calling to him.

The romance sequence of the highborn lady smitten with love for the knight is reproduced in two consecutive parts: Maritornes' seduction of the knight on behalf of her "lady" and Rocinante's seduction by a recently arrived mare. The actions of the participants of each dramatic segment mirror one another and in turn reflect back on the romance sequence the knight wishes to imitate.

The first segment begins as the knight falls for Maritornes' practical joke. He believes her and the innkeeper's daughter to be beauteous damsels, the common hayloft a magnificent castle, and the hole in the hayloft from which she and the innkeeper's daughter call him a window with a gilded grating. Flattered by their attentions, Don Quixote approaches to tell the ladies that he cannot be unfaithful to Dulcinea. When Maritornes claims that her lady will be satisfied with merely touching his hand, the knight finally acquiesces. He stands on Rocinante and puts his hand through the hole. Maritornes seizes it, ties a rope around his wrist and secures the rope to the hayloft door. This first scene ends as the giggling Maritornes and the innkeeper's daughter make their exit. The knight is left standing on his horse, held tight by the wrist to the hayloft hole as Maritornes had previously been held tight by the wrist by Don Quixote. Rocinante's conduct in this first segment is crucial, for the knight's only possibility of not being left hanging above the ground is contingent upon Rocinante not budging even an inch.

The second scene begins as several horsemen ride up to the inn. During a brief interchange between the horsemen and the knight, one of the traveler's mares smells Rocinante and the latter moves to reciprocate the act. The narrator's ironic commentary underscores Rocinante's role as inadvertent adversary of his master. He first reiterates Rocinante's gentle nature, stating that the knight's fears that Rocinante might move are unfounded "puesto que de la paciencia y quietud de Rocinante bien se podía esperar que estaría sin moverse un siglo entero" (I, 43: 528-529). He adds that when the mare initially smelled Rocinante, he was standing "melancólico y triste, con las orejas caídas" (44: 531). The narrator then contrasts this lifeless image with a description of Rocinante's uncontrollable animal urge, creating the "carne"/"leño" paradox: ". . . y como, en fin, era de carne, aunque parecía de leño, no pudo dejar de resentirse y tornar a oler a quien le llegaba a hacer caricias" (531). Both the conduct of death-like inaction that negates human passion and the blind submission to one's instincts are set in opposition to the ideal of human love the hero wishes to imitate and defend.

Rocinante's single movement is the culminating point of both dramatic segments. He thrusts downward his master's attempt to exalt human love with the display of his natural instincts. At the same time he literally causes his master to fall, collaborating with and completing Maritornes' action against the heroic task. As he moves towards the mare, the knight loses his sole means of support and is left hanging a small distance from the ground, again by his wrist. The still portrait of the hanging knight represents the transformation of the idealized hero into an inanimate carnival "pelele" or "monigote," the carnival dummy. This figure, a symbol of death and evil, is hung in the center of the marketplace where it is made target of various rites of expulsion and persecution.[15] The scene ends as dawn breaks and the knight's loud protests cause the entire inn to awaken. Maritornes, guessing the reason, rushes to the loft and unties the knight, causing him to plummet to the earth, his usual destination.

Inevitably, the comic imitation of the ideal hero leads to the hero's unmasking. As the objects that give birth to the knight (arms, armor, and steed) are projected into action, the identity the protagonist hopes to attain, that of defender of the needy, is substituted by its opposite, the persecuted sacrificial victim. Paradoxically, the birth of the carnival hero/clown is inseparable from his death. This duality finds its most characteristic expression in the comic image of the body.

In contrast to the classical image of the finished, completed man, the comic body is portrayed in moments of copulation, pregnancy, birth, old age, disintegration and dismemberment. In the bellicose action of carnival, human bodies and members are transformed. Joints are dislocated, arms battered, noses flattened, eyes knocked out, ribs smashed, members and organs wounded, thrashed and smashed into pulp. Such action has an "anatomizing" function. It transforms the body into meat that can be devoured and thus give new life. The enemy is slaughtered like hogs, his intestines are seen coming out, and after the slaughter a banquet is held. The intestines of the dead animals and their carcasses are seen roasting on the spit:

---

[15] As Caro Baroja points out (63), since carnival is a "play" or a dramatic representation of what was originally an act of "murder," the central figure of carnival activities is often a doll or dummy, substitute for the human figure.

The fighting temperament (war, battles) and the kitchen cross each other at a certain point, and this point is the dismembered minced flesh. Culinary images accompanying battle scenes were widely used in the fifteenth and sixteenth centuries; they were frequent precisely in the sphere where literature was connected with the folk tradition of humor. Pulci compared the battlefield of Ronceveaux to "a kettle filled with blood-stew of heads, legs, and other members of the human body. (Bakhtin, *Rabelais* 193-94)

In Cervantes' work, all of the components of the dying and devouring image of the comic hero are present: the knight's teeth are knocked out in the battle with the armies of sheep; in the meeting with the merchants from Toledo he is beaten; in the duel with the Basque, he loses half an ear; in the battle with the Yanguesans, his ribs are battered; and in the duel with the muleteers from Arévalo, his ribs are trod on. Yet the action of becoming, the renewing and regenerating aspect of the comic, is neutralized. In Cervantes' work, the action focuses principally on the rites of expulsion and the uncrowning of the hero, while the regenerating images that accompany such scenes are absent.

The images of the body rent to pieces are accompanied in Cervantes' work instead by images of hunger and deprivation. The feasts and banquets are replaced by fasts or by the frugal diet of Lent. In the battle with the wine bags, the blood of the hero is indeed transformed into wine, but the regenerating drink spills out onto the ground and is wasted. While the abstinent knight is regenerated by the balm of Fierabrás, Sancho practically dies from it. The concoction is made primarily out of oil. The replacement of wine by oil represents a shift from carnival's indulgence in the life-giving forces to Lenten abstinence. While wine liberates and introduces the carnival participant into the gay world of laughter and new truth, oil is symbol of official seriousness, of the old world, of the *agelasts*, those who do not know how to laugh (286).

The image of the body most frequently presented in Cervantes' work is that of the body subject to hunger. Don Quixote's imitation of the more ascetic side of chivalry works against his task of knight errantry by eventually weakening his physical condition. The carnival clown is frequently transformed into sacrificial victim by being denied food. He is prohibited from participating in the feast and is thus turned into a figure of Lent, symbol of maceration, solitude and affliction (Adrados 400-450; Redondo, "El personaje de Don Quijote"). In the text, Don Quixote turns himself into victim, rejecting the feasts and warm beds of the court knight. His first sally takes place on Friday, the day of penance. After fasting all day, he arrives an an inn where he is offered codfish, a food identified with Lenten starvation. On his second sally the knight continues his abstinence. He wishes to sustain himself exclusively on the sweet memories of his lady and requests that Sancho serve him foods that are conventionally offered to the carnival victim and associated with Lent, cheese, onion, bread, and dried fruit.

Since indulgence in food and drink forms an essential aspect of carnival, the mouth is the most important human feature. The comic face is actually reduced to the gaping mouth. Examples of comic masks with the large, gaping mouths are typically found in the Commedia dell'Arte. The gaping mouth and the long jaw form part of the portrait of Don Quixote, but these features have lost their function. They are disconnected from the generating activities of eating and drinking.

At the beginning of the novel, the narrator explains that perhaps the gentleman's name is "Quijada," a word that alludes to the image of the long jaw. As the knight passes to his task of knight errantry, the mask of the long jaw becomes more accentuated. In the midnight duel with the mule carrier from Arévalo, the latter discharges a blow on the narrow jaws of the knight and leaves them in a weakened condition. The loss or absence of the teeth contributes to the process of disfigurement of the jaw, causing it to lose its functional value, for the toothless mouth transforms the image of the gaping or engorging jaw into the "sagging" jaw. In the knight's battle with the warring armies of sheep, a good number of his teeth are knocked out. Sancho later informs him that only two molars remain in the lower jaw and none in the upper one. The knight expresses his dismay as he tells Sancho that "la boca sin muelas es como un molino sin piedra y en mucho más se ha de estimar un diente que un diamante" (I, 18: 227). Indeed, the tooth is also referred to as "hueso," a term employed to connote the male sexual organ. The tooth is associated with masculinity while toothlessness is linked with the crib or death.[16]

---

[16] On the concept of decay of the human body and its relation to the comic and the grotesque, see Iffland, I: 146-148.

The knight's jaws are rendered completely dysfunctional in what should be the culminating moment of his heroic quest: his encounter with the duke and duchess. During his first day's stay at their palace, the knight is treated for the first time as if he were truly of royal lineage. His ideal self-image is promptly neutralized when he removes his armor. The narrator describes him as "seco, alto, tendido, con las quijadas, que por de dentro se besaba la una con la otra" (II, 31: 276). The jaws are described as coming so close together that it seems that neither food nor drink can be ingested. He is the image of Lenten death.

The image of the skinny body and the sagging jaw is accompanied by another image of decay and death in the text, that of the deathly color and texture of the skin. The knight's skin is described by the narrator and other characters as the skin of a dead or mummified body, withered, wrinkled, dried up, and yellowish in color. These descriptions appear towards the end of Part I and at the beginning of Part II. They are important because they confirm the cumulative negative results of Don Quixote's imitation of the ideal knight's bellicose action, an imitation that forms the core of the knight's quest in Part I. In Chapter 37 of Part I, Don Fernando and his companions are surprised by the appearance of the knight: "Suspendió a don Fernando y a los demás la extraña presencia de don Quijote, viendo su rostro de media legua de andadura, seco y amarillo, la desigualdad de sus armas . . . " (458). A young lad that witnesses the knight's entrance to his village describes him to the housekeeper and niece as "flaco y amarillo" (I, 52: 602). Finally, at the beginning of Part II, the priest and barber pay a visit to the knight and they find him "tan seco y amojamado, que no parecía sino hecho de carne momia" (II, 1: 42).

The successful completion of the chivalric adventure serves as proof of the chivalric knight's heroic identity. Don Quixote's inability to comply with the authority of the written word and represent his role well, and the systematic uncovering of his essential fraudulence underscore the ephemeral, fictitious character of the model – of the model's strength, passion, purity, and suffering. The double-directed, dialogical discourse of Cervantes' work aims its violence not only at the figure of Don Quixote, but also at genres that veil the false or fictional nature of the idol behind the *areté* of the hero. The comic reconstruction of the romance hero functions to neutralize the power of romance to reflect a transcendental truth. By exposing the "fiction" of romance, Cervantes is able to bring to the reader's consciousness the resilient power of human deception, a power of which Don Quixote, reader of romance, remains ignorant.

The circle of birth and death that is repeated throughout the narration, initiating and terminating the narrative sequences as well as each sally, is reproduced in the last chapter of the narration, in a final description of the knight's decay. The description appears, ironically, at the moment that Cide Hamete reflects on his "creation" and the "birth" of Don Quixote.

With the appearance of the publication of Avellaneda's *Quixote*, the Arab historian/narrator's mask of "chronicler" is stripped off, unveiling his difference with respect to his model, the scribe of romance. Avellaneda's false continuation of the text reveals the "artist" behind the mask of scribe and causes the historian to make arbitrary changes in his work in order to avoid any similarities with the text of another rival, that "escritor fingido y tordesillesco." Avellaneda's act of aggression places Cide Hamete in a position of victim and instills in him an attitude of sympathy and alliance towards Don Quixote. His sense of dominance over his work and character and his pride in his artistry cause him to take measures to prevent any future threat against his creation. In an act of self-defense and revenge against Avellaneda, the narrator ironically turns against his character. Addressing his pen, he offers a final portrait of Don Quixote in complete decay as he advises his pen to let the knight rest:

> ... que deje reposar en la sepultura los cansados y ya podridos huesos de don Quijote, y no le quiera llevar, contra todos los fueros de la muerte, a Castilla la Vieja, haciéndole salir de la fuesa, donde real y verdaderamente yace tendido de largo a largo, imposibilitado de hacer tercera jornada y salida nueva. . . . (II, 64: 593)

The tale ends as the idealized image of the hero's soul rising up to Paradise, described in romance and the epic, is topographically reversed in the putrefied image of the hero's decaying cadaver. The desire of Don Quixote to be knight errant results in the renunciation of the knightly mask and in the biological death of the hero. His demise eternally reifies the chivalric hero turned surrogate victim in a manner that denies renewal, and the circle of the birth and death of the hero is finally closed.[17]

---

[17] Gump Stewart, 86, views the death of Alonso Quijano, on the contrary, as "the birth of a new understanding of heroism" a heroism which is "brought down to earth and humanized" and which affirms human existence, change, and renewal.

CHAPTER 3

THE HERO DIVIDED

Analysis of the ritual elements informing Don Quixote's character and action points to an underlying technique in the building of the comic hero, that of "condensation." In the figure of the knight, the old and the new, originally bearing a relationship of identification, are made to confront one another. In the comic, paradoxically, opposition and aggression always involve the use of methods of imitation and identification. The comic character may also be portrayed by means of a technique of "splitting," whereby at least two characters come to embody the model. The twin voices debate and dialogue with each other. As they do so, the double's conduct, in turn based on a technique of imitation, unmasks the ideals to which they both lay claim.

The figure of the double has been linked to primitive fertility rites by Frazer and Cornford.[1] Frazer explains that in primitive ceremony, the king's roles and duties are split between two characters who are clearly identified with each other but who become "contenders" in order to fulfill the demands of the ceremony. In the rite, the old king identified with the dying year was sacrificed because he was invested with the divine power of the gods and represented a threat to their power. The guilt feeling of the tribe that arose from carrying out such a "crime" caused the action to be diverted or transferred to another figure, a double of the king. The king maintained his power and control, while his more unpleasant duties were performed by a secondary figure, often a member of the tribe, a simpleton, a fool, an outcast. He was accompanied by other figures wearing animal masks that represented their gods.

---

[1] For a discussion of Frazer's and Cornford's theories on the relation of primitive myth to the literary work, see Sypher, 21-51.

As civilization progressed, the murder was eventually substituted by a mere contest, dialogue, or debate between the mock-king or *alazon*, an Imposter ("He Who Dares to Look") and the young king who was to replace him. The young king's role as "antagonist" was sometimes assumed by another figure, the *eiron* or Questioner ("The Ironical Man"). The contest was followed by the expulsion and sacrifice of the former.

At the heart of Old Comedy is the reenactment of the ancient fertility rite.[2] The duty of the young king *eiron* is to bring the *alazon* to confusion, deflate the "boaster" or "unwelcome intruder." The king or father figure is venerated and reviled, crowned and sacrificed, and finally converted into "clown," alter ego of the *eiron* himself. On the other hand, the *eiron* is similar to the god-imposter, for as he transforms the king/god into fool, he is seen as wise, even divine. As his counterparts in the fertility rite, he is made victim of other participants in the representation. Like the *alazon*, his character encloses a double possibility.

Ritual action and characters are present in New Comedy as shown in Aristotle's *Ethics* (VII, 4, lines 7-8). Aristotle mentions Socrates as the "mock modest" character who understates things. He is the Questioner who uses philosophical buffoonery to seek the truth and wears the ugly mask of the satyr or clown. His tactic is that of gaining victory by professing ignorance. Pretending to be stupid, he asks supposedly innocent questions of the "Impostor," the so-called wise men of Athens. His false disingenuousness intends to mislead its hearers. He is a wise guy (socarrón), an entertainer, although at times he is considered sacred and holy. He is a master of disguise. His irony defeats the enemy on his own ground, for in the course of the debate, the wisdom of the *alazon* is reduced to absurdity. Socrates thus corrects the folly of those who claim to know the "truth," and he, the clown, devil, jester, buffoon and tempter, proves to be wiser than the wisdom of the world.

The Renaissance tradition of the fool is patterned after the model of Socrates as well as the tradition of the carnival fool. He manifests all the attributes of the natural fool. As descendent from primitive myth and medieval spectacle, he is a simple, pot-bellied dim-wit whose life is governed by his creature comforts. Walter

---

[2] Frye discusses the comic characters *eiron* and *alazon* and traces their evolution from Old Greek Comedy through the present, 172.

Kaiser describes him as "the most playful creation of 'homo ludens'." He "comes to us as Brueghel painted him out of the village festival and the dramatic antics of rude mechanicals. He is the spirit of Carnival" (172).

Kaiser further describes the fool's development, departing from the medieval conception of the fool, not only as it became manifest in the ideal world of carnival, but in the real world as well.[3] In the Middle Ages, he was called a "natural fool." The artificial fool, that is, he who "played" the fool, did not exist until the fifteenth century. The medieval fool was considered to be natural because, unconscious of the rules of propriety, he performed his natural functions "naturally" and without sophistication. When he was hungry he ate, when he was happy he laughed, when he was sad he cried. Because he was not intelligent enough to remember the past or think of the future, he had no cares or fears and was believed to be happier in his simplicity than others in their wisdom. Because he did not comprehend society's conventions, he disregarded them. For this reason, he was considered a potentially subversive element. Because he was a fool, finally, he was tolerated and even given a certain privilege or "license" to speak, a privilege that was to be passed down to the artificial fool.

Not only was the fool countenanced by the society against which he rebelled, but also by the religious authority to which he was irreverent. He was tolerated by the church, Kaiser explains, because the profound simplicity of his childlike speech indicated a special affinity with Christian truth. He was granted license to speak because it was possible that when the fool's babbling was not idiotic, it was "theopneustic" or divinely inspired (8). Theologically this attitude was sanctioned by Saint Paul who taught that men must become fools for Christ's sake. He had preached that those who were considered wise by the world should become fools in order to become truly wise. This paradoxical concept of the "wise fool" finally allows the figure of the fool to acquire spiritual stature. It was not, however, until the end of the Middle Ages, with

---

[3] Swain and Welsford have documented the social, historical and literary importance of the Renaissance fool. Because Kaiser does incorporate their findings in his study, and makes an effort to go beyond them to define the relationship of the learned tradition of Renaissance Humanism and the figure of the fool, I will refer henceforth exclusively to his study.

the emergence of the northern school of mysticism associated with the names of Eckhart, Ruysbrock and Groot, and the movement known as the *devotio moderna*, that Pauline theology was extended and justified.

Two other men were finally to lend greater philosophical complexity to the fool: Thomas Kempis, with his paradoxical notion of "holy simplicity," and Nicholas Cusanus, with his paradoxical concepts of *docta ignorantia* (learned ignorance) and *coincidentia oppositorum* (the concord of opposites). The teachings of Cusanus laid the groundwork for what were to become the major preoccupations of Renaissance ideology.[4] His teachings centered on the problem of how man is able to attain knowledge of the world and a true perception of reality. In the sixteenth and seventeenth centuries, these concerns would give rise to skepticism, an important school of thought for both theologians and humanists. Cusanus concluded that wisdom is derived from the antithesis between the irrational absolute and logical reason. Wisdom can be acquired by being conscious of such contradictions, by rejecting rational theology and attempting to find the middle road between two extremes. The figure of the "wise fool" embodied this philosophy of wisdom.

Cusanus directly influenced the philosophical assumptions upon which Erasmus' fool was conceived. Erasmus' work in turn had an important influence on such writers as Rabelais, Shakespeare and Cervantes. His work, *In Praise of Folly*, is an examination of the values of the Renaissance, values that had been passed down from the Middle Ages: the concept of vices and virtues established by the church, and the values and conventions of society established by laws and institutions. The technique that Erasmus uses to break down these values in order to criticize them can be explained by means of Edgar Wind's discussion of the concept of "transvaluation of values" in his work *Pagan Mysteries in the Renaissance* (53-80). According to Wind, Western ethics continuously alternates between stoicism, that is, law, custom and convention, and the epicurean standard of "nature," a corrective to excessive stoicism. The

---

[4] Panofsky, 234-234, affirms that the idea that one must put reason into doubt in order to achieve wisdom is characteristic of Renaissance thought, and that this idea can already be found in Cusanus' paradoxical philosophy. Cassirer, 7, asserts that in order to understand the philosophy of the Renaissance, the works of Cusanus must be taken as a point of departure.

revival of epicureanism in the sixteenth century and its confrontation with stoicism constitutes an integral part of the transvaluation of values. Wind exemplifies the concept of transvaluation in his discussion of the sin of irascibility:

> So much has been written in recent years on the continuation of the Middle Ages into the Renaissance, and of medieval modes of thought in Renaissance platonism, that we are apt to underestimate the decisive "transvaluation of values" which Ficino and some of his Florentine friends effected in the theory of morals. A noble form of irascibility, for instance, remained a contradiction in terms as long as *ira* was classed irrevocable as a deadly sin. Yet under the influence of Seneca's *De ira*, although the medieval classification continued, a "noble rage" was separated off from the common vice and defended as a virtue by Florentine humanists, in particular by Bruni, Palmieri, Politian and Landino. (68)

It should be noted that the transvaluation of values could, in the same manner that it transmutes vices into virtues, convert virtues into vices. The accepted values of wisdom, honor and virtue, the concepts of the stoics upon which humanism since Petrarch had based its premises, could thus be put into doubt. An image that is emblematic of Dame Folly's entire speech and one that reflects the direct relation between Erasmus' "philosophy of the fool" and the concept of the comic in general is that of the *Silenus*. Erasmus' source is Alcibiades' comparison of Socrates in the *Symposium* to a grotesque figurine of a *Silenus*, which opened up to reveal the image of a god inside.[5] In Erasmus' work, Dame Folly tells us that all human affairs are like the *Sileni* of Alcibiades and have two aspects, so that for any given truth, the opposite may equally be true. If you open up a *Silenus*, you will find everything reversed. The mask must be stripped off in order to arrive at the esoteric meaning contained within. This is the principle of arcane literature. The entire concept of the transvaluation of values is based upon this simple premise. No longer are vice and virtue or jest and earnestness placed in antithesis. In the Renaissance, the one is concealed within the other (Kaiser 19-91).

---

[5] The *Silenus* is discussed by Plato in the *Symposium*, 215 a-b and by Rabelais at the beginning of *Gargantua and Pantagruel*.

In Forcione's insightful analysis of the influence of Erasmus on Cervantes' thought, he shows how Erasmus relates the question of sin and virtue to the problem of nature, in a manner that reconciles the epicurean standard of nature and stoic law (*Cervantes and the Humanist Vision* 160-169). For Erasmus, man is a being who bears within his reason a spark of the Creator. The Creator has imprinted on man's spirit a natural virtue, which is a replica of the divine spirit. Thus, man is inclined by nature to fit into this "mold" of goodness. By exercising his "right" reason, which could include the passions if directed towards creative purposes, and by rejecting the "law" of scholastic philosophy in favor of the value of observation and experience, man acquires knowledge of self and the world and acts in harmony with what the Creator has unfolded in the universe.[6]

The dynamics of the relationship between Don Quixote and Sancho can be grasped by comparing their actions and interaction with the behavior of the *alazon/eiron* pair both in its primitive and its Renaissance development. The values the knight espouses are inverted, questioned and redefined as Sancho expresses his bodily desires and inadvertently or intentionally ridicules his master's actions and words.

The transvaluation of values emerges naturally in the text as the initial similarity of goals that cause the knight and squire to become peaceably identified with each other gives way to an ensuing incompatibility. Sancho's consequent aggression toward his master, based on mimetic devices, will ultimately hold up to scrutiny the merit of his master's role as knight errant and the worthiness of the heroic world he wishes to restore. While tracing this development in the pages that follow, the extent to which Sancho may or may not embody an ethical norm of natural reason and wisdom and offer an alternative code of conduct to his master's rigid adherence to the dogma and authority of chivalric law, humanism, and neoplatonic philosophy will be assessed.

---

[6] The influence of Erasmus on Spanish writers and on Cervantes in particular has been studied by Abellán, Avalle-Arce, "Cervantes and the Renaissance" in *Cervantes and the Renaissance*, 5-6, Bataillon, Castro and Vilanova, 423-433. For an overview of the disparate theories on the influence of Erasmus on Cervantes, see Forcione, *Cervantes and the Humanist Vision*, esp. 13-20. His study, which is completed with *Cervantes and the Mystery of Lawlessness*, attempts to seek a configuration of ideas that link the two writers. It is an invaluable contribution to Cervantine criticism.

In Chapter 7 of Part I of *Don Quixote*, Sancho begins to undertake adventures with Don Quixote. The narrator tells us that he is a farmer and neighbor of Don Quixote, and describes him in terms that align him with the dim-witted natural fool: "hombre de bien ... pero de muy poca sal en la mollera," (I, 7: 125). Sancho's behavior and actions in the first adventures with his master seem to bear out the narrator's initial assertion and reveal the many facets of the natural fool's personality. He is portrayed as gullible and superstitious, for he believes in the "miracle" Don Quixote offers him in order to persuade him to serve him as squire – the possibility of becoming king: "... bien podría ser que antes de seis días ganase yo tal reino que tuviese otros a él adherentes, que viniesen de molde para coronarte por rey de uno de ellos" (127). Proof of his belief in the existence of giants can be found in the episode of the windmills when, on his master's insistence of their presence, Sancho naively asks "¿Qué gigantes?" (I, 8: 129). He is shown as greedy as he rushes in to collect the spoils of battle after the confrontation with the Benedictine friars in the adventure of the corpse and in the winning of Mambrino's helmet; a glutton in the aftermath of the battle with the warring armies of sheep when he is ready to abandon his master upon discovering that the pack saddle containing the *alhajas* is missing; lazy and unrefined in the meal with the goat herders in Chapter 11 of Part I, when he would rather go to sleep than listen to the love poetry read by one of the enamored goatherds; and cowardly in the two nocturnal adventures, the adventure with the corpse and the adventure with the fulling mills.

Sancho seeks an easy road to wealth and fame.[7] Given that he lives only to fulfill his present desires and to avoid physical pain and suffering, his relationship with Don Quixote seems to have an intrinsic explosive quality to it. His acceptance of the duties of squire causes him to form an alliance with the knight, but one whose benefits are, at least initially, unequally distributed. Don Quixote's adventures, successful or not, allow him to play out his fantasy of becoming a knight errant. From the very beginning, his task of knighthood is at least partially self-fulfilling. Sancho, on the

---

[7] Charney, 160-161, explains that the natural fool is recalcitrant to carrying out any type of moral obligation, an implicit part of any human commitment. He lives for the moment and wit becomes a lifestyle that replaces any moral, ethical, or religious consideration.

contrary, enters into the alliance performing a sacrifice. He gives and performs services for a reward he believes he will receive in the very near future and in exchange for physical protection he believes he will receive in the present.

As he enters into situations in which he is subjected to hunger, fear, physical assaults, and defeat in battle, Sancho experiences disillusion in his master's ability to carry out his promises and seeks retribution. In the ensuing episodes, linked together in a chain of cause and effect, either Sancho is turned into victim by Don Quixote as a result of the latter's failure to defend or reward him, or Don Quixote is turned into victim by Sancho.

In one of the earliest adventures, the battle with the Benedictine friars, Sancho's physical comforts are threatened. After "defeating" the friars, Don Quixote quickly moves on to challenge the Basque to a duel while Sancho lingers on in order to claim the spoils of the battle, the friars' habits. A servant boy approaches, throws the squire down and gives him a beating. Having escaped punishment for his error in mistaking the friars for demons, Don Quixote forgets about Sancho. The boaster thus flaunts the gods and even his own destiny.[8] He is oblivious to danger and to all human limitations. He is like the high wire equilibrist who by some magical effect seems to be free from the law of gravity, who cannot fall because the illusion of his "heroism" will then be broken. The unpleasant duties of his office are assumed by Sancho, the fall guy, who pays for his master's error by sacrificing his creatural well-being.

After the battle with the Basque is over, Sancho asks for compensation for his suffering: "–Sea vuestra merced servido, señor don Quijote mío, de darme el gobierno de la ínsula que en esta rigurosa pendencia se ha ganado. . . ." Instead of satisfying his squire's demand however, Don Quixote frustrates any hopes Sancho might harbor about having it fulfilled. He prolongs payment of his debt to an unknown future date and indicates to Sancho that more beatings are in store for him in the immediate future: "–Advertid, hermano Sancho, que esta aventura y las a ésta semejantes no son aventuras de ínsulas, sino de encrucijadas, en las cuales no se gana otra cosa que sacar rota la cabeza o una oreja menos" (I, 10: 147).

---

[8] On the concept of comic illusion and the comic hero, see Charney, 144-45.

Sancho's bodily suffering is further compounded with his fear of being imprisoned by the Holy Brotherhood as a consequence of his master's aggression against the friars and the Basque. The knight assures his squire that he will defend him, but his failure to have done so instills in Sancho a more aggressive attitude towards his master. When Don Quixote asks Sancho if he has ever read of a knight more valiant than he, Sancho, assuming the disguise of ironic deflater, gives a seemingly straightforward response, but one that disguises a subtle aggression, for his replacement of his master's word "valiant" for "daring" ("atrevido") elicits the latent negative quality of the virtue of bravery, that of foolhardiness:

> –La verdad sea –respondió Sancho– que yo no he leído ninguna historia jamás, porque ni sé leer ni escribir; mas lo que osaré apostar es que más atrevido amo que vuestra merced yo no le he servido en todos los días de mi vida, y quiera Dios que estos atrevimientos no se paguen donde tengo dicho. (I, 10: 148)

Sancho's foolishness continues to challenge the "wise" behavior of the knight as some humble goatherds, enjoying a country meal, invite the pair to join them. When Don Quixote picks up some acorns at the end of the meal, he recalls the utopian world of the Golden Age, citing all of the components of the myth: a world of plenty, an egalitarian society, where peace, friendship, and harmony reign, and where a natural and spontaneous respect exists among people, rendering superfluous the necessity of written law and its enforcement.[9] He closes by stating that his task as knight errant is to resurrect this world.

In the encounter with the goatherds, Sancho juxtaposes the comic representation of the myth of the Golden Age with the classical one his master upholds in his speech. Unlike the classical myth, the Golden Age of carnival is represented as a world lived in the body as well as the heart. As a time of feast and revelry, all codes and conventions governing social customs, from decorum in eating and drinking to customs distinguishing rank and class, are temporarily abolished (Adrados 350-90; Bakhtin; *Rabelais* 48; Caro Baroja 289).

---

[9] On the classical myth of the Golden Age in Cervantes' work, see Dunn, "Two Classical Myths in Don Quixote" and Levin, 140-43.

Sancho alludes to the comic myth, this time prior to his master's exposition of the classical one, and underpins the knight's ideals even before he pronounces his discourse. As the two begin to enjoy the meal set before them, Don Quixote begs Sancho to sit down and share his plate with him, expressing his desire to forgo the usual hierarchies that separate them. He will thus exemplify how the profession of knight errantry puts into practice the virtue of equality, and exalts anyone who may come into contact with that profession. Sancho rejects his master's offer because he would rather be alone and free to carry out his bodily functions than to have to observe the proper etiquette of the king's table:

> ... mucho mejor me sabe lo que como en mi rincón sin melindres ni respetos, aunque sea pan y cebolla, que los gallipavos de otras mesas donde me sea forzoso mascar despacio, beber poco, limpiarme a menudo, no estornudar ni toser si me viene gana, ni hacer otras cosas que la soledad y libertad traen consigo. (I, 11: 154)

Sancho unintentionally makes fun of the social codes of good etiquette as he opposes his ideal of the freedom of the body to his master's ideal of the freedom of spirit. His master responds to this threat to his authority by forcing the squire to be his equal: "–Con todo eso, te has de sentar; porque a quien se humilla, Dios le ensalza. Y asiéndole por el brazo, le forzó a que junto dél se sentase" (I, 11: 154-55). Don Quixote's justification of his actions is based on the authority of a biblical maxim. He will help Sancho to be humble so that later Sancho might win the greatest of all kingdoms. Yet such a philosophy is rendered ludicrous when one realizes that humility is an attitude in which one freely and actively engages.

This first dialogue between master and squire introduces the country meal. Don Quixote's speech on the Golden Age ends it. Both are equally bewildering to the humble goatherds. Yet they become comprehensible to the reader when the one is seen in light of the other. The sublime wisdom of table talk in the antique symposium echoed in the knight's speech is brought down and redefined as it is reproduced in Sancho's on the material bodily level.

Don Quixote's speech on the Golden Age does more than look backward toward the conversation between knight and squire. It is a pivotal point that closes the discussion between Sancho and Don

Quixote on their own ideal relationship, and introduces the pastoral drama of Marcela and Grisóstomo. Sancho takes the role of Adversary to his master's ideals before his master's discourse; Maritornes takes the role of Adversary after it. Just as Sancho's ideals of equality and freedom serve as contrast to his master's, Maritornes' ideal of freedom contrasts with Marcela's conduct of free will, supported by the knight. While Marcela defends her freedom not to correspond to the desires of another, Maritornes freely decides to engage in an erotic adventure with the muleteer. In his interaction with Sancho and Maritornes, the knight reverses his ideals. He twists Sancho's arm and forces him to sit down beside him while espousing the ideals of equality and freedom, just as he later seizes Maritornes' arm, forcing her towards him against her will when only shortly before he had been defending Marcela against the sway of another man's desires.

Sancho is again turned into his master's scapegoat in Chapters 16 through 20 of Part I in a series of misadventures that occur during their stay at the inn: the struggle between Don Quixote and the muleteer, the drinking of the balm of Fierabrás, and the blanket tossing.[10] In order to cure their wounds from the midnight struggle with Maritornes and the muleteer from Arévalo, Don Quixote has Sancho ask the innkeeper the following morning for the ingredients necessary to concoct the balm of Fierabrás, a medicine used to relieve bodily suffering. Sancho is intrigued by the powers of the drug. The acquisition of a miraculous balm that can provide him economic well-being, immortality and creature comfort seems more promising to Sancho than a governorship.

Don Quixote takes the cure in imitation of his hero, Fierabrás. The cure seems to meet with success, for after throwing up and sweating copiously for two hours, he feels restored and is ready to depart from the inn. Sancho's imitation of the heroic action is not so successful. The knight's movement towards immortality is contrasted with Sancho's vomiting, sweating, diarrhea, suffering spasms and death throes.

The scatological images of sweat, vomit and diarrhea are a grotesque imitation of the near-death/resurrection action of ro-

---

[10] On the inn as an ideal location for the practical joke, and how it serves as a comic convention in literary works, see Joly, *La bourle et son interpretation*, 331-486, 523-47.

mance. The comic image of the body is oriented in relation to the upper stratum (the mouth, teeth and gullet) and the lower one (the womb, genital organs and intestines). The body's movements and functions are seen as a system of flights and descents into the lower depths, where life and death forces meet. Actions and movements in traditional folk humor are a mimicking of the three main actions in the life of the grotesque body: "sexual intercourse, death throes (in their comic presentation . . .) and the act of birth" (Bakhtin, *Rabelais* 353-54).

Don Quixote is resurrected, at least for the time being, by the power of the concoction. Sancho is left in a state of near-death. That which rises must also fall, as we are reminded by Sancho's prostration. The announcement of bodily pleasure, sexual potency and immortality can be replaced by the announcement of bodily suffering and death, in the form of the elimination of residual, dead matter, which leads to the disintegration of the body, its being rended apart and swallowed, and sickness associated with this process. As Marthe Robert affirms, Sancho's body is there to remind Don Quixote of a reality that he refuses to recognize. Concerned exclusively with living his life as art, "Don Quixote shifts the baser responsibilities of his nature to Sancho" (19).

While his squire is still suffering from the effects of the balm, Don Quixote decides to depart from the inn. He advises the innkeeper that as knight errant, he is entitled to lodge anywhere without paying and is miraculously able to leave the inn without being prevented him from doing so. Sancho receives his next punishment, the blanket tossing, when he tries to follow suit. The movements of Sancho's body on the blanket are a repetition of his body movements under the effects of the balm. In the grotesque image, bodily topography is the human imitation of cosmic topography:

> The system of these movements is oriented in relation to the upper and lower stratum; it is a system of flights and descents into the lower depths. Their simplest expression is the primeval phenomenon of popular humor, the cartwheel, which by the continual rotation of the upper and lower parts suggests the rotation of earth and sky. This is manifested in other movements of the down: the buttocks persistently trying to take the place of the head and the head that of the buttocks. (Bakhtin, *Rabelais* 353)

Blanket tossing is a common activity of carnival, as the narrator indicates when he compares Sancho to a "perro por carnestolendas."[11]

Sancho reaches the lowest point of his descent in the following adventure of the warring armies of sheep, a point which necessarily engenders ascent and reversal. The squire's belief in his master's promise of a kingdom wavers with the beatings, stonings, defeats, and hunger. He is thus able to move from *pistis* or "illusion," the belief in laws and habits fixed by an older character, to *gnosis* or "reality," which negates at least certain aspects of the laws of the world (Frye 169-70). Sancho can now free himself from the world of the older character, and in order to implement this change, he will follow a new set of strategies and goals, but one which practically always entails the mimetic repetition of his master's words or actions.

The turning point in the knight and squire's relationship occurs in the episode of the warring armies of sheep. Sancho's faithful warning that two herds of sheep are approaching is ignored by the knight. Instead of receiving economic compensation for his attention to his master's wounded jaw, his master throws up the residue of the balm on him. He further discovers that the saddlebags are missing and along with them, all of their provisions. Sancho is now resolved to leave his master and return home without pay.

When Sancho next finds his creature comforts threatened, in the adventure of the fulling mills, he decides to fight back. In the dark and solitary forest, where the pair have entered in search of drinking water, they suddenly hear a terrible noise of clanking iron and chains, and the roar of water. Sancho implores his master to postpone the adventure until morning. Howard Mancing has signalled the conformity of Sancho's speech to classical rhetoric (*The Chivalric World* 74-78). Sancho begins with an *exordium* in which he states his purpose to dissuade his master from undertaking the adventure. The *narratio* follows, in which the squire describes the facts behind his purpose. He explains that since it is dark, no one will see them and later say they were cowardly. Sancho then appeals to recognizable authority, the local priest, who had said that he

---

[11] Caro Baroja, 47-63, tells us that one of the most popular expulsion rites of carnival is the blanket tossing of dogs and cats, as well as of other animals believed to incarnate evil forces; see also Ziomek, 116-18.

who seeks danger will perish in it, and that it is not right to tempt God.

When Sancho sees that his logical petition fails, the *logos* of classical rhetoric, he turns to other techniques, that of *pathos* and *ethos*. He tries to dissuade the knight from pursuing the adventure by saying that he should recall his moral responsibility to his squire. He adds that he has left his home and family to serve him, and now finds himself being deserted. All of this is accompanied by stylistic devices or the *elocutio* of classical rhetoric, such as the synonymous pairing of adjectives, verbs and nouns, preplaced adjectives, and parallel constructions. When this does not achieve the desired effect, Sancho employs chivalric archaisms: "que non se me faga tal desaguisado" (I, 20: 239).

Mancing suggests that Sancho's imitation of his master's pompous speech-making could have been learned from Don Quixote's speech on the Golden Age, or from Marcela's speech at Grisóstomo's funeral, both given previously. One need not return so far back as to Chapters 10 and 11 to find a model for Sancho's discourse. Sancho's speech is a replica of the knight's speech that introduces the adventure. Don Quixote begins his discourse with the *exordium*, stating that he is a true hero: ". . . yo nací . . . en esta nuestra edad de hierro, para resucitar en ella la de oro. . . ." He then proceeds to the narration. His describes the fearful night, but in a more detailed fashion than Sancho, in order to persuade the listener of his courage. The more fearful the adventure, the more glorious the hero's triumph. He then uses *ethos* and *pathos* in order to strengthen his argument. He opposes the two in order to prove his heroic distinction. He states, as Sancho will later, that other ordinary individuals and even heroic figures would be frightened by such a situation. But while Sancho will use this as an excuse to flee, the knight contrasts his own reaction to that of other mortals by adding that such a situation only moves him to undertake the adventure. His speech contains all of the classical rhetorical embellishments later found in Sancho's discourse, and closes with chivalric archaisms: ". . . por hacerme merced y buena obra, irás al Toboso, donde dirás a la incomparable señora mía Dulcinea que su cautivo caballero murió por acometer cosa que le hiciesen digno de poder llamarse suyo" (I, 20: 239).

Sancho's discourse appears immediately after his master's and is a re-elaboration of it. The two discourses are a dialogue or contest, the primitive *agon*, about how to behave when threatened by danger. The function of Sancho's imitation of his master's discourse is to qualify the absolute truth of his master's premise, namely, that one must face danger courageously. Simultaneously, his display of fear, hidden behind his words, qualifies his master's actions.

Sancho's specious use of sentential statements acts as a complement to the absence of them in his master's speech and echoes the false morality in his master's use of biblical maxims in his speech on the Golden Age. Sancho removes the maxim "Quien busca el peligro perece en él" and "No es bueno tentar a Dios" from their Christian-stoic context where they are used to reflect that one should flee from moral danger, such as gambling houses and houses of prostitution. By facing such dangers, one risks succumbing to temptation and sin. The squire uses them here for his own personal reasons, to justify his desire to escape from physical danger.

The squire's insistence on escaping from physical danger can further be interpreted as an exemplification of classical authority and its concept of "prudence," which permits the withdrawal from danger when its threat is insurmountable. Evidence of this authority can be found in his plea ". . . así que no es bien tentar a Dios acometiendo tan desaforado hecho, donde no se puede escapar sino por milagro . . ." (239).

Sancho's speech succeeds once again in signalling his master's foolhardiness, and his lack of "prudence." It also serves as a mask for Sancho's true motivation for withdrawal, that of fear, evidenced by his incontinence, his concern that others may see them flee and in his insistence on clinging to his master's side, which the narrator thus underscores: ". . . quedó abrazado con el muslo izquierdo de su amo, sin osarse apartar dél un dedo: tal era el miedo que tenía a los golpes que todavía alternativamente sonaban" (I, 20: 241).[12] More importantly, Sancho's discourse, although drawing on inverse premises, doubles the manner in which Don Quixote employs the so-called "truths" of classical authority to disguise his own fear. The narrator exposes their fear by means of a combined use of word play and the plural subject and object marker: ". . . oy*eron* a deshora otro estruendo que *les aguó* el contento del *agua*" (emphasis

---

[12] Sancho's defecation from fear in this episode and the aggressive acts that Sancho carries out against his master as a result of it have been linked to the grotesque by Molho, 217-336.

added). He then ironically emphasizes the knight's fear. He juxtaposes the word play with the affirmation of the knight's courage, stating that the poundings "pusieran pavor a cualquier otro corazón que no fuera el de don Quijote" (237). The knight's fear can also be noted in his unusual acquiescence to delay the adventure until morning, when he discovers that his horse does not budge.

The repetition of words, images, and stylistic devices in the twin discourses can be found as well in other elements within the episode, causing it to be one of the most humorous and most perfectly structured of the narration. After Sancho unties Rocinante's hooves the following morning, knight and squire approach the area from which the terrible noise issues to discover six fulling hammers striking against stone. The "giant" against whom the hero is to duel has been replaced by a pre-industrial, mechanical, and inanimate object. Sancho's next action is to convert his master into an object that repeats the same action over and over again, incapable of progress, like the fulling hammers he has before him. Sancho, the jester, turns to his master and mimics him by repeating his initial speech for a second time, now reproducing his master's words exactly: "–'Has de saber ¡oh Sancho amigo! que yo nací por querer del cielo...'" (248).

Don Quixote had used the speech to convince the audience of the truth of his heroism. Sancho employs his master's words to reveal the mad boaster and imposter, who tries to prove his courage in situations where no danger is present. The radical change in context between the two speeches discovers the ambiguity of language, a characteristic that prevents language from acting as the repository of a single authority of knowledge or truth, as the knight believes. Sancho's repetition reveals that words never produce the same meaning, even when they are repeated exactly. Moreover, repetition and imitation cause what is imitated to grow and proliferate to such a degree that any possibility for the continuity of the original word or deed is finally choked off. The final effect is not simply one of accumulation, but of snowballing, that rolls the reader along with the action or words to a catastrophic conclusion.[13]

The episode ends as Don Quixote punishes Sancho for making fun of him by dealing him two lance blows on his back, and demanding that he obey the standard hierarchies between knight and

---

[13] For a review of the concept of comic repetition, see Charney, 87.

squire. Sancho is once again subordinated to his master's will, but Don Quixote achieves this only at the expense of reversing his own ideals. By inadvertently bringing the punishment upon himself Sancho causes his master to go against a fundamental tenet of the Golden Age, that of equality. His final reminder to Sancho to take into consideration the difference in rank between them undermines his earlier petition to Sancho at the country meal with the goatherds, when he invited him to be his equal in order to prove to Sancho how glorious the world of chivalry is.

Thus far I have analyzed how Sancho undermines his master's embodiment of chivalric and humanist ideals, both in words and deeds. His questioning of his master's imitation of the enamored knight further provides an occasion for the reader to reevaluate the conventions of the courtly love tradition. The discussion between knight and squire on the objectives of the knight's penance in Chapter 25 of Part I exemplifies the manner in which the comic novel and its carnivalesque literary variants elaborate daring fantasies, actions or events that are internally justified by a purely ideological end: to create extraordinary situations in which to test a philosophical idea (Bakhtin, *Problems* 94).

The knight tells Sancho that he will do penance for his lady Dulcinea in imitation of Amadís, and that his imitation will cause him to rise to the highest level of heroism. The courtly behavior the knight imitates is based on the notion of an amatory service involving meditation and self-mortification, following a code which posits the mistress as a cold goddess and the lover a martyred devotee. Sancho intervenes in the episodes where his master tries to carry out this behavior to question the authenticity of such conventions. He begins by questioning his master about the motivation for his penance: "¿Qué dama le ha desdeñado, o qué señales ha hallado que le den a entender que la señora Dulcinea del Toboso ha hecho alguna niñería con moro o cristiano?" (I, 25: 305). Don Quixote justifies himself by telling Sancho that if he could do all of this without cause ("en seco"), he could demonstrate just that much more valor on an occasion when he must truly confront danger ("en mojado"). But Sancho's questioning makes clear that his master's conduct is merely a farcical rehearsal of a heroic act. While many actions can be imitated, it is inherently false to imitate in matters of love and spiritual suffering (Close, "Don Quixote's Love for Dulcinea"; Roberts).

The conversation now centers on the problem of how to notify Dulcinea of the heroic act that is to be performed on her behalf. Sancho is eager to return to his village to pick up the three donkeys his master has promised him. Don Quixote replies that before delivering the letter containing the news of his penance to Dulcinea, he would rather have him wait a few days in order to describe better to her his acts of folly, such as the tearing out of his hair and his head banging. Sancho's seemingly well-intentioned response, in which he suggests to his master that he hit his head against against something soft, belies his scornful opinion of his master's behavior:

> ... ya que a vuestra merced le parece que son aquí necesarias calabazadas y que no se puede hacer esta obra sin ellas, se contentase, pues todo esto es fingido y cosa contrahecha y de burla, se contentase, digo, con dárselas en el agua, o en alguna cosa blanda, como algodón.... (309)

Don Quixote thanks him for his "good" intentions but rejects the suggestion. Relying on the authority of the codes of chivalry, he explains to Sancho that a knight must never lie, and therefore his head banging must be authentic. Believing Sancho to be concerned for his welfare, Don Quixote interprets his advice to mean, 'I'm concerned that you might hurt yourself' when what Sancho is really suggesting is 'I do not care particularly if you get hurt, but since I see that your spiritual suffering is false, I wonder why you do not also make your physical suffering that must accompany it false also.' Sancho acts like Socrates, who, by his questioning, provokes the words of the other speaker, forcing him to state his opinions and thus expose his weak points, incompleteness or falsity.

From questioning the value of performing the formal convention of penance, devoid of content, it is only one step to question the value of the convention itself, even when truly motivated. When Sancho asks Don Quixote what childish act Dulcinea has committed with Moor or Christian, he directs the reader's attention to Roland's act of penance and, by extrapolation, to Amadís'. Between the lines he is saying that the unfaithfulness of Angélica and the disdainful attitude of Oriana are such trifles as to not warrant going mad, or suffering a penance involving a physical and spiritual suffering that often lasted for years. The reader thus comes to perceive the disproportion between cause and effect and to question the value of complying with the demands of a preestablished code, and ultimately if true sentiment is compatible with such codes.[14]

Before the penance occurs, Sancho turns to another topic of conversation: the details concerning the two letters he is to take back. He tells Don Quixote that he should consider that the three days have passed and promises to tell Dulcinea of his penance as if he had been an eye-witness. He then begs him to write the two letters. One is to go to Dulcinea. The other is the bill of exchange for the release of the donkeys. The juxtaposition of the knight's love letter and the squire's bill of exchange serves to uncover the artificiality of the former. The concern Sancho expresses for concrete legal aspects of the bill of exchange, such as the signature, the dictation, and the transcription of the letter, acts as a foil to the vagueness of the epistles found in romances of chivalry, in which all such details are left out. Sancho's questioning further insures the satisfaction of his desire, the retrieval of the donkeys. Don Quixote signs the bill of exchange and assures Sancho that the signature will be recognized by the housekeeper and niece.

Sancho's interrogations also undermine his master's courtly concepts, for his questions force Don Quixote to make several assertions which reveal the vulgar origin and identity of his lady, and the lack of true sentiment in their relationship. Under the fire of Sancho's interrogations, Don Quixote admits that his signature on the letter to Dulcinea is not important because his lady does not read; the letter will have to be read to her. He also admits that she would not recognize his signature anyway because she has never received a letter from him. Their love is platonic. He has only worshipped her from afar. Indeed, he has only seen her four times in twelve years, and she has never seen him. He concludes with the mention of her family name. The knight's attempt to justify his vague manner of letter writing by framing his behavior within the courtly and platonic love traditions suggests that a platonic expression of love can easily be represented as an emotion that is nonexistent.

The letters are finally written and Sancho departs. Passing the inn where he had been given the blanket tossing, Sancho encounters the priest and barber, who are in search of Sancho and Don

---

[14] Herrero, in his study "Sierra Morena as Labyrinth," views the entire action transcurring in the Sierra Morena as a criticism of the destructive force of Renaissance love as embodied in the courtly Petrarchan and Neoplatonic traditions.

Quixote in order to take them back to the village. Their presence at the point where Sancho feels to be close to achieving some compensation for his services, a necessary stimulus for the continuation of them in the future, is disastrous for Don Quixote. In order that Sancho might reveal the whereabouts of his master, the priest and barber accuse their neighbor of having robbed Rocinante and harmed his master. When they finally threaten to have him sent to jail, Sancho quickly replies by providing the facts that only minutes before he had vowed to himself to conceal. He betrays his loyalty to his master completely when he realizes that he has forgotten to bring the letters. The priest assures Sancho that he will help him retrieve the donkeys and attain the governorship, but only if they manage to prevent his master from continuing his useless penance. Sancho breaks his pact with Don Quixote and forms a new one with the priest. His other mission, to advise his master's lady of the knight's heroic act of penance, is replaced by a new one, to tell him a lie. He must now convince Don Quixote that he has completed his assignment and has returned from El Toboso with a message from Dulcinea in which she orders the knight to give up his penance and visit her in El Toboso immediately.

The adage that one lie leads to another is proven true in the actions Sancho suddenly finds himself being forced to carry out. Although the original plan to get Don Quixote back home via El Toboso is abandoned in favor of a new ruse in which the knight's chivalric fantasies are re-elaborated, Sancho's lie remains, and he is about to be caught in it twice. The first time is in Chapter 30 of Part I when Don Quixote asks Sancho to describe his interview with Dulcinea in detail. The second time is in Chapters 7 and 8 of Part II when Don Quixote and Sancho finally visit El Toboso, and the knight expects Sancho to be able to lead him to his lady's "palace." On both occasions Sancho invents and transforms reality in order to suit his needs, as does his master. While doing so, he subverts the knight's desire to deify his lady in compliance with the codes of courtly love.

In his description of his meeting with Dulcinea in Chapter 30, Sancho's description of Dulcinea corresponds to what he had previously said of her to Don Quixote in the Sierra Morena upon learning her identity, namely, that she is a brawny country girl, lacking the sensitivity necessary to appreciate the refined sentiments of his master. The invented description of their conversation is based on his true knowledge of who she is and how she would act in such a situation as well as on his own country experiences. The enchantment of Dulcinea in Chapter 10, on the contrary, represents a turning point in Sancho's aggressive techniques against his master. His truthful assertions no longer contrast with his master's alteration of reality. He now imitates his master's lofty poetic style as he himself transforms reality.

After a first turn about the town of El Toboso, Sancho has his master wait in a wood outside the village while he promises to find Dulcinea's dwelling. He spots three peasant girls approaching on their donkeys and remembers that his master barely has any notion of what Dulcinea looks like. He will make his master believe that these girls are Dulcinea and her ladies-in-waiting. He then calls his master and informs him that Dulcinea and her ladies are approaching and describes his lady's beauty to him:

> Pique, señor, y venga, y verá venir a la princesa, nuestra ama, vestida y adornada; en fin, como quien ella es. Sus doncellas y ella todas son una ascua de oro, todas mazorcas de perlas, todas son diamantes, todas rubíes, todas telas de brocado de más de diez altos; los cabellos, sueltos por las espaldas, que son otros tantos rayos del sol que andan jugando con el viento. . . . (II, 10: 108)

Sancho's description of the damsel is an imitation of the ones found in courtly love poetry, in which the facial features, hair, bust, and other visible parts of the lady are exalted. The features are compared to valuable objects, or to perfect elements found in nature. His description reveals his basic understanding, if not subtle mastery, of the metaphorical techniques he has often heard his master employ in his praise of his lady.

The context in which Sancho's description appears, however, provides a new vantage point from which to perceive the idealized image of the lady found in love poetry. As the three peasant girls finally come into sight, their vulgar physical appearance and coarse manners create an ironic shock for the reader as well as for the spectator, who suddenly see the perfection of art grotesquely debased as it converges with prosaic reality. Don Quixote sees reality as it is, and cannot ignore the discrepancy between Sancho's exalting description and the "specter" before him.

At the conclusion of his description of the "princess," Sancho begins to discuss the identity of the lady's horse. He affirms that the ladies are riding on palfreys: ". . . y sobre todo, vienen a caballo sobre tres cananeas remendadas, que no hay más que ver" (108). Sancho's transformation of the donkeys into palfreys can be understood as a type of persuasion based on a technique of identification; in other words, Sancho tries to convince his master that the peasant girl is a highborn lady by convincing him that this work animal is a steed. The success of Sancho's lie only makes sense, however, if we do not make this type of identification.[15]

The technique Sancho employs to convince his master of the girl's identity has its origins in the rhetoric of carnival, where illogical and incoherent ideas are introduced and supported as a means of parodying the *logos* of classical rhetoric. Sancho begins his argument with the false statement that the country wench is a highborn lady. Then, distracting his master from the question of the viability of this premise, he builds up equally fallacious arguments in support of it and causes his master to argue about the truth of these smaller arguments. When Don Quixote replies that he only sees three peasant girls on their donkeys, Sancho remains silent with respect to his mention of the peasant girls, while verbally insisting on the identity of the three animals as palfreys:

> –¡Agora me libre Dios del diablo! respondió Sancho–. Y ¿es posible que tres hacaneas, o como se llaman, blancas como el ampo de la nieve, le parezcan a vuesa merced borricos? ¡Vive el Señor, que me pele estas barbas si tal fuese verdad! (109)

If Sancho's aim were to convince Don Quixote that the girl is highborn by means of her identification with the palfrey, he would certainly have failed to achieve it, for Don Quixote never believes the beast is a palfrey. His concluding remark reflects his continued belief in his original assertion: "–Pues yo te digo, Sancho amigo –dijo don Quijote– que es tan verdad que son borricos, o borricas, como yo soy don Quijote y tú Sancho Panza; a lo menos, a mí tales me parecen" (109). Sancho's strategy is more subtle; it consists in the idea that it really does not matter whether or not he wins the point he is arguing. By merely causing his master to argue about the iden-

---

[15] For a different point of view on the hacanea-borrica argument, see Johnson.

tity of the beast, he wins the crucial point of not having to justify the original premise and take the risk of not being able to do so. By not arguing the point, Don Quixote is persuaded to or lets himself be persuaded to accept it.[16]

After the peasant girls depart, Don Quixote laments the transformation of his "princess" into "peasant," and curses the evil enchanters that he believes responsible for such devilry. Sancho responds by admonishing the enchanters, but while doing so, he overturns his initial portrait in which he had exalted the peasant girl:

> –Bastaros debiera, bellacos, haber mudado las perlas de los ojos de mi señora en agallas alcornoqueñas, y sus cabellos de oro purísimo en cerdas de cola de buey bermejo, y, finalmente, todas sus facciones de buenas en malas, sin que le tocáredes en el olor. ... (112)

The metaphors of love poetry are comically reversed here when Sancho substitutes the exalted object normally employed to describe a feature of the lady's body for one that has less than human value, taken from the plant and animal world. He compares the color and texture of her hair to that of an ox tail and the form of her eye to the gall nut of the cork tree. The gall nut, a growth formed in the branches of the cork tree, creates the image of the "bug eye." The image of the gall nut further signals the counterfeit nature of Dulcinea. Cork, a lightweight, porous material connotes an object without substance. The image makes a cross reference as well to Aldonza's last name, Corchuelo, suggesting not only a quantitative difference with respect to the true love object, but a qualitative one as well, as the pejorative diminutive "-uelo" indicates.

In the following chapter, Don Quixote continues to muse over the enchantment of Dulcinea, and corrects Sancho's second description of Dulcinea as highborn lady:

> ... he caído Sancho, en una cosa, y es que me pintaste mal su hermosura; porque, si mal no me acuerdo, dijiste que tenía los ojos de perlas, y los ojos que parecen de perlas antes son de be-

---

[16] The idea that Don Quixote knows that he is merely playing at being knight, and that Dulcinea is the fabrication of his imagination is suggestive. For a more detailed discussion of this point, see Torrente Ballester.

sugo que de dama; y a lo que yo creo, los de Dulcinea deben ser de verdes esmeraldas, rasgados, con dos celestiales arcos que les sirven de cejas; y esas perlas quítalas de los ojos y pásalas a los dientes; que sin duda te trocaste, Sancho, tomando los ojos por los dientes. (II, 11: 114)

The comment reveals Don Quixote's desire to exalt Dulcinea once again by means of the metaphors that Sancho has employed: "esmeraldas," "celestiales arcos" and "perlas." Sancho's lack of virtuosity in metaphorical techniques suddenly acts as a strategy that maliciously reverses his master's ideal of feminine beauty. When Don Quixote corrects his flaw, he reveals the true sense of it, that the image of pearls for eyes creates the image of the bug eye, and identifies the "queen" with a bream fish.

The knight then affirms that a better image to describe the beauty of his lady's eyes would be that of green emeralds, and that Sancho should take the image of the pearls from the eyes and put it where the teeth are, in accordance with standard metaphorical comparisons of love poetry. The purpose of metaphorical figures in love poetry is to create a portrait of perfect beauty by means of a harmonious mixing of each part of the lady. The comic reversal of this portrait is achieved, as Anthony Close has shown, with the complicity of Don Quixote. By correcting Sancho's foolish imitation, the knight dismembers the face of the beloved, and puts the pieces back together in a different way, as if features of the face could be removed and reinserted in alternate locations ("Don Quixote's Love").

The final consequence of Sancho's enchantment is the reversal of roles, the essence of the comic relationship. By means of the imitation of his master's language, Sancho rises to control his master, as his master had previously controlled him. This inversion of roles, often described in Cervantine criticism as the "Sanchificación" of Don Quixote and the "Quijotización" of Sancho, has been occurring all along. Almost from the beginning, Sancho imitates his master's speech, actions and values.[17]

---

[17] Traditionally, the term has been used to indicate not just Sancho's ability to transform reality but his process of spiritualization as well. See Brenan, 187, Entwistle, 133 and Madariaga, 127-135. On Sancho's role in the metamorphosis of Dulcinea and of this episode in general, much has been written. For an overview of this criticism, see Herrero's helpful article, "Dulcinea and her Critics."

The difference between Sancho's employment of his master's discourse in the enchantment of Dulcinea and in previous episodes is that prior to the enchantment, his imitation never implied control over his master. Before the enchantment, Don Quixote was able to punish Sancho for his tendentious imitation of or opposition to his ideals and could bring him under his control by employing one of a number of methods of force. After the enchantment, Don Quixote falls under Sancho's transformative powers, an imitation of his own, and is unable to free himself without openly admitting that Dulcinea, alias Aldonza Corchuelo, probably looks pretty much like the ugly specter they had before them, and that he has transformed her by his own poetic words just as Sancho has done. The ultimate trick of the enchantment is that Sancho's imitation of his master's transformation, in turn based on the artifice of the platonic love poets, puts Don Quixote face to face with the fiction of art and with his own lie, and reminds him that he cannot extricate himself from Sancho's powers without falling into the worse trap of having to own up to the invention of art and to his own role as Impostor.

Transforming himself from ally into adversary, Sancho finally emerges as the Trickster and puppeteer, the Tempter of the ancient fertility rites.[18] Wylie Sypher explains in his discussion of this figure that the *eiron*-Tempter disguises himself as devil or "enchanter," wearing as need arises the garb of buffoon, ironist, and madman. He leads us into a situation where the god within us (our own ideals and values) confronts the Adversary, our other Self. As the dialogue between them develops, the god is left dying before us:

> This Adversary . . . is the despiser of a morality we have never examined. To feel the spell of this "Tempter" we must take the awful risk of entering into a "boundary-situation" where nothing is taken for granted and where all our values must be found anew, without help from "the other." Here we walk alone upon the margin of Reason. The Adversary goes with us to this highest precipice of comedy. The Comic Feast of Unreason is a test and a discovery. . . . (41-42)

---

[18] Edith Kern explains that the "trickster" or "Prime Mover" is the instigator of carnival activities and usually displays saint and sinner qualities. He is a clownish figure that is unpredictable and changeable. He is a creator and destroyer, a giver and a negator, he dupes and is duped.

Prior to the enchantment, Sancho's quest to acquire a governorship was established for him by Don Quixote. Now Sancho actively elaborates the quest for Don Quixote: the rescue of a highborn damsel from bondage. In doing so, he controls the movements and thought of his master, and creates the infrastructure for the action contained in the rest of the narration, which can be seen in its most composite form in Don Quixote's descent into the Cave of Montesinos.

The action of the rescue of a lady from bondage belongs to a series of dying-god myths disseminated in the structure of romance fiction, the most common one being the St. George or dragon-slaying quest and the myths of the Leviathan and of Perseus (Frye 189-92). Similar to each myth is an action that involves the hero's struggle with a force associated with evil and death. In the St. George quest, a land ruled by a helpless old man is laid waste by a sea monster. The hero comes and kills the dragon to whom the king's daughter is to be sacrificed. He then marries the princess and succeeds to the throne. The hero thus advances from a state of conflict and near-death to one of rebirth by means of a great struggle with the forces of evil.

In the myth of the Leviathan, the hero also confronts the forces of evil. The monster represents the fallen order of nature over which Satan has some control. In the book of Revelation, the Leviathan, Satan, and the Edenic serpent are all as one. Northrop Frye suggests that if the Leviathan is the fallen world, sin, and death, the tyranny into which Adam fell, it follows that Adam's children are born, live, and die in his body. If the Messiah delivers us by killing the Leviathan, he releases us. In many folk tales of dragon-killing, the struggle and victory of the hero take place inside the monster's belly, from which the hero emerges alive after it is killed. The hero travels downward into the inside of the dragon and he returns by an upward movement. We have here, Frye suggests, all of the symbolism of the Harrowing of Hell, normally represented in iconography by the toothed gullet of an aged shark.

The dying god myths also have their place in comic fiction, where the dragon-killing quest of romance is carried out in reverse (Bakhtin, *Rabelais* 377-97). The underworld is organized as a typical carnival. Everything in hell is inverted in relation to the outside world. All who are highest are debased and all who are lowest are crowned. In Rabelais' narration of Epistemon's journey to the Underworld, we can find a carnivalesque travesty of antique and medieval heroes. The doomed hero is given new assignments and occupations. Epistemon explains that in the rule of hell, all who had been great lords and ladies on earth were condemned to struggle for the most ignoble and miserable livelihoods below, while philosophers and such who had been needy on earth became lords in hell. Finally, the heroes of folk humor, like their epic and romance counterparts, often descend into the underworld. Harlequin, for example, a devil in his pre-literary past, in a work called *The Gay History of the Feats and Adventures of the Italian Comedian, Harlequin*, reveals his dreams and visions and is seen turning somersaults, leaping, and sticking out his tongue.

The meaning of Don Quixote's descent into the Cave of Montesinos can be grasped by viewing it as a reenactment of the comic hero's mythical descent into hell.[19] The first incongruous detail is that Don Quixote begins his quest to rescue his damsel without any conscious knowledge of what he is doing. Only as the vision develops is it revealed to him that his messianic mission is to deliver Dulcinea and the other heroes of romance occupying the cave since their enchantment by Merlín. The quest is undertaken as Don Quixote descends into the cave in the guise of student, in order to satisfy his curiosity about the wonders of the cave.

The vision is divided into two parts, Don Quixote's conversation with Montesinos and the appearance of the enchanted Dulcinea. The two parts merge as the action within them thwarts the knight's mission to resurrect his mistress and the other inhabitants of the cave from their fallen state of enchantment. Don Quixote narrates the vision in order to compare his transformed mistress to other fallen heroes and heroines of the chivalric world and justify to his squire the hellish vision of the figure of Dulcinea in El Toboso. Inadvertently, however, he complies with his Adversary against his own ideals as he uncrowns and travesties the entire chivalric world.

Don Quixote begins the narration of his experience in the cave with the description of his encounter with Montesinos and with the

---

[19] Don Quixote's descent into the cave has been linked to folklore and myth. See for example, Riley, "Metamorphosis, Myth, and Dream in the Cave of Montesinos." Riley applies Jungian psychology to dream transformation here. See also Redondo, "El proceso iniciático." Redondo studies such folk motifs as the liberation of the enchanted princess and the search for the deceased wife.

other characters that belong to the legend, Durandarte and Belerma. Disguised as a tourist guide, Montesinos shows the knight the wonders of the cave. First he takes him to the crystalline palace, where the hidden faces of Don Quixote and the heroes he imitates are reflected. Inside the palace, Montesinos shows Don Quixote his dead cousin, Durandarte, lying in a tomb and explains that upon his cousin's last request, he had cut out his heart and delivered it to his mistress, Belerma.

Don Quixote's imitation of the ideal love of the enamored heroes and heroines of romance is grotesquely transformed as he reveals unheroic aspects of his models in his vision. Durandarte, the hero without a heart, is identified with Don Quixote. The enamored heart, inspired with heroic courage by means of the spiritual powers of his mistress's love, is converted into a dead organ weighing over two pounds, and subject to bodily decay. It must be salted in order to reach Belerma in a preserved state. Here we have the grotesque image of dismembered flesh turned into a piece of salted meat.

The mistress of the legend, Belerma, is portrayed in Don Quixote's vision with the same physical traits as Sancho's enchanted Dulcinea, the flat nose and the large mouth. The "specter" of the peasant girl chosen to embody Dulcinea and the "specter" of Belerma in the hellish vision of the cave are the double selves of Dulcinea and her romance counterparts. In the figure of Belerma, Dulcinea's eternal youth and maidenhood are seen as subject to eternal bodily decay. The bags under Belerma's eyes and her sallow and withered skin show not only a loss of maidenhood, but of her biological femininity as well, for the narrator's irony indicates that these signs of decay are due more to her menopausal decline than to the lady's grief. Don Quixote clings to the temporal rhythms of chivalric romance with its recurrent restorative cycles and its suspension in "a season of perpetual spring-like summer" (Murillo, *The Golden Dial* 18).[20] But the images of the destructiveness of time emerge from his inner self in this vision of decay.

The virtue of the loyal and chaste mistress of romance is reversed in the travesty of Belerma.[21] The change of costume serves

---

[20] For the divergent conceptions of time in this episode, see Sieber.
[21] The intrusion of incongruous and prosaic details into the dignified and exalted action of epic and/or romance, linked with costume and the body has often been

the function of uncovering the hidden self of the hero and heroine of romance. Belerma appears in the underworld cave in a funeral procession, mourning for her lost love, Durandarte. She is dressed in black and white, the proper colors of mourning, but her white veil is so long that it not only covers up her entire body, but drags on the ground. The veil is symbol of chastity and spirituality. The cloth frames the head and is used to conceal the mundane beauty of the damsel, symbolized by her hair. Belerma's veil nullifies her body and its exaggerated size signals the hypocrisy of her seemingly religious reverence for her beloved.[22]

Further description of Belerma's headgear underscores her immoral conduct. Like her ladies-in-waiting, Belerma is wearing a turban. The headdress of the Turk, the greatest enemy of the Catholic faith, is symbol of the lady's infidelity towards her beloved. Her part-time mourning for Durandarte, carried out only four times a week, comes to confirm a real basis for the symbolic turban. Finally, Belerma's turban is described as being twice as big as the biggest turban worn by Belerma's ladies-in-waiting. Here we have the image of the highborn lady turned into fool, wearing the clown's oversized cap.

Montesinos' costume further travesties the heroic figures of romance. Montesinos, like Don Quixote in his descent into the cave, is deprived of his identity as the hero of romance, and is shown in disguise as a schoolboy, wearing the collegian's bands of green velvet. Montesinos wears a counterfeit rosary just as Don Quixote did

---

signalled in this episode. For the most complete analysis, see Percas de Ponseti, *Cervantes y su concepto del arte*, 2: 417-19 and Dunn's classic article, "La cueva de Montesinos por fuera y por dentro: estructura épica, fisonomía."

[22] The image of the oversized veil reappears in the episode of the meeting of the knight with Doña Rodríguez. Here, her veil is so long that it covers up her entire body. The veil, a symbol of religious reverence when worn by the nun or widow, is given a reversed function. The religious hypocrisy represented in the exaggerated length of the veil is underscored by the narrator's use of the augmentative "-ísima" to describe the lady: "reverendísima dueña." Indeed, the comic irony of the meeting develops around the motif of the veil. Don Quixote, concerned that the lady might make sexual advances towards him, reads and interprets the super veil, as he does the romances of chivalry, at face value. Believing that the bigger the religious object is, the more religious or reverent the person wearing it, his fear of the lady is dispelled. He allows her to remain in his room, even though it is in the middle of the night: "... dadme, señora, la mano, que yo no quiero otra seguridad mayor que la de mi continencia y recato, y la que ofrecen esas reverendísimas tocas" (II, 35: 399).

in his penance in the Sierra Morena. The beads are the size of walnuts and every tenth one is the size of an ostrich egg. The oversized beads of Montesinos' rosary and the knight's cloth rosary reflect the hypocrisy behind their pretension of heroic action. Finally, like Don Quixote, Montesinos is portrayed as an authority figure. He is a venerable old man. His long grey beard is a physical trait that conventionally connotes authority and gravity. Yet like Belerma's veil, it is exaggeratedly long, reaching all the way down to his waist. The authority of the wise man that the beard symbolizes is suddenly transformed into the folly of the clown. The figure of Harlequin in the Commedia dell'Arte often thwarts official authority by means of the travesty of his long beard, which he often tucks in under his belt.

In the second part of his vision, the figure of Dulcinea appears, accompanied by her ladies-in-waiting, just as she had appeared before Don Quixote in El Toboso. Don Quixote narrates how the ladies jump and leap with acrobatic grace, just as the peasant girl portraying Dulcinea had done. Sancho, on the way to the Cave of Montesinos, deciphers the meaning of such movements, transforming Dulcinea into a fallen angel, when he affirms to the humanist cousin and to Don Quixote that Lucifer, the metamorphosed angel, was the first acrobat of the world.

The vision ends as Dulcinea sends one of her ladies-in-waiting to the knight to request a loan on her behalf of a dozen royal crowns. Don Quixote confesses that he does not have the amount requested and promises not to rest until he is able to disenchant her. The presence of money plays an important role in comic action. The essential goal of comic action is the acquisition of something, such as a woman or a successful job. When all means used to accomplish the desired end fail, money is always a final alternative. Its presence serves as a contrast to the accomplishments of the true hero. The essential inefficacy of the comic hero is discovered in situations where money cannot help, or, in this case, where the hero cannot even come up with the money requested, and thus come to the aid of his lady.

The effect of Sancho's enchantment culminates in Don Quixote's vision of the double of the "double" of Dulcinea in the Cave of Montesinos. Don Quixote is unable to punish Sancho for his aggression and subordinate him once more to his power. New characters are introduced that will take on the role of "tricking the trickster": the duke and the duchess. As George McFadden indicates, the logical unfolding of comic repetition of action occurs in the form of its own reciprocal, in that the initial aggressive act carried out by a character is repeated in a manner that aggression is eventually turned back on the aggressor (110-20). In the comic work, this becomes manifest in several common themes: the cheater cheated, the biter bitten and the robber robbed. The duke and duchess will appear to put this comic law of just retribution into effect, to the detriment of Sancho. Molho explains Cervantes' use of this comic law:

> La técnica que emplea Cervantes . . . consiste en invertir la situación angustiosa de un personaje propulsándole en dirección de un triunfo liberador, sin perjuicio de reconducirle después a una nueva situación angustiosa asímismo reversible. (297)[23]

More significantly, in the act of retribution that he is made to undergo, he will imitate his master's quest in a manner that identifies Don Quixote with the ritual character of the Impostor.

The noble couple meet knight and squire on the road. Having read Part I of *Don Quixote*, they are well acquainted with their guests' folly. They invite the pair to their "casa de placer" and decide to have some fun with them. After learning of the enchantment of Dulcinea in El Toboso and of her reappearance in the Cave of Montesinos, they plan a series of pseudo-adventures with the intention of transforming the aggressor back into victim. The result is that the puppeteer enters the mad world he has created and becomes controlled by it when he is made to carry out the heroic quest of rescuing the damsel that he himself had conjured up. Heroic quest action is displaced to Sancho, the Ironist/*eiron*. He now imitates the enamored hero's suffering and will begin to assume the unpleasant duties of his office.

The so-called heroic action he undertakes, like his master's penance in the Sierra Morena, are parodies of the romance hero's

---

[23] For Molho, the most salient fact about the folkloric and carnivalesque character represented by Sancho is his reversibility. Within the action of the tale, Sancho continuously alternates between the role of the simple or natural fool and that of the artifical fool, that is, he who plays the fool; between the dim-wit and the scoundrel. For a similar point of view, see Alonso, Hendrix and Márquez Villanueva. Of these, only Molho links the figure of Sancho to the folkloric tradition.

trials that are to prove his moral superiority. All of the pseudo-adventures planned by the ducal pair prior to Sancho's departure to the territory he is to govern serve to morally prepare the future prince. Sancho is to learn to be courageous when threatened with danger in the episode of the hunt so that he may protect his subjects when threatened by the enemy; he is to learn to be charitable and do good works by carrying out the penance of Dulcinea as the duchess points out:

> . . . menester será que el buen Sancho haga alguna diciplina de abrojos, o de las de canelones, que se dejen sentir; porque la letra con sangre entra, y no se ha de dar tan barata la libertad de una tan gran señora como lo es Dulcinea por tan poco precio; y advierta Sancho que las obras de caridad que se hacen tibia y flojamente no tienen mérito, ni valen nada. (II, 36: 320)

Finally, Sancho is to learn humility in the "flight" on Clavileño.[24] The humor of these adventures is derived from the fact that they are designed to expose the squire's subversion of these moral qualities.[25] The deceits thus contrast the ideal ruler's qualities of humility, courage and charity with Sancho's ambition, self-interest, fear, and indifference to his master.

The preliminary step in devising the adventures is to convince Sancho that what Don Quixote saw in the Cave of Montesinos is really true and that the peasant girl they saw in El Toboso really was Dulcinea. This achieved, the planned third appearance of Dulcinea will have the desired effect. After Sancho confesses his trick of the enchantment, the duchess suggests to him that perhaps he is the one tricked in believing himself to be the enchanter:

> . . . y créame Sancho que la villana brincadora era y es Dulcinea del Toboso, que está encantada como la madre que la parió; y cuando menos nos pensemos, la habemos de ver en su propia figura, y entonces saldrá Sancho del engaño en que vive. (II, 33: 301)

The first group of pseudo-adventures the ducal pair invent are a re-presentation of the adventure in the Cave of Montesinos in

---

[24] For the carnivalesque tradition in this episode, see Redondo, "De Don Clavijo a Clavileño."

[25] For another point of view, see Brantley.

which the same themes and images appear. Six days after knight and squire arrive at the ducal palace, the duke and duchess plan a hunting party which will conclude with two surprise activities: a battle and the appearance of Dulcinea. The hunt and the battle scenes introduce the theme of the art of governing. The duke informs Sancho, who is reticent to participate in the hunt, of the importance of the sport of hunting for the ruler:

> ... el ejercicio de la caza de monte es el más conveniente y necesario para los reyes y príncipes que otro alguno. La caza es una imagen de la guerra: hay en ella estratagemas, astucias, insidias para vencer a su salvo al enemigo; padécense en ella fríos grandísimos y calores intolerables; menoscábase el ocio y el sueño, corrobóranse las fuerzas, agilítanse los miembros del que la usa.... (II, 34: 307)

The Machiavellian concept of the role of king is given a comic perspective here. Indeed, the activities of battle and hunting are by their very nature (conditioned by rules, schemes, and astuteness) prone to a ludical interpretation. In carnival, both the battle and the hunt involve the pursuit, catching, and sacrifice of a scapegoat figure, to whom evil forces are transferred or attributed (Adrados 450-90; Caro Baroja 278). Collective battles between Catholics and Turks or Moors are ludically represented, the latter embodying destructive forces. The hunt also forms an important activity of carnival. In Galicia, for example, several members of the community dress up as wild savages and run and jump as if possessed. Then the chase begins and continues until the savages are caught, attacked and ritually sacrificed. In the duke and duchess's planned adventure, comic action gets underway as the would-be prince/hunter is transformed into the one hunted. As the hunting party travels towards the site of the hunt, the scenery of the Cave of Montesinos is reconstructed. The duke and duchess's staff, evenly distributed about the area, begin to make loud noises with their horns and the barking: "... repartida la gente por diferentes puestos, se comenzó la caza con grandes estruendo, grita y vocería, de manera que unos a otros no podían oirse, así por el ladrido de los perros como por el son de las bocinas" (305).

The hunt begins in a wood that is sunken between two very tall mountains, the image of a cave. The narrator tells us that "llegaron a un bosque que entre dos altísimas montañas estaba" (307). The duchess places herself at the side of the path where she knows that wild boars will pass and other members of the party follow suit. Don Quixote anxiously joins them, but Sancho is somewhat less enthusiastic and follows only in order not to be left without protection. A wild boar is soon heard approaching "crujiendo dientes y colmillos."

The duchess's behavior, who is most eager to confront the wild beast, is opposed to Sancho's, who in his attempt to escape up a tree, finds that the branch supporting him has broken. He is left hanging above the ground as his tunic gets caught on the stub of the branch. Don Quixote's "heroic" harrowing of hell in the Cave of Montesinos is refracted through the figure of Sancho in retreat, the hunter hunted, who is hanging from a branch and crying for help as if from inside the gullet of a monster. The narrator describes the scene thus: "Todos los que le oían y no le veían creyeron que estaba entre los dientes de alguna fiera" (II, 34: 308).

After the boar is hunted and captured, Don Quixote approaches to unhook Sancho. The second surprise activity begins as it gets dark. The images of the Underworld are again present. The confusion and havoc of hell are produced by means of the instruments of war and the great explosions and lights caused by the arms, and by the loud screams of the "Moors" as they enter battle.

The struggle of the Christian armies against the Moors reenacts the theme of the expulsion of the scapegoat, a rite which Sancho is made to under go in these pseudo-adventures. The theme is treated ludically here, for the supposed battle consists only of sounds, unaccompanied by substantive action. The scene acts as a bridge between the hunt and the emergence of Dulcinea from the underworld that follows, which the horns, shouts and lights announce.

As night closes in, a procession of carriages begin to file by, occupied by figures disguised as demons and devils. Finally a carriage bigger than the previous ones appears carrying eighteen penitents and the figures disguised as Dulcinea and Merlin, her enchanter. The presence of the penitents beside Dulcinea reintroduces the courtly love theme of romance: the knight's amatory service for his lady, based on spiritual and bodily suffering. A figure incarnating death stands up and identifies himself as Merlín. He explains that in order for Dulcinea to become disenchanted, Sancho must be whipped three thousand, three hundred times, "de modo que le escuezan, le amarguen y le enfaden" (II, 35: 314).

The ideal of the gratuitousness of love, the motivating factor behind the knight's penance in the Sierra Morena, is comically echoed here in Sancho's penance for Dulcinea. Although Merlín tells Sancho that his punishment should be an act of free will and that he may carry out the act of whipping himself according to his own time limits, the duke imposes the penance on him, threatening to withdraw his offer to make him governor if he does not comply with what is requested of him: "En resolución, Sancho, o vos habeis de ser azotado, o os han de azotar, o no habéis de ser gobernador" (318).

The "criminal" and "Adversary," who tells his master the lie in the Sierra Morena that he has been to El Toboso in order to prevent his master from continuing a penance that threatens his governorship, is finally caught and returned to the scene of the crime. Yet as he goes, he seizes the opportunity to unmask the *alazon*. His false penance underlies the fraudulence of his master's. Sancho whips the bark of trees instead of his back, as he had suggested to Don Quixote that he bang his head on cotton or water instead of on rocks, a punishment more in keeping with his false spiritual motivations.

Although the aggressor has been converted into victim, the duke and duchess's ruse allows Sancho to continue maintaining control over his master. Where before the attainment of Sancho's goal of becoming governor was dependent on Don Quixote's heroic action, now Don Quixote's goal of rescuing Dulcinea is dependent on Sancho's "heroic" penance, the execution of which is so slow that he completes it only shortly before they arrive home to their village, after the knight has renounced his knightly identity. Indeed, the entire heroic endeavor is removed from Don Quixote's hands in the latter part of the narration. The hero is estranged from his self-imposed prostration as well as from his task to rise to become acclaimed hero as the action deviates towards his counterpart.

Sancho finally receives his long desired governorship, not by means of the heroic action of his master, but as a result of a pseudo-adventure planned for him by the duke and the duchess. Sancho has no direct role model to imitate, for his master does not acquire a kingship in the narration. Yet indirectly Don Quixote does provide a paradigm for Sancho, in his famous "Advice" to Sancho in chapters 42 and 43 of Part II. Here Don Quixote espouses moral standards commonly enumerated in the manuals on the art of governing so popular in the time of Phillip the Second: fear of God, humility, good manners, courtesy, impartiality, constancy, compassion, and mercy (Bleznick). These values are held up to scrutiny as they are projected in a context that turns their logic inside out: Sancho's governorship (Redondo, "Tradición carnavalesca").

The first illogical event of Sancho's reign is that he is proclaimed governor of his "ínsula," a real township possessed by the ducal pair, when he has yet to prove himself worthy of such a position. Indeed the name of the "isle," "Barataria," indicates the cheap price at which it was given to Sancho. On the first day of his reign, the governor-elect is given judicial cases to solve as a means to establish his moral stature and shrewdness. The test of his austerity follows as he is made to undergo a gastronomic penance at the banquet. The night watch that follows tests his skill for handling chance encounters. On the following day, his discretion is tested as a number of riddlers are brought before him. The activities that are planned for him, like the hoaxes devised during his stay at the ducal palace, test the values that the knight has advised him to embody, as well as some traits of the squire seen previously. The outcome of the planned adventures will bring to light the governor-elect's contradictory qualities of peasant simplicity or shrewdness.

The three cases of the first day, like the questions posed to Sancho throughout his seven day reign, deal not with the implementation of justice, but with the unmasking of deception. Sancho compensates for his lack of knowledge of universal principles with his excellent memory and imagination, which allow him to apply his experience of one event to another by analogy, and his innate ability to solve riddles with common sense (Joly, "Ainsi parlait Sancho Pança"; Morón Arroyo 227). Agustín Redondo has shown the place of these riddles in a long tradition in European folklore. Each represents fraud masquerading as truth. All of this is, of course, very appealing to Sancho's ability to perceive and denounce fraudulence.

The first case involves a dispute between a distrusting farmer and a tailor about the advantage that could be made of the farmer's cloth. Sancho's decides that the miniature capes should be given up to the needy. With one stroke, Sancho undercuts the distrusting farmer, the tailor's greed and vengeance, and Don Quixote's serious ideal of charity, since the capes are doll size and can be of no use to anyone.

The case involving a woman's claim that a man has raped her is a reenactment of a popular trial celebrated at festival time, which mockingly censured attacks against women's virtue by unmasking women's conjugal infidelity and the promiscuity of single girls.[26] The defense of the victimized virtuous woman against her aggressor, as practiced by Don Quixote, is transformed into an exposure of the woman's guilt as Sancho discovers the brute power of the lady, capable of preventing any man from forcing her against her will. This representation of women is a commonplace in Golden Age literature.

The serious wedding ceremony, in which the physical and moral virtues of the bride are enumerated, are comically transformed in the first court case of the afternoon. A farmer appears before the governor to ask for a dowry for his son, and comically exaggerates the physical and moral defects of his son and bride-to-be, Clara Perlerina.

The banquet scene, in which Sancho is deprived of food by the Doctor Recio Agüero de Tirteafuera, forms part of the scapegoat ritual of hunger. Sancho has come to the isle expecting to satisfy the needs of his belly, as kings do. He requests to eat the "olla podrida," a favorite carnival meal composed of several types of meat, but is made to continue his Lenten penance. The "court" doctor, Pedro Recio Agüero de Tirteafuera restricts his diet to lenten foods, such as quince, grapes and wafer rolls.

The evening activities involve the governor's night rounds. The rounds of the clown-king form part of carnival activities. The king-elect of carnival is given his cane and the book of laws and walks around the town meting out punishments, usually in the form of fines. In the course of the rounds, local gossip is discovered, such as illegal business dealings, illicit affairs, and secret actions in general (Caro Baroja 289-300). Sancho's deliberation over a dispute between a gambler and the man who throws in his favor in hopes of gaining a tip which is not given to him, certainly reveals that he can envision moral reforms. However, his desire to abolish gambling

---

[26] The platonic tradition which idealizes women's virtue and beauty is contrasted in the comic work with the Gallic tradition. Bakhtin, *Rabelais*, 239, tells us that within the Gallic tradition, there exists a topos of the Middle Ages and the Renaissance, "La querelle des femmes," which offers a negative view of women, and is manifested in such themes as cuckoldry and the promiscuity of single girls.

houses does not go beyond the vague advice commonly made by the populace to the governors and kings, collected in the literature of "arbitrios" of the period.

Finally, the riddle of the bridge and the gallows, as Joseph R. Jones as shown, is a reproduction of traditional pedagogical material used to teach teen-age baccalaureate students the elements of formal logic. Sancho's resourceful resolution of the riddle, in accordance with his master's advice to be merciful, functions less to exalt the governor-elect than to out-trick the tricksters by revealing the puerility of the so-called "educated" courtiers who surround him.

On the seventh day, the clown-king's reign comes to an end. The duke and duchess as well as the members of their staff that form Sancho's cabinet plan a mock battle, advising Sancho beforehand of a possible invasion of the territory by their enemies. On being advised of the enemy's assault, Sancho rejects the role of soldier and defender of his people, the most important guise of the great ruler, and confesses his lack of knowledge and skill on such matters: "–¿Qué me tengo de armar –respondió Sancho–, ni qué sé yo de armas ni de socorros?" (II, 53: 441).[27]

Sancho's brief rule is truly remarkable. Here, more than anywhere else in the narration, the reader comes to identify with Sancho, spokesman and defender of the values he or she admires, such as charity, mercy, compassion, free will, and justice. Indeed, his reign has often been signalled as the culmination of Sancho's progressive intellectual and moral education at the side of his master (Brantley; Oëlschlager; Romero Flores). Yet the evolution of Sancho's character should not be confused with a true education. What Sancho does learn from his master is how to manipulate superficial formulas, clichés, and speech patterns generating a value system the reader abides by. In imitation of his master, Sancho exemplifies these values in situations that render them ambiguous, either because they are misapplied or exemplified in a manner that suggests their falsity, or because they are proven to be useless or ineffective. As witness to this ineffectuality, the reader is forced to reject the ab-

---

[27] The reign of the governor-elect conforms to the structure of the clown-king's reign at carnival time. The clown-king's domain is restricted to a single township and develops within the time limit proscribed by the duration of the town's festival, anywhere from three to seven days. At the end of the reign, the clown-king is ritually uncrowned and "killed." On the king-fool's uncrowning, see Bakhtin, *Rabelais*, 197-200 and Caro Baroja 284-300.

solute nature of these values, question as to when and under what conditions they can be applied and to what end.

At the close of the narration, Sancho comes to eclipse the quest of his master, but only as a half-figure, the fragmented other self of his master. By means of his different guises – jester, buffoon, Tempter, and Ironical man – Sancho comes to lay bare the inner guises of Don Quixote and his heroes. Sancho and Don Quixote's masks are like those of the characters in the Commedia dell'Arte, in turn derived from the *alazon/eiron* masks of primitive ritual. These masks are never complete in themselves. They come in pairs and act as mirrors. Harlequin has a very different character and nature from Scapino, and yet the inner being of Scapino is refracted in the external actions of Harlequin and those of Harlequin in Scapino (Nicoll). Similarly, Don Quixote's external actions mirror the inner selves of the chivalric heroes he imitates, while Sancho's actions mirror the interior self of Don Quixote, double of Amadís: his fraudulent suffering, penance and fear, masked behind the rhetoric of chivalry and/or classical wisdom.

If selfhood, according to the Christian Humanists, consists in the freedom of moral choice, based on a natural capacity that distinguishes man from the beasts, the inverted image of this "right" reason is the figure of the frightened Sancho, whose "uncrowning" consists of being armed in a manner that transforms him into the image of the tortoise as well as into the inanimate objects of a slab of bacon between two boards and a boat upturned and caught in the sand. At the fall of his reign, as he continues to reproduce proverbial, dogmatic truths in justification of his fear, he reveals his inability to engage in the human activity of individualized thinking.

In his effort to find a confluence of thought in Erasmus' and Cervantes' works, Alban Forcione affirms in *Cervantes and the Humanist Vision* that throughout the *Quixote*, Sancho Panza is the embodiment of Erasmus' ideal of natural reason, "linked to that primal period before writing, philosophy, and the numerous confusions of civilization, when nature's norms were clearly apprehensible to man" (166-67). As spokesman for empiricism, Sancho "rises to challenge the vanities of man's prideful intellect" (307). He represents true wisdom as opposed to mere knowledge, as demonstrated in his governorship, his use of common sense to outwit the "primo humanista," in his ridicule of Don Quixote's reading of the mysterious prophecy of the fleeing rabbit and in his insistence on the truth of his senses in the enchanted boat episode (308). There is no doubt that his common sense logic acts as a corrective to his master's obedience to the authority of the word. Yet as I have shown, his uncritical obedience to learned or popular authority, transmitted to him orally by his master or the collectivity in general and imprinted if not on the written page, on the slate of his well-endowed memory, is equal to that of his master's.

Following Américo Castro, Forcione suggests that Sancho's charitable and humane character is posited as an ideal substitute for his master's bookish knowledge.[28] His humanity can be found in his resolution of the paradox of the bridge and the gallows, his indignation as he beholds the rowers whipped in Barcelona, and his compassion for the old galley slave who is being led in chains to his death (313). The adage that "charity begins at home" would be well worth remembering here. Viewing the galleyslaves from afar it is easy for Sancho to feel compassion, just as it is easy for him to opt for mercy, in compliance with his master's Advice. His virtuous action serves as a clever solution to the seemingly inextricable dilemma of the riddle of the bridge and the gallows. Yet his charity towards his master is always on the verge of being transmuted into its opposite, as has been shown, where his "valientes posaderas" are involved. Nowhere is this more eloquently revealed than in his inconclusive self-inflicting penance, a trial which was to prove his charitable spirit and moral preparation for his governorship. The cruelty of his deceits and trickery in view of his professed friendship far surpasses the ruses of the priest and barber, or those designed in the ducal palace.

Sancho's sacred wisdom or "tología" derives instead from his capacity to: imitate, refract and expose his master's protean embodiment of varying dogmas as it behooves him; master a self-enhancing situation or extricate himself from a difficult one; and to veil a range of illicit, libertine conducts and attitudes in contexts that reveal his master's partial adherence to chivalric virtue or classical wisdom and the limitations of the codes on which they are based. It is in his divergence from what can be understood as an "individuated personality" that Sancho discloses his ritualistic origins.

---

[28] For a similar point of view see Close, "Sancho Panza: Wise Fool" and R. M. Flores, 138, who defends the seriousness and complexity of Sancho's wisdom.

CHAPTER 4

WORD PLAY

Like the characters and situations, the discourse of *Don Quixote* is constructed by means of an irreverent mimesis. This chapter on word play, and these following on argumentation and the speaker-listener relationship, will show how attitudes and point of view are transmitted, and explore how discourse contributes to the creation of the comic character and situation, and the inversion of classical and chivalric romance ideals.

In his work on the grotesque, Philip Thomson asserts that there is a strong play urge in the grotesque work of art, and that word play is the defining characteristic of the grotesque in language (98). For him, the presence of word play signals an unresolved confusion of distinct attitudes. While language should be a vehicle at the service of direct communication of an idea, this normal relation of reader to language is lost in the grotesque work of art. Hidden meanings of words and utterances are brought out, as if against the will or consciousness of the speaker, transforming the message he or she is trying to communicate.

Other theorists on the comic coincide with Thomson. As Maurice Charney affirms, a major function of word play is to to cause the reader to doubt logical assumptions and values created and transmitted by the normal use of language (19-48). From there it is only one step to the reader's reflection on the fallibility of reason and the difficulty of communication. Bakhtin's concept of "dialogue" also offers a description of how meanings are layered in words. In his study on Dostoevsky, he explains that there are two types of discourse in European narrative, monological and dialogical (63-82).[1] The first is defined by its closed universe. It has only one consciousness. The ideology of the author is absorbed and assimilated in that of the characters, resulting in a single projection of ideas and values. Language is fixed, tending to move on one plane and in one direction, and is given a single tone and style. In dialogic discourse, language is open, moving on several planes and directions and a combination of points of view is offered. The form of the discourse is open, unstable, and undetermined, and a variety of experiences and events is allowed to enter its sphere. Language and writing produce multiple levels of intention and meaning.

The origin of dialogic discourse can be found in the serio-comical genres which arose at the close of classical antiquity: the Socratic dialogue practiced by such figures as Plato, Xenophon, Phaedo, and Antisthenes – and Menippean satire, allegedly invented by the Greek cynic Menippus (Bakhtin 87-100; Frye 309-12; Parr 124-39). His works were lost, but his philosophy was transmitted by his disciples, the Greek Lucian and the Roman Varro, and by the tradition of Varro, as well as by Petronius, whose *Satyricon* best exemplifies the genre. Both Socratic dialogue and Menippean discourse ran into opposition with serious genres, such as the epic, tragedy, history, and classical rhetoric, and were set apart from them by virtue of their bond to carnivalistic folklore, literary variants of oral carnival folk genres.

While these comic genres contained strong rhetorical elements due to the influence of serious genres, the carnivalesque attitude that prevailed in these works produced a weakening of one-sided rhetorical seriousness, of rationality and singularity of meaning. In these genres, the carnivalesque vision of the world emerges as the mythical and historical figures of the past are deliberately substituted by contemporary figures. The values of that time are provided with a new space and time, and the action is allowed to develop freely, finding a new basis in the experience and free imagination of the author. These works contain a deliberate multifariousness and discordance that resist stylistic unity. There is a mixture of the high and the low, the serious and the comic. Finally, the form and composition of these works are heterogeneous. We find a patchwork of

---

[1] For a summary of his concept of dialogical discourse, see Socrate, 22-28 and Kristeva, "Word, Dialogue, and Novel," 80-83.

many genres, such as the introductory genre, the letter, the convention of the discovered manuscript, the reconstructed quotation and the use of slang.

In his chapter on the "word" in Dostoevsky, Bakhtin explains that the words of a speaker enter into dialogic relationships when they act as the sign of another speaker's semantic position, that is, another speaker's "voice" (150-64). He calls these utterances "double-voiced." The logic of the science of linguistics alone is powerless to explain the difference between the double-voiced word and the word of monological discourse. Normally, extra or metalinguistic elements, irreducible to logic, are also at work at the moment a word is suddenly infused with new meaning. These would encompass such factors as change in tone, style, change of time or space, or other conditions which invest the utterance with a new, "foreign" accent, a new valuation, a new understanding. Bakhtin does not rule out the possibility of a speaker entering into a dialogic relationship with one of his or her own utterances, if in some way the speaker separates himself from his utterance or one of its individual parts, maintaining a distance, as if dividing him or herself in two.

Dialogic discourse is double-directed as well as double-voiced. Words or utterances refer simultaneously to an object of speech, like an ordinary word, analyzable in terms of its relationship to other words appearing with it in the passage, or in the work at large, and to another person's speech. When a text makes reference to the words of a speaker, it antagonizes the other person's speech, and this antagonism determines the speaker's word no less than the object. This is what Bakhtin calls the "hidden polemic" of the double-voiced word.

In the text of *Don Quixote*, we find that the scope of word play is so extensive that it can easily be considered one of the primary features in the style of the work, and has been studied by several critics (A. Alonso; Corley; Hatzfeld; Read; Rosenblat; Spitzer). All speakers engage in wordplay. We can find examples of word plays made by only one speaker, and those made by at least two speakers, each one eliciting a different meaning or intention.. Both types abound in the text, and in both, new perspectives are offered on the ideals belonging to the world of chivalry that Don Quixote tries to restore.

Sound play, including such devices as alliteration, assonance, rhyme play, and play with word roots, is even more frequent in the text than simple sense play. Finally, under the category of word play, a concept broad enough to include a variety of devices that transform the sense of an utterance, the presence and usage of devices involving word and phrase substitution, such as error and word permutation, and those involving word and phrase repetition, such as the synonymous word pair, will be considered.[2]

Practically all plays on the meanings of words are oriented towards objects, characters, or ideals that form part of the world described in chivalric romance. One such object is the hero's horse, the magical and mythological creature that aids the suffering hero in his effort to reach his triumphant destiny. At the very beginning the narrator tells us that the hero's horse had "más cuartos que un real" (I,1: 75). Double meaning is brought out by one speaker and the word is not repeated. "Cuartos" is a type of skin disease contracted by horses, but also, as the final words in the sentence reflect, a coin representing monetary value.

The first meaning of the word forces the reader's attention towards the transformation the narrator has carried out as he substitutes the mythological image of the hero's horse for the grotesque image of a horse in decay. The second meaning of "cuartos" as a coin fabricated by the state, a modern object, jolts the reader out of the exotic past when knightly adventures were carried out and creates a time that is incongruent with the mythology the hero is trying to restore as he collects his heroic trappings. Finally, the comparison enhances the word play. The word "más" asks the reader to compare the number of "cuartos" in the horse's flesh with the number of "cuartos" in the "real." The reader is led to conclude that the horse has more of the first than of the second (there are thirty-four "maravedíes" in one real and four of these make a "cuarto"). Such a conclusion forces the reader to perceive a comic contradiction within the terms of the comparison "más," since the more "cuartos" his flesh contains, the fewer "cuartos" he represents in monetary worth.

---

[2] I have used Olbrechts-Tyteca's work *Le comique du discours*, 55-99, as a basic theory for my analysis of word play in *Don Quixote*. Her book has specifcally been useful in regard to the division and organization of material and definition of terms and techniques.

Sansón Carrasco frequently employs word play to make fun of the knight's heroic endeavor. The knight asks his neighbor if a second part of the narration of his exploits is forthcoming and Sansón replies that he is not sure but that "algunos que son más joviales que saturninos dicen: "Vengan más quijotadas . . .' " (II, 4: 68). When Don Quixote asked about a second part, he was referring to the poetic narration of his deeds. Sansón's claim that the jovial readers are those who ask for more "quijotadas" seems to suggest another meaning, the narration of the rash and foolhardy deeds of Don Quixote.

In a conversation with the housekeeper immediately preceding the knight's third sally, Sansón alters the image Don Quixote attempts to project from hero to fool. Noticing the housekeeper's affliction, he asks her what is troubling her. She replies:

>—No es nada, señor Sansón mío, sino que mi amo *se sale*; ¡*sálese*, sin duda!
>—Y ¿por dónde *se sale*, señora? –preguntó Sansón–. ¿Hásele roto alguna parte de su cuerpo?
>—No *se sale* –respondió ella– *sino por la puerta de su locura*. Quiero decir, señor bachiller de mi ánima, que *quiere salir otra vez*. . . . (II, 7: 85, emphasis added)

In this conversation, multiple word play is brought out as the dialogue develops. At least three meanings can be detected. The first, intended by the housekeeper, is simply that her master is going to leave again on his third sally. Sansón, feigning not to have any knowledge of or complicity in the knight's decision to undertake another sally, pretends to understand something else, that the knight is wounded. In response to this the housekeeper offers a third meaning, that he has lost his wit. The qualification of the housekeeper "quiero decir" strengthens the relationship of cause and effect between loss of wit, "no se sale . . . sino por la puerta de su locura," and his sally,"quiere salir," already established by word play.

Word play also offers new perspectives on the ideal of feminine virtue. When in the Sierra Morena Sancho learns the identity of his master's lady, he tells the knight that he is acquainted with her and then describes her: "Y lo mejor que tiene es que *no es nada melindrosa*, porque tiene mucho de *cortesana: con todos se burla* y de todo hace mueca y donaire" (I, 25: 312, emphasis added). The meaning of "cortesana" as a lady pertaining to the king's court is lost as the meaning of courtesan is emphasized by the allied phrases that precede and follow it.

The physical perfection of the highborn lady of romance is described in a new light by virtue of word play. In a midnight meeting with Don Quixote, Doña Rodríguez reveals to the knight the existence of certain open wounds, "fuentes" in the duchess's leg. She means "fuentes" in the medical sense. The narrator later refers to these as the "Aranjuez de sus fuentes" (II, 50: 415). The hyperbole "Aranjuez" elicits the meanings of "fountains," as it refers ironically to the renowned beauty of the fountains in that locality. The narrator's word play underscores the disparity between the beauty of those "fuentes" and the ones in the duchess's legs, representing physical decay and deterioration.

Sound play is even more abundant in the text than simple sense play. Play with prefixes and suffixes is a device frequently deployed in literary works of the time as a means of embellishing the text. When the device is employed excessively, however, it can destroy the poetic effect. Most of the examples of plays on prefixes and suffixes generate conflicting attitudes within those words normally used to construct the idealized world of romance (García de la Torre).

The narrator plays with the prefixes of words in order to undermine the image of the triumphant hero in the episode narrating Don Quixote's duel with the Knight of the Mirrors. The narrator seems to be describing the riding talents of the horseman and the excellence of his horse, such as the knight's agility and the horse's quick response to his master's spurring. Word play, however, reveals that the horse's quick response to the spurring is due to the horse's deathlike thinness rather than to his reflexes or the knight's talents. The rough spurring into his skeletal flanks cannot fail to produce an effect:

> Don Quijote, que le pareció que ya su enemigo venía volando, arrimó reciamente las espuelas a *las trasijadas ijadas* de Rocinante, y *le hizo aguijar* de manera, que cuenta la historia que esta sola vez se conoció haber corrido algo.... (II, 14: 142, emphasis added)

The knight's helmet also becomes the object of sound play. The narrator ironically emphasizes the counterfeit nature of the helmet when he describes the fully armored knight: ". . . puesta su mal-compuesta celada . . ." (I, 2: 79).

The criminal exploits of knight and squire are accentuated by the narrator by means of word play. Sancho finds a case in the Sierra Morena, and empties its contents, stuffing them into his sack. The narrator describes his action: ". . . *desvalijando* a la *valija* de su lencería, la puso en el costal de la despensa" (I, 23: 281, emphasis added). The verb "desvalijar" does not mean simply to remove the contents of the case or "unpack, but to swindle or rob the case of its contents.

The narrator's word play in the adventure with the dead body reveals that the knight's victory is due to the adverse circumstances of his enemy. The knight's opponents cannot defend themselves against their assailant because they are unarmed, but also because their long robes inhibit their liberty of movement, leaving them helpless to escape from or confront the knight. The narrator describes their plight: "Los enlutados asimesmo, *revueltos* y *envueltos* en sus faldamentos y lobas, no se podían mover; asi que, muy a su salvo, don Quijote los apaleó a todos, y les hizo dejar el sitio mal de su grado . . ." (I, 19: 231-32, emphasis added).

Two words in the text are continually subject to changes of prefix and suffix, both pertaining to Don Quixote's profession: "aventura" and "andanza." Play on these words allows the reader to hear a new, unheroic "voice" in these words. For example, after Sancho's blanket tossing and suffering under the effect of the balm of Fierabrás, the squire expresses his distrust in the knightly adventure as a means of gaining a governorship. He does this by means of word play: "Y lo que yo saco en limpio de todo esto es que todas estas *aventuras* que andamos buscando al cabo al cabo nos han de traer a tantas *desventuras* que no sepamos cual es nuestro pie derecho" (I, 18: 216, emphasis added). The change of prefix shifts the meaning of the word from "exploits" to "misfortune."

A similar play is made by Alonso López in the adventure with the dead body. The unfortunate student accompanying the twelve priests who were transporting a dead body to Segovia is attacked by the knight. Lying on the ground with a broken leg, he tells the knight how unfortunate he was for having encountered someone looking for adventures: ". . . harta *desventura* ha sido topar con vos, que vais buscando *aventuras*" (I, 19: 233, emphasis added). The student's play on prefixes reveals how the knight reverses his concept of adventure from a means to aid the needy and the innocent to one of bringing misfortune and need to the innocent.

This student, as well as others in the text, is a prolific word player. As he continues to speak to the knight, he plays on the word "andante": ". . . suplico a vuestra merced, señor *caballero andante* (que *tan mala andanza me ha dado*), me ayude a salir de debajo desta mula, que me tiene tomada una pierna entre el estribo y la silla" (I, 19: 233, emphasis added). The first use of the word "andante" conveys the conventional meaning of the word, simply that of "errantry." The change of suffix to "andanza" preceded by the adjective "mala" produces a change in meaning. Perhaps even two new meanings can be brought out: a figurative meaning, the bad fortune brought upon him by the knight, and a literal one, that he has crippled him.

The addition of a prefix or suffix can give rise to false cognates and plays on the roots of words. Kneeling before the peasant girl in El Toboso, Sancho plays on the word "alta" in a manner that puts his alleged attempt to exalt the lady into doubt. He addresses her with the words "vuestra altivez" (II, 10: 109). His unfamiliarity with or feigned ignorance of the correct address to a noble lady, "alteza" causes him to employ the word "altivez" which means "arrogance."

The narrator employs the augmentative suffix ironically on several occasions. For example, he calls the ceremony in which Don Quixote is to be knighted "armazón" (I, 3: 90). The narrator's feigned purpose of employing the utterance is to exalt the ceremony. Yet his choice of suffix serves to remove the action in which the knight is involved from the hierarchy of such ceremonies. The word "armazón" refers to the external part of a structure or its framework. When the narrator employs this word, he implies that the only similarity between the ceremony celebrated by the knight and those described in romance is the external structure or form, one totally devoid of content.

Plays on etymologically related words abound in the text. The narrator plays on words of the same root to describe the Yanguesan muleteers' escape after they had beaten the knight and squire with their stakes: "Viendo, pues, los gallegos el *mal recado* que habían hecho, con la mayor presteza que pudieron cargaron su *recua* y . . ." (I, 15: 192, emphasis added). The word "recado" is conventionally employed to refer to the equipment used for the drove or "recua." The narrator employs it in a figurative sense, to refer to the damage the muleteers had done, but at the same time to the specific cause of the damage: the presence of the "recua" or pack animals owned by the muleteers, which had provoked the "erotic" desires of Rocinante.

As the episode continues, Sancho comments that his beast, suprisingly, has not received any wounds: ". . . de lo que yo me maravillo es de que mi jumento haya quedado libre y *sin costas* donde nosotros salimos *sin costillas*" (I, 15: 196, emphasis added). The parallel phrasing "sin costas" and "sin costillas" is deceiving since they represent phrases of opposite meaning. The first means that the beast was exempt from punishment and the second that they had to pay for Rocinante's attack on the mares with a beating in the ribs.

Other types of sound play found in the text involve such devices as alliteration, assonance, the repetition of words of like sound, and rhyme play. The entire pseudo-adventure involving the knight's meeting with the Princess Micomicona and their subsequent journey to her kingdom to rescue it from the giant is comically deflated by means of sound play. The narrator describes how the priest, masquerading as a damsel in distress, explains to the barber that in order to insure the successful outcome of his plan, he will tell the knight not to "quitar su antifaz, ni la demandase cosa de su *f*acienda, *f*asta que la hubiese *fecho derecho* de aquel mal caballero . . ." (I, 26: 326, emphasis added).

When Dorotea agrees to take over the role of princess and tells the knight of her mission to find him, the knight responds to her in the style of chivalric romance, employing the device of alliteration in order to convince her of his knightly identity: "–No os responderé palabra, fermosa señora –respondió don Quijote–, ni oiré más cosa de vuestra facienda, fasta que os levantéis de tierra" (I, 29: 364).

In the same sequence, the priest and Cardenio finally join the Princess, her squire, Don Quijote and Sancho. The priest approaches them from the opposite direction, kneels before Don Quijote and praises him as a great hero. When Don Quijote recognizes him, he begs him to mount his horse. The priest refuses the offer, saying that the knight will be able to perform great deeds if he remains on his horse: "–Eso no consentiré yo en ningún modo –dijo el Cura–: estése la vuestra grandeza *a caballo,* pues estando *a caballo acaba* las mayores fazañas y aventuras que en nuestra edad se han visto . . ." (I, 29: 367-368, emphasis added).

The word play involves a pun. The priest's play with the sound and sense of words enters into conflict with his supposedly serious intention to praise the knight's undertaking. In the entire sequence, the reader has the impression that everyone is playing a game and everyone knows it, including the knight. The alternating between contemporary speech and chivalric archaism, often marked by sound play, is precisely what distinguishes the style of romance from the "stylization" of *Don Quixote*.

The narrator employs the lofty style of romance to describe a prosaic object in his description of the loft or attic at the second inn. The knight sleeps in the loft for the night and imagines that the daughter of the warden of the "castle" will come to visit him. The narrator calls the loft the "estrellado establo" (I, 16: 201). The devices of assonance and alliteration strengthen the narrator's sense play. The word "estrellado" conveys a first meaning of "starry," an adjective often deployed to create a romantic atmosphere, the "starry sky" or the "starry night." The adjective clashes here, however, with the noun "establo," producing a violent change in meaning. The adjective now refers to the roof of the loft, and is used to explain the fact that the roof has so many holes in it that the stars can be seen through it. "Estrellado" also conveys the meaning of "ill-fated." The narrator employs the word with this intention in order to foreshadow the disastrous series of events that will ensue within the confines of the loft in the course of the evening, radically different from those that should develop in the knight's meeting with a damsel in chivalric romance. These would include the knight's struggle with Maritornes as he attempts to seize her against her will, his "duel" with the muleteer, Sancho's beating at the hands of Maritornes, and the cudgelling the knight receives by the Holy Brotherhood.

Sancho frequently uses like-sounding words such as "el hato y el garabato" and "perro con cencerro". Humor results from the confrontation of his country style and the learned and affected style of his master. Other speakers also employ these colloquialisms, however, and usually in the most unexpected circumstances. Don Quixote describes the enchanted sheep as well-built, proper men: ". . . son hombres hechos y derechos" (I, 18: 224). Observing the struggle involving practically all of the lodgers at the inn, dealing mainly with the barber's attempt to reclaim his basin and pack saddle, the knight is reminded of the discord described in *Orlando Furioso* in King Agramante's camp. The narrator's use of the colloquialism, incongruous with the poetic exaltation of the event, weakens the effect the knight is tryng to produce: "Y en la mitad deste caos, máquina y laberinto de cosas, se le representó en la memoria a don Quijote que se veía metido *de hoz y de coz* en la discordia del campo de Agramante . . ." (I, 45: 544, emphasis added).

Word repetition involving merely a change from masculine to feminine ending or vice versa can result in sense play. When knight and squire are in the Sierra Morena, Don Quixote asks Sancho to go to the other side of the mountain in order to find the owner of the case they had found. Sancho expresses his fear of leaving his master and Don Quixote replies that he is happy that his courage is of service to him, and assures him that he will continue to protect him in the future: ". . . y yo estoy muy contento de que te quieras valer de mi *ánimo*, el cual no te ha de faltar, aunque te falte el *ánima* del cuerpo" (I, 23: 285, emphasis added).

Don Quixote's affirmation of the continued usefulness of his courage to his squire is undermined by the qualifier "aunque" which introduces the repeated word "ánima." The inference of the second phrase is that if Sancho might be dead, that is, without a soul ("ánima") in his body, the knight's courage will have been of no use to him, and being of no use to him in life, it will be of even less value after he is dead.

Thus far I have examined the homonym. The synonymous word pair also produces double and multiple meanings within a single thought or idea and is therefore complementary to the homonym. Yet it involves a technique that is somewhat different. By means of the synonymous word pair, the idea or object is defined by at least two words of similar or apparently similar meaning. Used deliberately as a rhetorical device, it can add force and clarity to a serious argument. It can also be used as a poetic device, because the employment of repetition can give pleasure. In Cervantes' work, the device can be found in the speeches of the major characters as well in those of the narrator, but in a manner that transforms its poetic or oratorical use into a new double-voiced discourse.

The intended emphatic effect of the word pair can be weakened when the individual words of the pair, when joined together, cause the reader to grasp another meaning, at odds with the intended one. For example, the knight wishes to praise his lady as he stands guard at the entrance to the inn: "–¡Oh mi señora Dulcinea del Toboso, estremo de toda hermosura, *fin y remate* de la discreción, *archivo* del mejor donaire, *depósito* de la honestidad . . . !" (I, 43: 526, emphasis added). In the first word pair, the words "fin" and "remate" both convey the meaning of "extremity," and correspond to the phrase that precedes it, "extremo de toda hermosura." This is the meaning the speaker intends, and if either one of the members of the pair were employed separately, this meaning would be directly conveyed. The emphatic expression, however, expressed by means of the repetition, causes the reader to think of a second meaning conveyed by both words, that of "end " or "destruction."

The second word pair or phrase pair "archivo de . . . /depósito de . . ." functions in a similar manner. Both words convey the meaning of "store" or "treasure," Don Quixote employs these words in a figurative sense, in order to magnify the virtuous qualities possessed by the lady. However the juxtaposition of the two words and the emphasis it conveys causes the reader to think of the literal sense of the words. The effect is that instead of exalting the lady's virtue, the knight inadvertently depersonifies the lady, attributing to her an inanimate state.

Sancho employs his master's words in a manner that alters the attitude projected by them when his master asks him what opinion the readers of his exploits have of him. In the conversation, Don Quixote begs Sancho to tell him the truth about the readers' opinions because ". . . si a los oídos de los príncipes llegase *la verdad desnuda, sin los vestidos de la lisonja,* otros siglos correrían . . ." (II, 2: 55, emphasis added). Sancho replies by supplying the other member of the pair for his master:

> –Eso haré yo de muy buena gana, señor mío –respondió Sancho–, con condición que vuestra merced no se ha de enojar de lo que dijere, pues quiere que lo diga *en cueros, sin vestirlo de otras ropas* de aquellas con que llegaron a mi noticia. (II, 2: 55-56, emphasis added)

Don Quixote uses the expression "la verdad desnuda" in a figurative or metaphorical sense to mean the "pure" truth," while Sancho employs the expression in a literal one, that of "naked." The knight's high ideal of truth is destined to be conveyed by means of Sancho's colloquial expression, one which has the effect of weakening the sense of purity that the knight's metaphorical discourse intends to transmit.

Sancho employs the synonymous word pair in a similar fashion in his praise of his master at the initiation of the knight's descent into the Cave of Montesinos. The word play involves a fixed form of speech, "flor y nata." Sancho seems to employ the expression in this laudatory sense when he praises his master's heroic descent. But as he adds another synonym to the pair, "¡. . . flor, nata y *espuma* de los caballeros andantes!" (II, 22: 209, emphasis added), he elicits a new sense that transforms his praise into abuse. The term "nata" is employed figuratively in the fixed form of speech to mean "the best." Sancho reminds us of the literal meaning of the word, that of "cream," a sticky, liquid substance, as he joins it with the word "espuma." The presence of the last word transforms the exalting effect of "nata," for the "espuma" or foam is constituted of a light, porous texture, without substance. The knight is no longer portrayed as the best of knight errants. Instead his inauthenticity as exemplary knight is foregrounded.

The narrator employs the word pair disjunctively as he puts word pairs in opposition to each other in his description of the knight's vigil of his arms. The narrator has previously told the reader that the innkeeper has told all the other lodgers at the inn about Don Quixote's madness. After Don Quixote defends his arms against two muleteers who have moved his arms in order to water their beasts, the other muleteers lodged at the inn begin to throw stones at the knight. The narrator describes the effect of the knight's angry response on the muleteers:

> Decía esto con tanto *brío y denuedo*, que infundió un terrible temor en los que le acometían; y *así por esto como por las persuasiones del ventero*, le dejaron de tirar, y él dejó retirar a los heridos, y tornó a la vela de sus armas, con la misma *quietud y sosiego* que primero. (I, 3: 92, emphasis added)

Word repetition in the first pair is unincremental and ironic, for the narrator's assertion that the boldness of the knight instilled fear in his opponents is immediately mitigated by the following phrase in which he implies that the muleteers were persuaded to withdraw more by the innkeeper's words. The second word pair stands in contrast to the first one, weakening it further. While the noble rage of the true hero can only be appeased gradually, the Manchegan knight shows a radical shift in attitude from extreme ire to extreme calm. Such fluctuations are more indicative of madness or childishness than of heroism.

The repetition of words is complemented in the text by the repetition of entire phrases. One type of repetition involves only a change in the order of the second phrase repeated, and is conventionally employed with poetic intention. It is frequently found in *cancionero* and *romancero* poetry of the same period and prior to the publication of *Don Quixote*, contributing to the playful quality and the musicality of the poems in these collections. The device is also used in rhetoric, of course, for purposes of emphasis. In Cervantes' text, we find such repetition in the most unexpected circumstances.

Don Quixote most frequently employs this device. After being beaten by the muleteer from Arévalo and cudgelled by an official from the Holy Brotherhood in the stable at the second inn, Don Quixote attempts to exalt one of the most unheroic situations narrated in the text by speaking in a poetic style to his squire: "Sancho amigo, ¿duermes? ¿duermes, amigo Sancho?" (I, 17: 207). The context in which the words are spoken mitigates the poetic force the repetition is to transmit.

Don Quixote frequently employs the device of phrase repetition as a means of persuading his audience of his deeds or ideals. Trying to persuade his audience of his heroic ire, he says: "*–¿Leoncitos a mí? ¿A mí leoncitos*, y a tales horas? Pues ¡por Dios que han de ver esos señores que acá los envían si soy yo hombre que se espanta de leones!" (II, 17: 160, emphasis added). The phrase "¿leoncitos a mí?" has become proverbial in Spanish and is employed to indicate the confidence one has to carry out a task successfully under adverse conditions. The knight employs the device of repetition in order to prove his superiority with respect to the lion and the use of the diminutive obviously serves the same purpose. The effect of the knight's speech, however, is different from that intended.

The knight's use of the diminutive "leoncitos" indicates the speaker's lack of certain heroic attributes, such as prudence, a quality that aids the hero in judging the opponent's strengths and weaknesses, and humility, a quality that allows the hero to be aware of his own limitations. In this episode, carnivalesque actions replace those of romance as the roles and identities of animal and hero switch. Now the lion demonstrates heroic qualities. Proving to be prudent and generous, the lion does not attack the poor knight:

> Pero el generoso león, más comedido que arrogante, no haciendo caso de niñerías ni de bravatas, después de haber mirado a una y otra parte, como se ha dicho, volvió las espaldas y enseñó sus traseras partes a don Quijote, y con gran flema y remanso se volvió a echar en la jaula. (II, 17: 164)

The lion's behavior only takes on meaning when we compare it to that of the knight and vice versa. The knight's attempt to minimize the lion's grandeur by use of the repeated phrase is met with the lion's refusal to even recognize the knight as a potential threat. The fact that the lion looks all around before returning to the cage, without resting his eyes on any particular object or person, reflects the total insignificance of the knight as a possible opponent. This fact further explains the calm and placid condition of the lion, his yawn, and his exposure of his back side, In these gestures, the lion reveals his total lack of fear that the knight might possibly attack him from behind. The knight's bravado juxtaposed with the lion's eloquent pantomime prove true the adage that gestures speak louder than words. Indeed, the tame conduct of the lion says much more about his power than his fierceness could have, and inversely, the knight's "persuasive" rhetoric, implemented by means of phrase repetition, has the effect of underscoring his own physical inadequacy.[3]

Another type of phrase repetition that frequently appears in the text is the synonymous phrase pair, by virtue of which a description, action, or idea is stated in at least two ways. The repeated phrase does not strengthen the truth of the first one, but comes into conflict with it and often disproves it entirely. It is often employed in the text for the purpose of comic emphasis, in order to underscore unheroic aspects of Don Quixote. In all cases where the device appears, the idea, action, or description is first stated affirmatively, and then restated by its opposite. This type of negative

---

[3] In her analysis of this episode, Rogers concludes that our laughter is directed towards the lion, and issues from the elements of surprise and comic relief.

restatement or "litotes" is, of course, a form of understatement. One understates an idea to such a point of exaggeration that the opposite comes to be understood.

The priest uses litotes in the Sierra Morena in imitation of his master's pompous speech. In order to provoke a reaction from the knight in front of the Princess Micomicona, the priest describes how a madman and criminal released a group of dangerous galley slaves. He ends by saying that "[Q]uiso . . . hacer un hecho por donde *se pierda su alma y no se gane su cuerpo*" (I, 29: 371, emphasis added). The priest's jesting imitation of the knight's rhetorical style emphasizes the knight's fallen moral state, resulting from his criminal action, as well as his physical deterioration, resulting from the beating he received at the hands of the criminals.

The narrator employs the synonymous phrase pair in order to create comic emphasis. He tells us that Sancho was reluctant to mount the flying horse, Clavileño, not only because of his fear of flying, but also because of the discomfort of sitting on the wooden horse. Referring to the back part of the horse ("las ancas"), he tells us that Sancho "las halló *algo duras y no nada blandas*" (II, 41: 348, emphasis added). The understatement in the affirmative phrase as well as the exaggeration obtained by restatement in the negative one comically underscore the conflict between Sancho's constant desire for enjoying physical comfort and his obligatory accommodation to bodily suffering on the wooden horse. The narrator's rhetoric serves the purpose of highlighting the comic aspects of the trial elaborated by the duke and the duchess in the design of this pseudo-adventure.

The narrator's employment of litotes further reveals Sancho's disloyalty to his master. On his mission to El Toboso to deliver the knight's letter to Dulcinea, Sancho encounters the priest and barber of his village and immediately swears to himself not to give away his master's whereabouts. When immediately the priest threatens to have the squire sent to jail for having robbed his master's horse on which he is mounted, the "medroso" Sancho quickly turns his good intentions around and reveals his master's location and business:

> —No hay para qué conmigo amenazas, que yo no soy hombre que robo ni mato a nadie: a cada uno mate su ventura, o Dios, que le hizo. Mi amo queda haciendo penitencia en la mitad desta montaña, muy a su sabor.

> Y luego, *de corrida y sin parar*, les contó de la suerte que quedaba, las aventuras que le habían sucedido, y cómo llevaba la carta a la señora Dulcinea.... (I, 26: 322, emphasis added)

The narrator's repetition comically reveals the squire's haste to betray his master, and shows that in spite of his earlier claim to never harm anyone, he gives information that will lead to the knight's capture, imprisonment, and temporary renunciation of his knightly identity.

A final type of phrase repetition is the pleonastic expression. This involves the use of superfluous words, added with the intention of expressing an idea more completely or with greater clarity. Although in some cases it can be used legitimately for the purpose of emphasis, more frequently it results in violation of correct grammatical usage. This device lends itself well to a comic use of rhetoric, for it underscores the limitations of rhetorical emphasis.

Don Quixote employs a pleonastic expression in his order to Sancho to withdraw while he fights for the acquisition of Mambrino's helmet: "*Apártate a una parte* y déjame con él a solas; verás cuán sin hablar palabra, por ahorrar del tiempo, concluyo esta aventura, y queda por mío el yelmo que tanto he deseado" (I, 21: 253, emphasis added). The knight's eagerness to prove his heroic worth to his squire after his humiliation in the adventure of the fulling mills is expressed in his rhetorical emphasis. His transcendence of the bounds of normal speech is opposed to but complemented by his total silence with respect to the man approaching them. The knight knows that if he stops to make inquiries, the response he receives might prevent him from carrying out his actions. For the reader, however, the knight's attempt to employ such rhetoric as a means to regain his authority is ineffective, because the narrator has already informed us that the man is not wearing a helmet but a barber's basin. The effect of his speech on Sancho is not much different. Even before he actually distinguishes the object on the man's head, he responds to his master in a manner that reflects a continued distrust of his master, that cannot be easily overcome by words: "–Yo me tengo en cuidado el apartarme –replicó Sancho–; mas quiera Dios –tornó a decir– que orégano sea, y no batanes" (I, 21: 253).

Don Quixote speaks pleonastically, when, after leaving the first inn on his first sally, he hears cries for help. The humor of the episode derives from the knight's error in judging the servant boy Andrés as innocent victim in need of help when he is really deserving of punishment. The knight's pleonastic expression in his reference to the origin of the cries, "son de algun menesteroso o menesterosa, que ha menester mi favor y ayuda" (I, 4: 95), has the effect of emphasizing his error in judgment, contrary to the knight's aim to exalt his heroic role.

Complementary to the device of word and phrase repetition is that of word and phrase substitution, whereby the word or utterance present in the text implicitly repeats the absent one it replaces. The word or utterance appears now in an altered form, in the "voice" of its substitute.

Neologism or word invention is one type of word substitution that appears in the text, albeit infrequently. The invented words are analogical, that is, based on familiar forms, words, or word constructions, linked to the world of chivalry. The new utterance projects a different perspective on that world. The narrator resorts to this device when he describes the masked and disguised Tomé Cecial as a "narigante escudero" (II, 14: 145). The invented word "narigante" seems to be a compound word including "nose" ("nariz") and "giant" ("gigante"). The implications are ludicrous. It appears that the closest the knight comes to duelling with a giant is having before him the Knight of the Mirrors' squire, with his giant nose.

The alderman employs the device of word invention when he praises his fellow alderman: ". . . que por el Dios que me crió que podéis dar dos rebuznos de ventaja al mayor y más perito *rebuznador* del mundo . . ." (II, 25: 232, emphasis added). The verb is changed into another part of speech, describing the person who realizes the action. As Spitzer pointed out in his article on linguistic perspectivism in *Don Quixote*, the ending is high-sounding and recalls the words "campeador" or "emperador" (165). However, the noble sound is drowned out by another voice, that of the hoarse braying of the ignoble beast.

Word permutation is another type of word substitution employed in the text. The device occurs in sentences that are constituted by symmetrical phrases, such as two nouns with their adjectives or two verbs with their objects, and consists of switching the adjectives or the position of the verbs. The narrator employs this device at the beginning of the adventure of Mambrino's helmet to advise the reader that, contrary to what Don Quixote has affirmed, the man riding towards them is a barber wearing his basin. The reason the knight thought the basin was a helmet was because "todas las cosas que veía con mucha facilidad las acomodaba a sus *desvariadas* caballerías y *malandantes* pensamientos" (I, 21: 253-54, emphasis added). The narrator's word substitution causes the reader to see as equivalent the noun "caballerías," which refers the knight's alleged chivalric action, and the noun "pensamientos," which refers to his fantasies about his identity. What links them is the fact that they are both erring, not in the sense of "errantry," but in the sense of being "mistaken," "foolish" or "mad."

The innkeeper of the first inn employs word permutation when he describes the "heroic" exploits of his youth. He says that he traveled all over, "haciendo muchos tuertos, *recuestando* muchas viudas, *deshaciendo* algunas doncellas . . ." (I, 3: 89). He reverses heroic action by replacing "deshaciendo" or "righting" in the first phrase with "haciendo" or "causing." His affirmation that he courts widows ("recuestar") is shown to have new meaning when juxtaposed with the phrase "deshaciendo algunas doncellas." The two phrases become synonymous as another meaning of "recuestar" is brought out, that of "to lie with". The speaker plays here with two verbs of like sound, and that even share some common conjugations, but are different in meaning: "recuestar" and "recostar."

Another technique of substitution employed in the text with some frequency is "false anticipation" (Olbrechts-Tyteca 67-68), in which the reader or listener, accustomed to a certain jargon, structure, or dialogue, expects a certain word to appear, but this word is replaced by an unexpected one. In all cases where this occurs in the text, the lofty chivalric discourse of the knight is debased, and the noble action he wishes to carry out is seen as low and prosaic.

Sancho employs this substitution in his conversation with the village priest and barber outside the inn. Reproducing the contents of the letter his master has written to Dulcinea, which began with the words "Alta y soberana señora," Sancho says that his master began the letter with the words "Alta y sobajada señora" (I, 26: 324). The first adjective "alta" now comes into conflict with the second one, "sobajada" which means "crumpled, "pawed," or "handled."

One final type of word substitution employed frequently in the text is that of word error. As Angel Rosenblat explains in his work on the language of *Don Quixote*, the employment of corrupted forms of speech is a technique already found in the learned theater of the sixteenth century as a stock comic device used to mock peasant speech and the speech of the illiterate in general.

Treatises on rhetoric written in the sixteenth and seventeenth centuries can also explain the humor of such devices. The canons of formal rhetoric stipulate two requirements for correct elocution. The first one is "latinidad." The opposite of "latinidad" is "barbarismo," which can mean the use of foreign words, but also refers to errors in syntax, spelling and pronunciation. The second requirement is "claridad." One should avoid using words that are unintelligible to the audience. If the audience cannot understand, the speaker's discourse is useless, and the speech will appear affected. Indeed, a speaker commits errors following the exposure to a discourse unadapted to his or her cultural level. Unsure of the meaning, the listener restates the word, but in doing so, alters it, exchanging it for a word that is more familiar, of like sound, but radically different in meaning.[4]

Comic discourse, produced by such corruptions in language, attracts attention to certain elements of language, such as syntax and spelling, and the rules that generate them, attacking the weakness of language and of all speakers. Finally, the presence of such corruptions in the text has the overall effect of casting a shadow on the knight's ideal of proper language and his attempt to embody that ideal by means of his discourse.

Sancho's discourse contains many word errors, although errors can be found in the speech of other characters (A. Alonso; Hacthoun). As the squire gradually comes to imitate his master, he attempts with greater assiduity to imitate his speech. But his unfamiliarity with the jargon of romance, his lack of knowledge on history, grammar, Latin, and other subjects related to humanistic studies, as well as his general illiteracy, cause him to commit grammatical errors that are common to the speakers of his linguistic community, including epenthesis, syncope, metathesis, and paranomasia.

Epenthesis involves the insertion of extra letters in a word. When the knight accuses his squire of citing so many proverbial statements that he cannot be understood, Sancho justifies himself, saying that he is sure that he has not said so much nonsense, and in-

---

[4] For the rules of classical rhetoric in Cervantes' time, see Rico Verdú and Lausberg, 1: 301-59.

sists that Don Quixote always acts as "f*r*iscal" of his words and deeds (II, 19: 181, emphasis added). The form of the squire's discourse tends to weaken the content, that is, his assertion that he has not said any nonsense. Other examples of epenthesis in Sancho's speech can be found in the text with similar results.

The error involving syncope reflects the inverse process of epenthesis. Here the speaker removes a letter or letters of a word. In the adventure of the enchanted boat, the knight tells his squire that the enchanter who is transporting them to such faraway lands ("tan *longuincuos* caminos") will also take care of their beasts (II, 29: 263, emphasis added). Sancho tries to repeat the word but because he does not know Latin, he leaves out letters. He tells his master that he does not know what "*logicuos*" means (263, emphasis added). Ironically, his error acts as a corrective to his master's affected speech that in turn results in "barbarismo," since he uses a foreign word in his discourse that his audience has no obligation to understand.

Errors involving metathesis occur when there is an inversion in the order of letters in a word, or the permutation of letters. In his conversation with the knight about the publication of their adventures, Sancho informs the knight that he has been told that he is one of the main characters in the tale: ". . . también dicen que soy yo uno de los principales p*r*esonajes della" (II, 3: 62, emphasis added). As in the example above involving the word "friscal," the form of the discourse weakens the content, in this case, the squire's intention to make himself seem superior to others.

The error of paronomasia consists in the replacement of certain letters by others present in the word. As a type of pun, this device allows for a play on words of like sound. The speaker repeats the words of another speaker erroneously, inventing a new word, or employs an existing word incorrectly. This unintentional paronomasia or "malapropism" occurs when Sancho tells his master that he has convinced his wife to let him leave on a second sally with his master: "–Señor, ya yo tengo re*l*ucida a mi mujer a que me deje ir con vuestra merced . . ." (II, 7: 86, emphasis added). Sancho substitutes the "l" for the "d." When his master corrects him, he becomes irritated and tells Don Quixote not to correct him unless he truly does not understand him, and when that is the case, he should ask him to explain what he means again. If the knight still does not understand him, he may then correct him because, the squire concludes, he is a very docile person: "que yo soy tan *fócil* . . ." (II, 7: 86, emphasis added).

The first error is the result of a word used incorrectly, but the knight is able to guess the word Sancho intends to say. The second error gives rise to a certain confusion, resulting in a lack of communication. The dialogue that continues between the pair comically testifies to the difficulty Sancho has in making himself understood:

> –No te entiendo, Sancho –dijo luego don Quijote–, pues no sé qué quiere decir 'soy tan fócil.'
> –Tan "focil" quiere decir –respondió Sancho– "soy tan así."
> –Menos te entiendo agora –replicó don Quijote.
> –Pues si no me puede entender –respondió Sancho–, no sé como lo diga; no sé más, y Dios sea conmigo.
> –Ya, ya caigo –respondió don Quijote– en ello: tú quieres decir que eres "tan dócil. . . ." (II, 7: 86-87)

The substitution of letters can also result in a mistaken communication in Cervantes' work. The intended word, usually a learned one related to the world of chivalry, is replaced by another word of like sound, but which projects a prosaic perspective on the word and on the world associated with it. In Sancho's discussion with the Knight of the Mirrors' squire over what arms they should use in their duel, Sancho's opponent suggests that they fight with linen sacks in order to avoid the risk of seriously wounding each other, but that they should fill the sacks with stones. Sancho objects to the statement that such a stuffing will prevent them from physical suffering: "–¡Mirad, cuerpo de mi padre –respondió Sancho–, qué martas *cebollinas* o qué copos de algodón cardado pone en las talegas, para no quedar molidos los cascos y hechos alheña los huesos!" (II, 14: 138, emphasis added). In Sancho's attempt to exalt their duel and put it on the same plane as the sword fight of their masters, he refers to the common stone as the exotic "sable skin," but inadvertently mispronounces "cebellines," calling it "cebollinas." He thus transforms the high-sounding "sable skin" into the prosaic "onion skin," a food product with which he is indeed more familiar. Examples of these errors abound in Sancho's speech and with the same results, including many errors on the difficult proper names of romance, such as "Fierabrás" to "feo Blas," "Catón Censorino" to "Catón Zonzorino" and "Cide Hamete Benengeli" to "Cide Hamete Berenjena" (Spitzer 155-57).

In my discussion of word play in *Don Quixote*, I have attempted to offer a representative sampling of the major types of word play and analyze the techniques involved to create them, the effects obtained by a word play in the particular sequence and context, as well as the effects it obtains within a wider network of word relationships in the text. While the enumeration and analysis of word plays have not been exhausted, they form a basis that will allow me to make a few conclusions about the use of word play within the imitative and creative processes of the text.

More than one critic has held that Cervantes' ideal language model consists of a clear, simple style.[5] Accordingly, Cervantes adheres to and exemplifies the perfect embodiment of the model of proper language, an ideal elaborated by humanists of the sixteenth century, such as Nebrija or Juan de Valdés.[6] Those who support Cervantes' subordination to such an authority have justified their point of view by citing certain parts of *Don Quixote*, such as Don Quixote's advice to Sancho, Maese Pedro's advice to his assistant to avoid an affected style and to speak in a clear, natural manner, and finally the general mocking and parody of the archaic language employed by the knight. However, analysis of the discourses of ro-

---

[5] Rosenblat, in the first chapter of his work, entitled "Actitud de Cervantes ante la lengua," affirms that Cervantes' reiterated ideal is simplicity of style ("llaneza"); and Bataillon says in his study on Cervantes that his prose is surprising for its "limpidez" and that when compared to the mixed style of Quevedo or Tirso, Cervantes' prose "tiene la sabrosa insipdez de la leche o del pan" and ends with these words: "Más que ningún otro escritor de la época de Felipe III, él permanece fiel al ideal de transparente sencillez que Juan de Valdés había formulado en el *Diálogo de la lengua*," 781-82.

[6] Nebrija's publication of the *Gramática Castellana* in 1492 and Valdés' publication of the *Diálogo de la lengua* in 1535 corresponded to efforts being made in Italy with Pietro Bembo's publication of his *Prose della volgar lingua* in 1525 and in France with Joaquin Du Bellay's *Deffence et illustration de la langue françoyse* in 1549. They established an ideal language model of the vernacular tongue which was to unify the language and fix and stabilize its norms of usage. In Spain, Castilian was still in a state of flux. The fragility of the model is manifested when language is spoken by individual speakers, human beings that inevitably commit errors and break rules, intentionally, or accidentally, as Sancho's discourse bears out.

Moreover, regional dialects, with their separate and independent set of rules of usage, came into conflict with the unified model of Castilian. As these speakers attempted to speak in Castilian, they commited all sorts of errors. The humor in the Biscayan's speech is due to such a conflict. According to treatises on rhetoric of the time, one of the serious errors a speaker could incur in is the "solecismo," that is, errors in the conjugating of verbs and in the use of adjectives. This is an error commonly made by Basque speakers.

mance, amatory poetry, and classical oratory reveals that such a conclusion is unwarranted.

Unlike the discourse of these genres, the double-voiced and double-directed discourse of *Don Quixote* does not attempt to persuade the reader into accepting a certain attitude or point of view, captured, fixed and transmitted by language. Indeed, there is a constant conflict between the knight's attempt to imitate perfectly the world of romance by means of his discourse and the discourse that issues from the contexts, circumstances, and speakers that the novel constitutes.

Don Quixote wishes to find truth by restoring an original unmediated relationship between words and things and consequently the world that rests on the belief in such a relationship, that of the Golden Age. His notion of truth is based on the longing for a mythic world in which there is no gap between the object and the word, between the expression and understanding of meaning.[7] And yet as the knight imitates the speech of chivalric romance, he calls attention to the impossible existence of unmediated discourse.

The knight's continuous attempts to find resemblances between his own circumstances and the situations narrated in romance, such as the lion episode, his cudgelling by the official from the Holy Brotherhood ("Sancho, ¿duermes amigo? ¿amigo duermes?"), and his encounter with a damsel-in-distress ("–No os responderé, fermosa señora . . ."), and fix the truth of them by means of his discourse only serve to make us forget the similitude and focus on the difference, so that *the* truth to be obtained is put into doubt. Language is used in order to consciously signal the arbitrariness of the word. As Robert Alter puts it, "the ontological doubleness of language in Cervantes is mirrored in the new kind of narrative structure he devised: the fictional world is repeatedly converted into a multiple regression of imitations that call attention in various ways to their own status as imitations" (11).

The discourse of all the speakers in the text splits language open and projects ideas that are in conflict with each other without looking for resolutions. As Ramón Saldívar has shown in his analysis of figural language in *Don Quixote*, Cervantes transcends the

---

[7] On the magical-religious concept of the name and of the word in general, its relation to the object in medieval culture, and how this relationship is transformed in *Don Quixote*, see Foucault, Robert, 152-56 and Williamson, 1-7.

bounds of Socratic knowledge, which purports to be able to "uncover" the truth. Cervantes seems to want the reader to realize that the interpretation of the sign is not a meaning, but another sign, and that this sign will lead us to another sign, but never to a final truth (5-13, 25-71). The double-voiced discourse of the text shows that the truth or value of an ideal, transmitted by the word, cannot be understood unless the word is continuously restated by other "voices" from other positions. Meanings are altered in the constant exchange of signs in daily life. The reader emerges in a new relationship with the discourse of the text. Situated at varying degrees of distance from the different poles of meaning, he or she is invited to actively analyze the logic and truth of them without having to accept or reject fully one or the other.

CHAPTER 5

COMIC ARGUMENTATION

> –Paréceme, ¡oh Anselmo!, que tienes tú ahora el ingenio como el que siempre tienen los moros, a los cuales no se les puede dar a entender el error de su secta con las acotaciones de la Sancta Escritura, ni con razones que consistan en especulación del entendimiento, ni que vayan fundadas en artículos de fe, sino que les han de traer ejemplos palpables, fáciles, inteligibles, demostrativos, indubitables, con demostraciones matemáticas que no se pueden negar, como cuando dicen: "Si de dos partes iguales quitamos partes iguales, las que quedan también son iguales"; y cuando esto no entiendan de palabra, como, en efeto, no lo entienden, háseles de mostrar con las manos, y ponérselo delante de los ojos, y, aun con todo esto, no basta nadie con ellos a persuadirles las verdades de mi sacra religión.
>
> *Don Quixote,* I, 33

The study of word play in the previous chapter serves as a basis to identify and define some underlying functions of dialogical discourse in a literary work. First, word play makes the reader aware of the multiple possibilities the word offers of conveying meaning, attitudes and values, enabling him or her to become dissociated from fixed ideals conventionally linked to a word in order to analyze their value. There is no total intelligibility of language. Words are inscribed in a network of relays and differences, more numerous than can ever be grasped by the speaker. Secondly, it serves to point out a curious paradox of semantics. The word can give rise to multiple meanings, thereby expanding its semantic possibilities. Yet if the word is to convey a specific meaning, it becomes subject to rigorous linguistic and metalinguistic restrictions.

On the one hand meaning is always necessarily inscribed in a pre-existent economy of sense, which it can never control. In the case of the *Quixote*, it is the discourse of chivalry. Yet on the other hand, this very condition, by creating such a complex background of constraints, makes it possible for other meanings to emerge. Meaning, thus, not only invests itself with structures, but with structures that are endlessly producing new possibilities of sense, all of which display the "opening" of the text. The constant susceptibility of speakers to fail to meet the requirements that condition meaning signals the difficulty of communication, and even more importantly, the difficulty of maintaining the status quo of the logical functions within language, by means of which conventional hierarchies, such as assumptions, facts, and values, indeed, knowledge itself, are transmitted.

While monological texts consciously or unconsciously suppress these possibilities, the dialogical discourse of Cervantes' work consciously exploits the layering of meanings into words. As speakers link words in order to form "arguments," the restrictions imposed on a particular speaker become more pronounced. Don Quixote and other characters employ rhetorical arguments in order to sustain their ideals, imitating rhetorical-literary conventions which governed the style, tone, and structure of the literary works of the time. Yet as they do so, a second, quasi-logical discourse joins itself with the classical one, and in dialoguing with it, reinscribes its "truth" in a new order of textual signification.

In order to retrace this dual inscription of argumentation in the text, I will begin by reviewing the notion of rhetoric within its historical context, according to the treatises written in the time of Cervantes, and analyze a set of rhetorical metaphors in order to show that the very language that theorists employed to support their ideas carries within it the "voices" of opposition, of contradictions and dislocations that turn reason against itself. The comparison of this analytical technique with Jacques Derrida's deconstruction of classical rhetoric will further articulate the process by which the rhetoricians' attempts to perpetuate stable and abstract hierarchies by means of language are self-defeating. Once the framework within which the double-voiced rhetorical discourse of Cervantes' text must be integrated has been established, I will then proceed to analyze the arguments.

One of the defining characteristics of the prose fiction of the Golden Age is the presence of a rhetorical discourse, which can be accounted for if we recall the formal education of the writers in that era. According to the studies of Kristeller, Garin, and other specialists on the period of Renaissance humanism, the major goal of humanism was to restore the "educative ideal" of antiquity. Humanists studies were to give man a general education via the language arts. The study of rhetoric was one of the subjects studied by humanists (along with poetry, grammar, history, and moral philosophy). Indeed, humanists were identified as "orators" or "poets" before the term "humanist" came into use. In a manner of speaking, the study of rhetoric was the study of literature in prose and consisted of the reading, interpretation, and oral and written imitation of ancient models.

The humanists believed that classical language and literature was the threshold to all knowledge and that correct speech and an elegant style was a prerequisite for any type of oral or written manifestation. With their focus on a linguistic and literary concept of education, the humanists created a program for literary production which limited artistic creation, for they subordinated the writer to a rhetorical apparatus by prescribing fixed models, genres, themes, style, and organization.

Spain bore witness to a flourishing of rhetorical studies during the Renaissance.[1] Treatises defining the purpose and techniques of classical rhetoric were written throughout the sixteenth and seventeenth centuries by leading figures of the humanist movement, such as Arias Montano, Sánchez de las Brozas and others. The major prose works of the period reveal the influence of humanistic teaching and theory. This influence is present in adjunct or accessory material, such as the use of prologues, in interpolated material such as laudatory descriptions, fables, apologues, sentential statements, letters, discourses, and philosophical digressions, and in the body of the works within the language of the characters.

According to the theory of the time, based on a long classical tradition, the function of rhetoric is to move the public by means of

---

[1] For an excellent overview of these treatises, see Rico Verdú.

reason or passion, in order to persuade it to accept the truth or falsity of something that is hypothetical. Logic is an abstract process that is based on empirical evidence and experience, and somehow preexistent to language, while rhetoric – speech and writing – is formulated in language. Yet according to Arias Montano and other theorists of the time, logic is the "hermana gemela" of rhetoric. Logic gives the orator "ideas" with which to persuade the audience, while rhetoric gives the orator the "afeites y colores" with which to dress up the ideas.[2]

While the figure "hermana gemela" suggests a relationship of equivalence, the following one, "afeites y colores," infers an elusive, inferior status of rhetoric, suggesting that it is relegated to a secondary or outside position to wisdom. It cannot be on an equal footing because "afeites and colores" can only "enhance" the preexistent truth. Yet the metaphor "afeites y colores" is self-revealing, and seems to question the priority of logic over rhetoric that it infers, because if the "afeites y colores" can bring out the "truth" of something that is preexistent but not self-apparent or comprehensible, they can also disguise what is "untrue" by 'dressing it up' as truth. Or what is more to the point, they can disguise the fact that the truth is hypothetical to begin with. Behind reason and morality, there is a fundamental will to persuade. Truth is a reductive process, maintained inasmuch as it can be successfully supported over the counter assertions of another. It is inseparably bound to the rhetorical devices that support it.

Derrida's study of language in his readings of the most influential philosophers of language from Plato to Saussure amasses evidence that signals a total suppression, from Socrates onward, of everything that threatened the sovereign power of dialectical reason, particularly, the insidiousness of writing. In his texts on Greek philosophy in *Of Grammatology*, Derrida traces some of the means by which writing or rhetoric is systematically opposed to speech, truth, self-presence and origin (11-93). The suppression of writing operates in Plato and his numerous descendants by means of a vehicle of self-perpetuating rhetorical or metaphorical devices. Yet the devices reveal contradictions and ruptures that undermine the truths they intend to support.

---

[2] These are Benito Arias Montano's definitions from his work *Rhetoricorum*, Libri III, cited by Rico Verdú, 83.

Derrida shows that Plato defends the inalienable status of reason and knowledge in a primary opposition, that between "lived truth" and "writing." Socrates "lived" the truth and thus his "experience" of truth, inevitably linked to his presence and the primal authority of speech, maintains its status as "the" truth only by avoiding submitting them to textuality, that is, to writing (*Of Grammatology* 6-13). In further pursuing the sanctions against writing within Plato's thought, however, Derrida picks apart one of Plato's key metaphors and reverses this hierarchy. He discovers a second opposition between "good" and "bad" writing. The first is figural or metaphorical and is viewed as "natural" and "inscribed" upon the soul by reason. The second is a debased and "literal" script which obtrudes its shadow between truth and understanding. In other words, the figurative or imaginative ('good') writing is a more real, immediate and powerful vehicle to reveal the truth than its "literal" counterpart. This fabricated or imaginative immediacy, made possible by writing, then becomes the source of all authentic wisdom and truth (15-18).

The hypothetical, the "fictional" or "metaphorical" nature of truth, becomes more self-evident when the nucleus of rhetorical discourse is examined, that of the argument. The argument is included in that part of rhetoric called *inventio*. The speaker who wishes to persuade the audience of something will have to invent a discourse that will best serve the purpose of the argument. The speaker will treat the matter from various viewpoints in order to "illuminate" the truth of it, solving all apparent contradictions. These viewpoints are called "arguments" and serve as "proof" of the orator's premise or hypothesis.

The treatises on rhetoric catalogue the varying types of arguments and the basis for the definitions and divisions of the catalogue underscore the metaphorical nature of truth. Arguments can be intrinsic and extrinsic (Lausberg, 1: 301-59). The intrinsic argument can be developed in two ways. The object or person on which the argument turns can be considered in terms of its own nature. Its truth is proven by means of one of several methods of *ratiocinatio*, the most perfect one being the syllogism. The syllogistic argument confirms the truth of its premise deductively: what is asserted as true, when contrasted with all to which it is opposed, is found to be not that to which it is opposed, and therefore the truth. The truth about an object or person can also be considered in relation to another object or person by comparison or antithesis. These can be real, taken from contemporary society or history, or fictitious, taken from already existing tales or invented by the orator. This type of argumentation constitutes "artistic" proof of the premises. Another type of linked argument is that providing "inartistic proof." In this type of argumentation, the truth of a premise is supported by considering it in light of existing legal or moral codes and customs. Finally, the truth of a premise can be supported when the thing or person is considered in light of extrinsic elements that condition it, including such factors as social or psychological states, geography and weather.

This review of the essence and purpose of arguments by classical theorists suggests that rhetoric is more than just "afeites y colores," a collection of classified devices reducible to a system, subordinate to and in service of the truth. With its identities and differences, explanations and fables, rhetoric is endowed with the powers of myth and poetry. Together they take us back toward the origin of thought in man's encounter with experience. The central purpose of all three is to *explain*, to *make sense of* humanity's experience by means of metaphor and analogy. Everything is metaphor and analogy (Derrida 15).[3] Logic is the product of a desire to understand, and selectively arranges the habits of thought so as to make some sense of immediate experience. The synthetic nature of human thought describes things according to the contingent qualities of their appearances and then generalizes and identifies them as essential qualities. This is a rhetorical or metaphorical process of false substitutions.[4]

In monological rhetorical discourse there is an intent to suppress the elements that would threaten the logic of argumentation and prevent the speaker from achieving the orator's goal: to move the audience with his or her eloquence, "teach" the audience to "understand" the truth by means of the reasoning processes, and "delight," by convincing the audience of a matter by means of a perfectly constructed speech. In Cervantes' work, the speakers,

---

[3] Nelson, in his analysis of Renaissance poetic theory, p. 49, underscores the link between poetic fiction with its claim to a higher truth, ancient myth and biblical parable and their relationship to rhetoric: they are all rhetorical devices for willing moral, religious or historical truths.

[4] For a review of these and other concepts of deconstruction, see Norris, *Deconstruction*, 22-83; and his most recent work, *Derrida*, 28-46.

while feigning or seriously attempting to imitate the rhetorical model in their speeches, produce a deviant figuration that weakens the "truth" of their premises, namely, the existence of the world of chivalry, the heroic conduct of the knight errant, or the personal defense of their moral conduct, and the rhetorical model.[5] This process can be confirmed by a close analysis of the arguments employed by the various speakers in the text.

It should first be remembered that when setting out to prove his or her premise, the speaker must be aware that an argument develops more successfully when the premise rests on assumptions already accepted by the audience. In comic argumentation, the force of the values, rules, codes and assumptions held by the collectivity to which the listener and speaker belong is stated or implied, only to be weakened by the development of the argument. There can be a discrepancy between the premise and the conclusion; the speaker can depart from a premise that is not real or possible; or other speakers can build on the speaker's arguments in order to reveal the falsity in them (Olbrechts-Tyteca 91-117). In my analysis of these discrepancies, I will examine not only the development of arguments that pertain to formal rhetoric, such as the syllogism, but also those that are implied in the speaker's discourse, often called "enthymeme." For example, a speaker states his ideas and expects his audience to accept them because of a common cultural heritage and moral code.

The listener's acceptance of facts or beliefs may be weakened when a rule is set up in the premise as fact or reality when it is not. The premise is accepted as true and its logic is played out. The logic is convincing or correct, but the premise is not. Don Quixote establishes a false premise in a conversation with his squire after his duel with the Knight of the Mirrors. The knight is eager to uphold the "fact" of his status as triumphant hero. Sancho questions the validity of this status by suggesting that his opponent was not a knight, but his neighbor, Sansón Carrasco.

The knight is not aware of his neighbor's plan to disguise himself as knight errant, defeat him in battle, and order him to renounce his knightly identity. He thus affirms to his squire that Sancho's premise is false. He claims that it could not have been Sansón.

---

[5] A few deconstructive critiques of *Don Quixote* are beginning to appear in collections or comparative studies. See Ralph Flores, 19-43, 88-115 and Saldívar, 1-66.

If they looked alike, it was because the evil enchanters who persecute him transformed his opponent into the figure of his neighbor in order to deprive him of his glory. The arguments he employs to back up his premise are sound: his neighbor is not his rival or enemy, nor is he a soldier:

> –Estemos a razón, Sancho –replicó don Quijote–. Ven acá: ¿en qué consideración puede caber que el bachiller Sansón Carrasco viniese como caballero andante, armado de armas ofensivas y defensivas, a pelear conmigo? ¿He sido yo su enemigo por ventura? ¿Hele dado yo jamás ocasión para tenerme ojeriza? ¿Soy yo su rival, o hace él profesión de las armas, para tener invidia a la fama que yo por ellas he ganado? (II, 16: 148)

As we can observe from the knight's arguments, comic rhetoric operates to remind us that the truth and logic of all arguments are limited by other people's counter assertions and by facts or knowledge unknown to the speaker which refute the speaker's assertions.

The knight's lack of knowledge of certain events causes him to believe in the truth of a false assertion immediately preceding his confrontation with the lion. Don Quixote has discovered that fresh cheese curds have been placed in his helmet. He is not aware that during his conversation with the Man in Green, Sancho had wandered off to ask a goatherd for some cheese, yet his knowledge of the squire's character causes him to suspect Sancho of having put them there. Sancho denies the knight's premise. He supports his innocence with logical arguments based on the nature of his own character, and therefore convinces the knight. He tells his master that not only does he not have any cheese, but if he did, he would have put it in his stomach: "... yo confío en el buen discurso de mi señor, que habrá considerado que ni yo tengo requesones, ni leche, ni otra cosa que lo valga, y que si la tuviera, antes la pusiera en mi estómago que en la celada" (II, 17: 159).

Sancho's arguments demonstrate that even knowledge that one has of the speaker's character does not serve as absolute proof of the truth or falsity of his or her assertions. Extenuating circumstances can intervene to temporarily alter a person's normal conduct. On this occasion, the narrator informs the reader of a fact that the knight is unaware of: Sancho had not eaten the cheese because his master ordered him to undertake an adventure before he could do so. In his hurry, the squire was forced to dispose of the cheese by placing it in his master's helmet, which he was carrying at the time.

Sancho employs a false premise in the braying episode, one of a number of false arguments in the text that are instrumental in weakening the domain of "history" as the only means of projecting truth. The squire is disillusioned with his master's promises to protect him and reward him with a governorship. Prepared to return home, he demands pay for the time he has served. Don Quixote then asks him how long he has been serving and the squire responds: "–Si yo mal no me acuerdo . . . debe de haber más de veinte años, tres días más a menos" (II, 38: 259). The squire's attempt at an almost scientific exactness is comically contrasted with his mistaken estimation, since only months have passed since the beginning of their first sally. However, Sancho's false premise shows the limitations of objective standards of time. As he lays forth his arguments, his recollection of his continuous beatings, physical suffering, and fear, he reveals that there is some truth in falsity:

> A la fe, señor nuestro amo, el mal ajeno de pelo cuelga, y cada día voy descubriendo tierra de lo poco que puedo esperar de la compañía que con vuestra merced tengo; porque si esta vez me ha dejado apalear, otra y otras ciento volveremos a los manteamientos de marras y a otras muchacherías, que si ahora me han salido a las espaldas, después me saldrán a los ojos. (257)

The limitations of our beliefs can be discovered when a premise is asserted that is true, but the arguments employed to support it are false. Such a discrepancy occurs in the priest's discussion with the innkeeper at the second inn about the books the latter possesses. The priest looks at four of the innkeeper's books: *Don Cirongilio de Tracia*, *Felixmarte de Hircania*, *Historia del Gran Capitán* and *La vida de Diego García de Paredes*. He declares to the innkeeeper that the first two works should be burned because they are "milesias" and "cuentos disparatados." They cannot delight or teach because the events they narrate are not believable, and therefore not exemplary. Yet, the other two are historically true. They are "good" because they narrate events that are inspirational, and they delight because we admire the conduct and actions of the heroic figure.

In order to prove his premise, the priest cites Diego García as an example of a true hero and claims that he had such great strength that he stopped the wheel of a mill in full force with one finger. The priest's premise that historical figures are "true" and therefore inspire and delight is put into doubt by the argument. The priest is moved not by the historical aspects of the hero's life, but by the fantastic feats that are attributed to him, just as the knight and the innkeeper are inspired by the fantastic feats narrated in chivalric romance.

Not only are our beliefs in facts or objective codes and rules put into doubt where there is a disparity between premise and argument, but our assumptions as well. We may assume that something will happen, and our interest in an event focuses on what we expect (Olbrechts-Tyteca 92-97). The speaker plays on that interest for his or her own benefit. The destruction of the reader's assumptions is the result of Sancho's narration of the tale of the shepherdess Torralba in the episode of the fulling mills.

In the tale, the unfaithfulness of the shepherdess causes the shepherd to scorn her and flee the village. He is forced to wait, however, when he comes to a river, until the ferryman takes his herd of sheep across, one by one. The tale is conventionally told to take children from a state of frustration to the relief of sleep, as a result of counting the sheep. For Sancho, the story is a means to express his hostile response to his master's intention of leaving him unprotected in a remote wood in the middle of the night in order to undertake an adventure. The knight becomes frustrated because he does not hear the end of the tale. Only after Sancho begins to narrate the crossing of the sheep and several have already passed does he tell the knight that the contingency for the continuation of the tale is the knight's ability to correctly count the number of sheep, when the compliance with such a request is no longer possible. The brusque ending of the story bewilders the knight:

> –Dígote de verdad –respondió don Quijote– que tú has contado una de las más nuevas consejas, cuento o historia, que nadie pudo pensar en el mundo, y que tal modo de contarla ni dejarla, jamás se podrá ver ni habrá visto en toda la vida.... (I, 20: 244)

The knight, avid reader of chivalric romance, had asked the squire to tell him a story that would "entertain" him, and he evidently has certain assumptions about this type of literature.

In reality, the conflict between the reader's expectations about the "story" and the actual story narrated to him in Chapter 20 is a microcosm of the conflict the reader of *Don Quixote* must face as he or she confronts the material of the text. The reader of the tale, like the reader of the text, is continuously baffled. Episodes follow, one after the other, like the sheep crossing the river, and in spite of the narrator's joking assertions scattered throughout the text that the knight was "almost" killed, the truth is that Don Quixote is never killed or even seriously wounded, nor is anyone else. The knight never rises from his initial position, never experiences a change of fortune, although at times he is made to believe so, and he is never joined, separated, or reunited with his mistress. The deviation in the text from romance ravelling and unravelling to comic "meandering" functions as a criticism of the reader's fallacious inflexibility toward what a "libro de entretenimiento" should be.[6]

Other assumptions played upon in the text pertain to values of a moral order rather than to a literary one. We assume a logical link between elements that constitute a value is guaranteed and conditioned by our customs, the nature of human beings and society. For example, choices and decisions are contingent on the actual value of an element. We decide to obtain an object or choose to carry out an act because the goal is worthwhile, even if we must suffer to achieve it. The decision is based on the premise "I choose to do this because it is good." Dialogic discourse operates to underscore the force of these links while trying to show their fallibility.

An example of a play on moral assumptions can be found in Sancho's conversation with his wife before departing for a second time with Don Quixote. Teresa tells Sancho she is sorry to see him go and face so many hardships. She then asks him why he looks so happy. He answers by asserting that he wishes he were not so happy as he seemed to be: "–Mujer mía, si Dios quisiera, bien me holgara yo de no estar tan contento como muestro" (II, 5: 73). Teresa responds by pointing out the incongruity of Sancho's assertion with certain social assumptions, namely that it is not logical to be unhappy about being happy, or conversely, to be happy about being unhappy: "–No os entiendo, marido –replicó ella–, y no sé qué queréis decir en eso de que os holgárades, si Dios quisiera, de no estar con-

---

[6] Charney discusses the concept of comic aimlessness and pointless meandering discourses, 32-34.

tento; que, maguer tonta, no sé yo quien recibe gusto de no tenerle" (73).

Sancho then explains what he means: he is happy at the thought of earning money, but he wishes he already had the money at home, and then he would not have to leave and be happy about doing so. He has to make quite a long paraphrase in order to explain the seeming contradiction. The humor of the interchange is derived from the condensation of Sancho's assertion, one which shows that our assumptions can sometimes follow a more hidden or indirect logic, escaping the bounds of the indirect linking to which we are accustomed.

Moral assumptions are further played on in the episode narrating the knight's confrontation with the galley slaves, in the criminals' narrations of their crimes. The first galley slave says that he is going to the galleys for being in love. The knight is baffled because according to an agreement of values held by society transmitted through writing, one assumes that love is a positive and exalting emotion, and certainly nothing which deserves punishment. The force of the link is weakened when the assumption that love is an exalting emotion is no longer applicable. What the criminal "loved" was a basket of clothes that was not his, and that he "hugged" and did not want to relinquish.

The second galley slave is going to the galleys for being a musician, "va por canario" (I, 22: 267). Singing, and music in general, is an exalted human activity, considered to be the purest form of human expression in practically every culture, even the most primitive kinds. The force of the link, namely, that singing is uplifting, is underscored by the knight's citation of a sentential statement, as he shows his bewilderment for the punishment: "que quien canta, sus males espanta" (267). The knight understands the words "canario" and "cantar" in their literal sense, simply "canary" and "to sing." The thief employs the terms in thieves' jargon, where "canario" or "cantar" means to confess one's crimes (note 12). When the knight cites the sentential statement as a means to justify his own reaction, the thief replies in a manner that reveals that his assumption is not always borne out: "–Acá es al revés ... que quien canta una vez, llora toda la vida" (267).

Assumptions on the value of honor are played on in the text criticizing the value on which the institution of chivalry is predicated. It is assumed that giving one's word or complying with a promise is "honorable." The narrator's discourse weakens this assumption by having Maritornes act honorably about fulfilling a dishonorable act:

> Había el arriero concertado con ella que aquella noche se refocilarían juntos, y ella le había *dado su palabra* de que, en estando sosegados los huéspedes y durmiendo sus amos, le iría a buscar y satisfacerle el gusto en cuanto le mandase. Y cuéntase desta buena moza que *jamás dio semejantes palabras que no las cumpliese, aunque las diese en un monte y sin testigo alguno; porque presumía muy de hidalga*.... (I, 16: 201, emphasis added)

The logical link between premise and argument is essential in what is considered the most perfect form of *ratiocinatio*: the syllogism. The syllogism attempts to establish the truth of a hypothesis by means of a process of deduction and argues by referring to the object or person itself. If one wishes to prove that virtue is good, he argues by defining virtue and its intrinsic value. Lausberg provides this syllogism:

> solum bonum virtus
> nam id demum bonum est;
> quo nemo male uti potest
> virtute nemo male uti potest;
> bonum est ergo virtus. (Lausberg, I: 310)

This kind of deductive reasoning is often used in mathematical equations as a means of defining, classifying, and categorizing objects.

In serious argumentation, the speaker must employ a hypothesis the truth of which is so powerful that it will naturally and instantly be acceptable to the audience, as in the example above, because of a common code of values or mores. If the speaker manages to achieve this, the succeeding links of the arguments will be accepted, and the listener will be carried from one point to the text, forced to admit the logic of the links.

The logical processes which constitute syllogistic reasoning break down when the speaker employs a hypothesis that is not accepted by the audience and then employs a logical linking of arguments to prove a "false" hypothesis. Some of the most important premises the knight attempts to establish in the text are argued on the basis of syllogistic reasoning. Don Quixote justifies the virtue of the chivalric hero as well as his own heroic identity by means of the syllogism. The narrator tells the reader in Chapter 1 of Part I that after assuming his knightly identity, Don Quixote sets about to choose a lady with whom to be in love because according to the knight, "el caballero andante sin amores era árbol sin hojas y sin fruto y cuerpo sin alma" (77). The syllogism is implicitly stated and could be loosely interpreted in these terms: all knights errant have ladies who are their "soul," that is, the seed containing their self-worth or virtue, just as the fruit and the leaves contain the value of the tree; the knight errant who does not have a lady is not virtuous; I am a knight errant and I am in love with a lady; therefore, I am a virtuous knight errant.

The very identity of the knight and the worthiness of his profession are founded on his argument, namely, that he is in love. Yet having read the first chapter of Part I, the reader is instantly aware of its flaws. Don Quixote has arbitrarily chosen a lady to love, a girl from a nearby village to whom he has never spoken. Vivaldo, who "era persona muy discreta y de alegre condición" and well-acquainted with chivalric tales, encounters the knight during the latter's visit with the goatherds in Chapter 13 of Part I. He sets out to disprove the knight's arguments by means of the knight's reasoning processes.

The traveler is surprised to see Don Quixote completely armed in such peaceful territory, and asks him the cause for it. The knight gives him an account of his profession, underscoring its risks and dangers, and describes the virtue of true knights. Knights carry out God's justice on earth and exercise their duty as good Christians. Vivaldo attacks the first point, and in doing so, signals not only the flaws in Don Quixote's argument, but in chivalric morality as well. He suggests that when a knight is at the point of risking his life in a dangerous adventure, he should be more concerned with commending himself to God than to his lady. The insinuation is that not only is the knight sacrilegious, but that he is so because of his love for his lady. He has set his love for Dulcinea above all other types of love, in accordance with the canons of courtly love. By attacking the first point of the syllogism, the second point is also questioned, namely, that the source of the knight's virtue is his love for his mistress, which inspires him and infuses him with the desire to do good.

As the traveler continues to speak, he questions another link in the knight's arguments, that all knights are in love, and all knights commend themselves to their lady in battle: "Cuanto más, que yo tengo para mí que no todos los caballeros andantes tienen damas a quien encomendarse, porque no todos son enamorados" (175). Before the traveler has a chance to justify his assertions, Don Quixote rejects his statement, affirming that all knights are in love, and if there were one who did not have a lady, he would not be a true knight, but an illegitimate one, an impostor, and a criminal. Without realizing it, Don Quixote has aided his opponent in disproving his own arguments, for Vivaldo then asserts that one of the greatest chivalric heroes did not have a lady:

> –Con todo eso –dijo el caminante–, me parece, si mal no me acuerdo, haber leído que don Galaor, hermano del valeroso Amadís de Gaula, nunca tuvo dama señalada a quien pudiese encomendarse; y, con todo esto, no fue tenido en menos, y fue un muy valiente y famoso caballero. (175)

Unless Don Quixote wants to admit that one of the greatest chivalric heroes is a common thief and "bastardo," he will either have to modify his premise, namely, that all virtuous knights errant are in love, a premise which is to confirm his own identity, or he will have to make up a lie. As dishonest as it may seem, Don Quixote opts to do the latter. He contends that Don Galaor was secretly in love, an affirmation which is ludicrous since a narration of his supposed devotion to a lady is non-existent.

After weakening the first links in Don Quixote's argument (all knights errant have ladies whose love causes them to perform virtuous action; those knights errant who do not have ladies are not virtuous and are not even legitimate knights errant, but criminals), Vivaldo attacks the final links, in which Don Quixote attempts to deduce that he is in fact a knight errant and that he is performing virtuous action. Vivaldo asks Don Quixote if he is in love: "–Luego si es de esencia que todo caballero andante haya de ser enamorado –dijo el caminante–, bien se puede creer que vuestra merced lo es, pues es de la profesión" (176).

He then asks to know what the lady's name is, as well as her country, pedigree, and a description of her beauty: ". . . le suplico, en nombre de toda esta compañía y en el mío, nos diga el nombre, patria, calidad y hermosura de su dama ..." (176). The knight responds by attempting to exalt his lady. He gives her an invented name and invented status of princess, and the name of the village of El Toboso. He then describes her beauty by means of the standard metaphors of amatory poetry, and supplies the lady's lineage, race and family at Vivaldo's request:

> –No es de los antiguos Curcios, Gayos y Cipiones romanos, ni de los modernos Colonas y Ursinos, ni de los Moncadas y Requesenes de Cataluña, ni menos de los Rebellas y Villanovas de Valencia, Palafoxes, Nuzas, Rocabertis, Corellas, Lunas, Alagones, Urreas, Foces y Gurreas de Aragón, Cerdas, Manriques, Mendozas y Guzmanes de Castilla, Alencastros, Pallas y Meneses de Portogal; pero es de los del Toboso de la Mancha, linaje, aunque moderno, tal, que puede dar generoso principio a las más ilustres familias de los venideros siglos. (176-77)

This question and answer dialogue is drawn directly from the preestablished arguments of classical rhetoric called the *loci* which the orator can choose from and employ in support of the truth he or she is asserting (Lausberg, 1: 312-19). The speaker must select the *loci*, however, that are appropriate for the premise and that will benefit his or her case. The *loci* referring to people provide the audience with concrete facts about the person that should serve as conclusive proof of what one has asserted about the person, such as name, country, pedigree, sex, age, education, body habits and fortune. In classical rhetoric these *loci* are closely linked to laudatory literary descriptions, such as the literary portrait, biography, and the eulogy.

The most important fact about the *loci a persona* is that they serve as extrinsic proof of what one asserts, that is, they refer to external elements acting directly over the individual and do not require a linking with other arguments in order for their "truth" to be proven. Don Quixote employs the comparison because he knows that the extrinsic proof of his premise is weak. There are no noble pedigrees in La Mancha. The comparison is destined to have an adverse effect. By naming the complete range of noble pedigrees in Spain, preceding each one with the phrase "no es" or "ni," he forces the reader to conclude that the lady is removed from the hierarchy of the highborn altogether. His finally assertion of her identity, "es de los del Toboso" is refuted by Vivaldo, who suggests that such a family is nonexistent: "Para decir verdad, semejante apellido hasta ahora no ha llegado a mis oídos" (177).

Vivaldo takes the bottom out of the knight's premise. Dulcinea is nonexistent, therefore, the knight does not have a lady, and he is not in love; if he is not in love, then he is not a virtuous knight errant; therefore, he is an illegitimate one, a "bastardo," an impostor, and a thief. The false syllogism throws into doubt the supposed "self-evidence" of reason by revealing its ostensible inability to justify its methods on other than purely tautological grounds.

Sancho imitates his master's syllogistic reasoning in Chapter 49 of Part I. The knight has been enchanted, placed in a cage, and is being driven back to his village by the disguised priest and barber. Sancho has recognized them and tries to convince his master that his enchantment is no more than roguery, but the knight refuses to believe this. The squire tells him he will prove it to him and asks him if he has any inclination to carry out his bodily functions. When Don Quixote replies affirmatively, the squire affirms that his response serves as "proof" that he is not enchanted:

> –¡Ah! –dijo Sancho–. Cogido le tengo: esto es lo que yo deseaba saber, como al alma y como a la vida. Venga acá, señor: ¿Podría negar lo que comúnmente suele decirse por ahí cuando una persona está de mala voluntad: "No sé qué tiene fulano, que ni come, ni bebe, ni duerme, ni responde a propósito a lo que le preguntan, que no parece sino que está encantado"? De donde se viene a sacar que los que no comen, ni beben, ni duermen, ni hacen las obras naturales que yo digo, estos tales están encantados; pero no aquellos que tienen la gana que vuestra merced tiene, y que bebe cuando se lo dan, y come cuando lo tiene, y responde a todo aquello que le preguntan. (575)

The squire's reasoning contains the four links of the syllogism: the major premise, no people who are enchanted perform their bodily functions; the thesis restated in the negative, all people who are not enchanted perform their bodily functions; the minor premise, you perform your bodily functions; deduction, you are not enchanted. Like his master, Sancho employs logical processes to explain extra-logical activities, such as the belief in magic and the power of evil enchanters.

The humor of the speech is derived from the fact that the credulous Sancho does not attempt to question the truth or falsity of the enchanted state itself, but only the possibility that the knight is enchanted. His citation of the sentential statement is to serve as authority or proof of his premise, that all enchanted people do not perform their bodily functions. The argument is falsely established, however, for the statement is only to be understood figuratively, as a manner of speaking. One says of people who do not eat or sleep that they look as if they were enchanted. When a person employs the saying, it cannot be inferred that he or she believes that people can really be enchanted.

Sancho's literal interpretation of the statement is no less comic than the knight's acceptance of his squire's syllogism. He is unwilling to admit his squire's premise, however, as he would then have to admit that he is not traveling as a knight who has been enchanted by evil sorcerers envious of his great fame, but that "va . . . embaído y tonto." He tells his squire that his enchantment is different from those narrated in chivalric romance. The exercise of such enchantments can change with the times:

> –Verdad dices, Sancho –respondió don Quijote–; pero ya te he dicho que hay muchas maneras de encantamentos, y podría ser que con el tiempo se hubiesen mudado de unos en otros, y que agora se use que los encantados hagan todo lo que yo hago, aunque antes no lo hacían. De manera, que *contra el uso de los tiempos no hay que argüir ni de qué hacer consecuencias.* Yo sé y tengo para mí que voy encantado, y esto me basta para la seguridad de mi conciencia. . . . (575; emphasis added)

The knight's refutation of his squire's arguments is firmly supported by classical canons of rhetorical argumentation, according to which it is paramount that the orator have a deep knowledge or life, human activities and thought, especially a knowledge of psychology and sociology. In order to obtain a credible and consequent argument, the orator must know that customs, activities, and beliefs are not always the same, but are transformed as a result of the era or region of the world in which they are expressed. Don Quixote's argument has persuasive power, but its force is mitigated by his immediate admission that he simply has blind faith in his enchantment, regardless of whether it is true or not, and which no logic can weaken: "Yo sé y tengo para mí que voy encantado. . . ."

Don Quixote's seeming indifference to Sancho's reasoning processes is contradicted in the episode of the Cave of Montesinos, where the knight restates the syllogism as a means of sustaining the projection of himself as hero. In the narration of his vision to his squire and the cousin, the knight has Dulcinea appear with him in the company of the enchanted chivalric heroes in order to justify his own misfortune: the enchantment of Dulcinea into an ugly peasant girl. He reasons that he is like other great heroes because he too, or what is the same, his lady, has fallen victim to evil enchanters.

In a question and answer dialogue about the events that developed inside the cave, the knight tries to prove that he has a similar identity and destiny to the heroes inside the cave by means of Sancho's reasoning processes:

> –Y ¿ha comido vuestra merced en todo este tiempo, señor mío? –preguntó el primo.
> –No me he desayunado de bocado –respondió don Quijote–, ni aun he tenido hambre, ni por pensamiento.
> –Y los encantados, ¿comen? –dijo el primo.
> –No comen –respondió don Quijote–, ni tienen escrementos mayores; aunque es opinión que les crecen las uñas, las barbas y los cabellos.
> –Y ¿duermen por ventura los encantados, señor? –preguntó Sancho.
> –No, por cierto –respondió don Quijote–; a lo menos, en estos tres días que yo he estado con ellos, ninguno ha pegado el ojo, ni yo tampoco. (II, 33: 219)

The knight's affirmations repeat the terms of his squire's syllogism in Chapter 49 of Part I. It can be postulated as follows: all of the people inside the cave are truly enchanted, as proven by the fact that they do not perform their bodily functions; I did not perform my bodily functions, therefore, I was inside the cave with the enchanted heroes and with Dulcinea, who is also truly enchanted.

Although Don Quixote has employed his squire's arguments, he does not prove his case, and neither Sancho nor the cousin are convinced by his arguments. The knight has failed to remember the advice he gave Sancho in Chapter 49 of Part I when the squire was proving he was not enchanted, namely, that times change, and an argument that is persuasive in one situation is not in another. Don Quixote has not considered that Sancho was at the very opening of the cave, and knows that his master did not perform his bodily functions because he was only down for an hour. Nor does the knight realize that Sancho knows that Dulcinea is not enchanted, for he was the one who made Don Quixote believe that the peasant girl they saw in El Toboso was the enchanted Dulcinea.

A serious argument can further be weakened by a technique referred to as "retortion" (Olbrechts-Tyteca 169-70). The first speaker, inadvertently or intentionally, tells the listener a fiction or falsity. The second speaker then builds on it, employing it for his or her own benefit, weakening the first speaker's assertions. No matter how convincing an argument may seem, when applied to others in other situations, or when employed by another speaker, the flaws in the arguments are made explicit. This is a technique that is often used in philosophy. One takes a philosophical system and employs its concepts in a manner that its flaws are revealed.

Sancho often resorts to the technique of retortion, revealing the flaws in his master's arguments. One of the arguments most frequently employed by the knight is that if he has been defeated in battle or has mistakenly believed that an adventure has been offered when it has not, it is because evil enchanters envious of his fame persecute him. In the episode narrating the events leading up to the knight's confrontation with the lion, Sancho employs this argument to his own benefit. In doing so, he shows how the argument functions as a pretext or excuse for not taking responsibility for a negligent action.

During his master's conversation with the Man in Green, Sancho goes to buy some fresh cheese from a shepherd he spots nearby. When Don Quixote observes a man driving a carriage covered with royal flags, he believes that an adventure is offered him and orders his squire to bring him his helmet. The Man in Green attempts to tell Don Quixote that the carriage is simply carrying money to the king, but the knight explains that it could be an adventure and that since he is prepared for it and "foresees" it, he has half the battle won: "–Hombre apercebido, medio combatido" (II, 17: 158). Don Quixote immediately puts on the helmet. When he discovers that the sticky, white liquid running down his face is not sweat but the cheese curds, he accuses his squire of the roguery: "–Por vida de mi señora Dulcinea del Toboso, que son requesones los que aquí me has puesto, traidor, bergante y mal mirado escudero" (159).

Sancho not only transforms the foresighted hero into the blind fool ("Dame, si tienes, con que me limpie; que el copioso sudor me ciega los ojos" [158]) and the hero's face into the whitened face of the clown, but he also refutes his master's accusations by using the knight's own arguments against him:

> A la fe, señor, a lo que Dios me da a entender, también debo yo de tener encantadores que me persiguen como a hechura y miembro de vuesa merced, y habrán puesto ahí esa inmundicia para mover a cólera su paciencia, y hacer que me muela, como suele, las costillas. (159)

Upon his return to the Sierra Morena, Sancho again employs his master's arguments for his own purposes. As previously advised by the priest and the barber, he tells his master he has been to El Toboso and that his lady requests his presence there. When the knight and squire later travel to El Toboso and Don Quixote asks him where his lady's dwelling is, Sancho realizes he must find a way not to be caught in his lie. He first tells Don Quixote that he should not be expected to remember where Dulcinea lives. He only visited her one time. It seems more logical to Sancho that Don Quixote should find it, since he must have visited her thousands of times. The knight responds with neoplatonic concepts. He has only loved her from afar:

> Ven acá, hereje; ¿no te he dicho mil veces que en todos los días de mi vida no he visto a la sin par Dulcinea, ni jamás atravesé los umbrales de su palacio, y que sólo estoy enamorado de oídas y de la gran fama que tiene de hermosa y discreta? (II, 9: 101)

Sancho replies that he has never seen the lady either. When the knight asks him how that is possible, when he had said that he saw her sifting the grain, the squire replies that his visit to her was *also* by hearsay: "–No se atenga a eso, señor –respondió Sancho–; porque le hago saber que también fue de oídas la vista y la respuesta que le truje..." (101).

Thus far I have focused my analysis on the speakers' attempts to support the truth of a hypothesis by analyzing the thing or person in terms of its own nature, and inscribing that truth in a preexistent economy of sense, the ethics of chivalry. Even more abundant in the text are the instances in which speakers support the truth of a matter by putting it into a logical relationship with something else. According to the canons of classical rhetoric, certain arguments offer a high degree of security to one's premises. These types of arguments are: legal codes, moral law, customs, common opinion, and objects, actions or events that can be observed by the senses (Lausberg, 1: 307-08).

Our agreements on moral and social values and hierarchies are transmitted and sealed via the paremiological expression, including the popular saying, biblical maxim, Latin precept and aphorisms. Such forms, fixed by usage and custom, act as a form of written "law" on moral conduct and thought, propagating the wisdom of the ancients as well as the experience of the collectivity. They are employed in rhetorical argumentation as arguments of authority. When inserted in a literary context, however, they can be consciously used as verbal strategies. It is not enough to simply glean the text for aphoristic expressions. We must, as Constance Sullivan underscores,

> . . . study the dynamics of their inclusion in the overall discourse for how and why they are used, for what they accomplish in the larger text, just as students of human communication and sociolinguists study the modifications of the meaning of a proverb within a particular conversational setting, examining relationships, power games, and possible ironic up-endings of usual or expected meaning. (93)

Several techniques are employed in *Don Quixote* for the purpose of weakening the authority of ancient and popular wisdom and the values they uphold, and they frequently appear in combination with each other: The speaker 1) transposes the citation in a surprising context in which the moral lesson it is to teach is shown to be inapplicable or immoral, 2) cites a moral statement and then follows it up with a series of contingencies that place its authority into doubt, 3) strings citations together, ordering them so that the truths that some affirm the others deny, 4) cites a moral statement in order to justify his or her action, and then cites one of opposing value and point of view in a similar situation, 5) corrupts the citation, 6) interprets the figurative language of the citation literally or vice versa and plays on the ambiguity of words, and 7) paraphrases, explains and interprets the citation, eliciting unexpected meanings.

Citations are frequently found in series in *Don Quixote*. These series are invariably constructed by Sancho, and employed by him in order to strengthen his premises. According to the canons of rhetoric, a strong argument can produce a greater effect when it appears alone, thanks to its intrinsic force. The weaker arguments gain force when they are accumulated. However, moral *exempla* are not the type of arguments that are appropriate for being put in a series because of their condensed form of expression. Moral citations create an excess of information, and the listener does not have time to evoke the themes referred to (Olbrechts-Tyteca 298). While in serious argumentation arguments that are strung together are consistent with each other and consequent with the premise, in Sancho's discourse of deviant figuration, arguments expressing opposing points of view are juxtaposed, resulting in a weakening of the premise and of the arguments employed.

Sancho's stringing together of citations is well illustrated in the episode of the wedding of Camacho. The student has narrated to Sancho and Don Quixote the story of Basilio and Quiteria's love and of Basilio's despair upon hearing the news of Quiteria's imminent marriage to Camacho. As Sancho comments on the story, he seems to express the desire to cheer up the two young lovers:

> –Dios lo hará mejor –dijo Sancho–; que Dios, que da la llaga, da la medicina; nadie sabe lo que está por venir: de aquí a mañana muchas horas hay, y en una, y aun en un momento, se cae la casa; yo he visto llover y hacer sol, todo a un mesmo punto; tal se acuesta sano la noche, que no se puede mover otro día.... (II, 19: 181)

The squire cites the first few sayings in order to express the idea that if the lovers are presently suffering some misfortune, they will find a remedy for it. Then Sancho employs arguments that reflect alternate points of view. The saying "en un momento se cae la casa" indicates that one's good fortune can fade when one least suspects. The following saying, "yo he visto llover y hacer sol ...," indicates that one can experience good and bad fortune at the same time. The final saying, "tal se acuesta sano la noche ..." indicates that one can have good fortune in one minute and bad in the next. Sancho's speech, more than the construction of a single argument and point of view, is an exploration of the problem of fortune, and of the manners in which good and bad fortune can combine and alternate.

Sancho's series of citations in a conversation with Sansón Carrasco and his master at the beginning of Part II underscore the role that personal interest has in the building of arguments, taking priority over the possible truth of an assertion. Sancho tells his master that he has no intention of fighting on their next sally. He will win fame by his show of loyalty. If his master wishes to compensate him for his conduct by giving him a countship, he will be pleased to accept it. If he chooses not to, however, Sancho does not care because:

> . . . nacido soy, y no ha de vivir el hombre en hoto de otro sino de Dios; y más, que tan bien, y aun quizá mejor, me sabrá el pan desgobernado que siendo gobernador; y ¿sé yo por ventura si en esos gobiernos me tiene aparejada el diablo alguna zancadilla donde tropiece y caiga y me haga las muelas? Sancho nací, y Sancho pienso morir; pero si, con todo esto, de buenas a buenas, sin mucha solicitud y sin mucho riesgo, me deparase el cielo alguna ínsula, o otra cosa semejante, no soy tan necio, que la desechase; que también se dice: "Cuando te dieren la vaquilla, corre con la soguilla"; y "cuando viene el bien, métela en tu casa". (II, 4: 71)

The first few citations back up the premise that Sancho puts forth of not caring if his master gives him the governorship or not. The saying "nacido soy" means that he is fine just the way he is. He is in God's world, and he will be taken care of (Note 13, 71). The second one, "no ha de vivir el hombre en hoto . . ." acts as a complement to the first, and indicates that one should not depend on another person's luck, but on God. The following saying, "¿sé yo por ventura . . .?," is a stronger argument in favor of the maintenance of the squire's present position. Not only is Sancho fine the way he is, but he could even be worse off than he is presently if he acquires a governorship. At this point, Sancho remembers that his interests are really quite different. He does care about the governorship. He is thus compelled to take the other side of the argument and makes the transition with the qualifier "pero" and the contingency, "si, con todo esto . . . ," followed by opposing arguments. Arguing from contrary sides, Sancho reminds us that the wisdom of experience and the truth it imparts by means of the popular saying is not absolute, but contingent on and conditioned by vested interest, a fact that the listener is made to forget in serious argumentation.[7]

Sancho puts feminine virtue into doubt, one of the most sacred tenets of the chivalric ethos, in a conversation with his master about Madásima, a chivalric heroine. The knight and squire have just received a beating from the mad youth Cardenio because the knight had threatened and insulted him for having put the virtue of Madásima into doubt. Reacting to his unpleasant plight, Sancho argues to his master that it was not necessary that his master defend the lady because Madásima is not his lady. Besides, one need not pay any attention to the words of a madman. The knight defends his conduct by affirming that it is his duty to defend the honor of all ladies, especially that of a queen, as Madásima was. He then adds that she was not only beautiful, but also virtuous and that anyone who might think or say anything to the contrary is a liar. Sancho responds to his master by setting up a premise of fact. He does not think anything other than what his master has affirmed. His premise involves two ideas: first his own exoneration. He is not a liar, nor is he slandering anyone. Secondly, he supports his master's premise that the lady is innocent:

> –Ni yo lo digo ni lo pienso –respondió Sancho–; allá se lo hayan; con su pan se lo coman; si fueron amancebados, o no, a Dios habrán dado la cuenta; de mis viñas vengo; no sé nada; no soy amigo de saber vidas ajenas; que el que compra y miente, en su bolsa lo siente. Cuanto más, que desnudo nací, desnudo me hallo: ni pierdo ni gano; mas que lo fuesen, ¿qué me va a mí? Y muchos piensan que hay tocinos y no hay estacas. Mas ¿quién puede poner puertas al campo? Cuanto más, que de Dios dijeron. (I, 25: 302)

The first *exempla* are employed by the squire as a means of defending his innocence, but at the same time imply the guilt of an-

---

[7] The incongruity between content and function is studied at the meta-paremiological level by Joly, "Le discours métaparémique dans *Don Quichotte*."

other party and thus function to slander Madásima. The saying "allá se lo hayan; con su pan . . ." indicates that one does not want to participate in some event because there might be some negative consequence. Covarrubias tells us that the saying "De mis viñas vengo" is an excuse that is employed in order to affirm that one is not involved in some bad action. Sancho then affirms that he is against murmuring, and that he would never say anything bad about others, an assertion which is denied with the following saying, "el que compra y miente . . . ," which indicates that if you have spent money, your purse is there to prove it, no matter what you may say to the contrary. In other words, one cannot hide what is evident. With this saying, Sancho contradicts both ideas implicitly in his premise. He does not think or say anything that would differ from what his master has affirmed about Madásima, and he supports his master's premise that the lady is innocent of the illicit affair.

The following group of citations contains the same kind of ambiguity. Sancho employs the saying "desnudo nací . . ." to indicate that he would have nothing to gain from believing the lady was guilty. He follows this saying with another which seems to support her innocence, "y muchos piensan que hay tocino . . .," but really does the opposite. Sancho seems to be saying that where many people may believe that some illicit affair has occurred betwen Madásima and Elisabat, nothing has happened. Such an argument would be an appropriate response to his master's earlier claim that the company the lady kept with Elisabat was simply a friendship or a teacher/student relationship, although it had been common opinion that she was living in concubinage with him. However the saying is conventionally linked to another type of premise.

The authentic citation is "donde hay tocinos, no hay ni estacas" and is employed to indicate that people are misled who believe that there is some great faculty in a person (Caballero 91). If we consider the absent uncorrupted usage, the defense of the lady's virtue against slander is suddenly transformed into an accusation, for it implies that where it might be believed (by Don Quixote) that there is great virtue in the lady, there is not. Indeed, the following saying "¿quién puede poner puertas al campo?" seems to confirm the accusation, for it indicates the difficulty in hiding certain things which cannot be closed off or fenced in, like the countryside (Caballero, 91). It seems that Sancho means that the lady's concubinage is so obvious that no arguments will suffice to deny it.

Although Sancho closes his speech with a saying that aligns the virtue of the lady with God's, "que de Dios dijeron," a saying that indicates that all virtue is slandered, even the highest and purest kind, his arguments have seriously put the lady's virtue into doubt and have revealed his own suspicions concerning her guilt. Don Quixote responds to his squire by asserting that he has said a bunch of nonsense. As he finishes his speech, however, he indicates that he has understood the sense of Sancho's insinuations, for he orders him to stay out of his affairs and to simply have faith in his master's actions:

> –¡Válame Dios –dijo don Quijote–, y qué de necedades vas, Sancho, ensartando! ¿Qué va de lo que tratamos a los refranes que enhilas? Por tu vida, Sancho, que calles, y de aquí adelante entremétete en espolear a tu asno, y deja de hacello en lo que no te importa. Y entiende con todos tus cinco sentidos que todo cuanto yo he hecho, hago e hiciere, va muy puesto en razón. . . . (302)

As Sancho's employment of popular sayings shows, the truth and wisdom of experience are not applicable with equivalent meaning. When employing the saying as an argument of authority, the speaker must remember the context to which the argument is linked if the premise is to be persuasive. The logic of deviant argumentation results when the normal linking of argument to premise, sealed by agreement of usage, is intentionally or inadvertently disregarded by the speaker.

Sancho again breaks the link between premise and argument after Don Quixote's narration of his vision in the Cave of Montesinos. The knight has explained that he has been down in the cave for three days, that during that time no one in the cave had eaten or slept or performed any other bodily functions and that he had not either. Sancho responds thus:

> –Aquí encaja bien el refrán –dijo Sancho– de dime con quién andas, decirte he quién eres: ándase vuestra merced con encantados ayunos y vigilantes: mirad si es mucho que ni coma ni duerma mientras con ellos anduviere. (II, 23: 219)

Don Quixote asserted that no one had performed bodily functions in the cave as a moral argument in order to support the premise that he and his lady are of the same superior fiber as the chivalric heroes he encountered in the cave. The flaw in his reasoning is that he employed arguments belonging to a physiological or biological hierarchy as "proof" of a moral premise. Sancho discovers the quasi-logical link between the knight's premise and argument as he repeats the same reasoning process by means of the popular saying. The saying "dime con quien andas . . ." is conventionally employed to indicate that one can be influenced morally by the company one keeps.[8] Sancho removes the saying from the moral hierarchy and places it in a biological one, confirming ironically his master's absurd thesis that one can be affected physiologically by another's company.

Frequently in the text the disparity between the arguments and the premise is so great that it becomes necessary for Sancho to explain the link that binds them and the moral lesson the saying is to impart. The paraphrase contradicts the concept of the sentential statement, which, as Don Quixote tells Sancho on more than one occasion, "son sentencias breves, sacadas de la experiencia y especulación de nuestros antiguos sabios; y el refrán que no viene a propósito, antes es disparate que sentencia" (II, 67: 551). The lesson of the saying, which should be self-evident, disappears altogether when moral statements are cited that do not seem to "venir a pelo," and Sancho has to explain the moral "proof" of his premise with the words "quiero decir" or "dígolo porque. . . ."

Sancho paraphrases moral arguments in a dialogue with his master, when they first encounter the duke and duchess. The knight tells Sancho to greet the noble lady on his behalf, and cautions him not to employ so many popular sayings in his speech. Sancho replies that he does not need advice on these matters: ". . . al buen pagador no le duelen prendas, y en casa llena presto se guisa la cena: quiero decir que a mí no hay que decirme ni advertirme de nada: que para todo tengo, y de todo se me alcanza un poco" (II, 30: 269). The sayings Sancho cites are conventionally used in a literal sense, that is, to indicate that one has material possessions (Caballero 190). Sancho employs them in a figurative sense to indicate that he possesses the necessary mental faculties to carry out the mission. He is thus forced to explain the link.

---

[8] The variations Correas cites underscore the moral use of the sentential statement: "dime con quién andas, diréte lo que hablas" and "dime con quién andas, diréte tus mañas," 324.

The moral lesson conveyed in the saying is weakened when the language of the saying is intended in a figurative sense, but the speaker interprets it in a literal sense, or vice versa, resulting in word play. In the episode narrating the knight's confrontation with the lion, Sancho tries to warn his master of the danger involved in such an adventure by telling him that he has seen the lion's nail through the bars of the cage, and if he can judge by the nail, the lion must be as big as a mountain. There is a reminiscence of the Latin proverb *Ex ungue leonem* in Sancho's advice. The proverb is conventionally employed with a figurative sense to indicate that by having knowledge of a partial action, conduct, or aspect of a person, one can make assumptions about his or her general character. By providing the proverb with a literal context and application, the general moral lesson to be derived from it is eliminated and replaced by a simple narration of what is taking place, albeit filtered through Sancho's optics of fear.

The meaning of a moral statement is transformed in similar fashion in the braying episode. The statement "No rebuznaron en balde el uno y el otro alcalde" (II, 27: 251) is written in big letters on one of the flags held by the group of men from the braying village. The statement is to be understood ironically to mean that someone carries out an action in vain (Caballero 217). As Cervantes supplies a story for the statement, he transforms the general or universal moral value of the statement into a mere summary or conclusion of the story. Play on the sense of the statement is carried one step further in the braying episode. New interpretations arise when it is shown that the men from the braying village have taken the saying literally, not ironically, and employ it to reaffirm to their enemy that their braying was indeed purposeful. Unfortunately, the enemy never appears and therefore cannot be convinced of its purpose, even by means of physical force.

Many of the sentential statements the knight employs to justify his conduct and actions are those linked to the ideals of heroism. The arguments employed to support these ideals are weakened when they are: 1) inserted in contexts that put their values into doubt 2) applied with contingencies 3) corrupted and 4) applied to justify opposing conducts. Some of these deviations can be illustrated in the knight's speech to the Man in Green, following his duel with the lion.

The knight justifies his confrontation with the lion by affirming that although he was rash, it is easier for a rash person to rise to show true valor than a cowardly person, and that it is difficult to reach the perfect mark of heroism in chivalric adventures:

> ... el acometer los leones que ahora acometí derechamente me tocaba, puesto que conocí ser temeridad esorbitante, porque bien sé lo que es valentía, que es una virtud que está puesta entre dos estremos viciosos, como son la cobardía y la temeridad; pero menos mal será que el que es valiente toque y suba al punto de temerario que no que baje y toque en el punto de cobarde; que así como es más fácil venir el pródigo a ser liberal que el ávaro, así es más fácil dar el temerario en verdadero valiente que no el cobarde subir a la verdadera valentía; y en esto de acometer aventuras, créame vuesa merced, señor don Diego, que *antes se ha de perder por carta de más que de menos*.... (II, 17: 167-68, emphasis added)

The knight's reasoning is specious. No one has asked him to consider if the coward or the rash man is "closer" to being heroic, and certainly no social agreements or assumptions cause the reader to believe, as the knight affirms, that the rash man is closer to heroism. Moreover, heroism, of course, is not a matter of "almost" or "close to."

The knight continues to support his rash conduct as he quotes the saying "pecar por carta de más o por carta de menos." The saying is employed in the jargon of card players in reference to the game of "twenty-one," and used to criticize those players who have not reached the desired number or those who have exceeded it, expressing the notion that the middle between the two extremes is best (note 20,168). The knight employs the saying to justify his rashness, but in order to do so, he must corrupt the saying, altering it to say that it is better to lose the game by a card too many than by a card too few. The knight forgets that in matters of heroism as well as in those of card games, one does not win or lose "more" or "less"; one simply wins or loses, and one loses just as much by not reaching as by exceeding.

While in the adventure of the lion the knight cites the *aurea mediocritas* argument, albeit with the contingency "pero menos mal será ...," in order to support his rashness, he cites the same ideal in the braying episode in order to justify an opposing conduct, that of fleeing from danger. The comic implications of what could otherwise be considered straightforward speeches emerge when the reader becomes aware of such contradictions. Don Quixote and his squire are attacked by the group of men from the braying village. Realizing that the danger is great and that he is totally outnumbered by his enemy, Don Quixote decides to flee rather than to face the danger. Since he is taking the other side of the argument in support of his premise of his heroic conduct, justifying the avoidance of danger, he simply substitutes the vice of cowardliness, a vice of which he does not want to be accused, for the virtue of prudence, and places it in opposition to the vice of rashness:

> –No huye el que se retira –respondió don Quijote–; porque has de saber, Sancho, que la valentía que no se funda sobre la basa de la prudencia se llama temeridad, y las hazañas del temerario más se atribuyen a la buena fortuna que a su ánimo. Y así, yo confieso que me he retirado, pero no huído; y en esto he imitado a muchos valientes, que se han guardado para tiempos mejores. . . . (II, 38: 257)

As the knight takes the other side of the argument, he puts his earlier premise into doubt, that rashness is close to heroism, and explains that his so-called triumph in the battle with the lion was purely a matter of luck.[9]

Other types of arguments of authority that must be put in relation to the truth to be proven are those that cite the authority of the law, the law of the state, of the church, of a profession, of a social class, or of any collectivity. These are used with some frequency in the text, but operate together and are joined with another type of argument called the *signum*, in Chapter 45 of Part I, appropriately entitled "Donde se acaba de averiguar la duda del yelmo de Mam-

---

[9] As I close my discussion of the comic use of the citation of sentential statements, I would like to note that an examination of poetic citation employed in the text by various speakers would show that poetic citations are analogous to the citation of sentential statements. Speakers employ poetic citations to support the truth of a statement, but in doing so, they undermine the truth to be proven by 1) employing a citation in a manner that the link between the general truth and the specific cause is so weak that he or she has to explain what the link is, 2) employing the citations in unexpected circumstances, resulting in the rupture of the listener's assumptions about poetic discourse, 3) corrupting the citation and 4) giving the figurative or metaphorical language of the citation a literal sense or vice versa.

brino y de la albarda y otras aventuras sucedidas, *con toda verdad"* (540, emphasis added).

Lausberg explains that while the arguments of authority of the law exist independently of the rhetorical process and have to be put in relation to the matter in question by means of the cognitive process, the *signa* are found together with the object, person, or event being debated. The *signum* can be defined as a sign perceived by the senses that normally accompanies the fact or event, so that by means of the sign, one can deduce the thing or event it signifies with more or less security. We would call the facts produced by the *signa* "evidence."

In serious argumentation, the arguments of the law and of the *signa* are offered as "proof" to convince the listeners of the truth that is being asserted. In the mock trial held on Chapter 45 of Part I, the listeners already know the identity of the objects being discussed, the pack saddle and the barber's basin. Their attention is thus directed towards the techniques of argumentation and the private interests and concerns of the orators. The listener consequently comes to perceive the arguments as "artifice" rather than as a vehicle by means of which the truth is transmitted.

The confrontation between the knight and the barber, true owner of the basin, begins in Chapter 44, when the latter arrives at the inn. He discovers his pack saddle on Sancho's ass in the stables, and comes into the inn to claim it and the basin. The knight refuses to return the objects on the grounds that the object in question is not a basin but Mambrino's helmet, which he won in fair battle. As proof of his premise, he employs the argument of the *signa*, ordering his squire to retrieve the object so that they can see with their own eyes that it is indeed a helmet:

> –¡*Porque vean vuestras mercedes clara y manifiestamente el error en que está este buen escudero,* pues llama bacía a lo que fue, es y será yelmo de Mambrino, el cual se le quité yo en buena guerra, y me hice señor dél con ligítima y lícita posesión! En lo del albarda no me entremeto; que lo que en ello sabré decir es que mi escudero Sancho me pidió licencia para quitar los jaeces del caballo deste vencido cobarde y con ellos adornar el suyo; yo se la di y él los tomó, y de haberse convertido de jaez en albarda no sabré dar otra razón sino es la ordinaria: que como estas transformaciones se ven en los sucesos de la caballería; para con-

firmación de lo cual, corre, Sancho hijo, y *saca aquí el yelmo que este buen hombre dice ser bacía.* (539, emphasis added)

It is important for the knight to prove his assertions because the winning of an object belonging to a great hero legitimates the knight's heroic identity. It is also to the squire's benefit that the knight prove the "truth" of his assertion, for he would like to keep the pack saddles. He communicates this interest to his master, while at the same time pointing out the limitations of the argument of the *signa*. He reminds him that in eyewitness testimony, it is the word of one witness against the other: "–¡Pardiez señor –dijo Sancho–, si no tenemos otra prueba de nuestra intención que la que vuestra merced dice, tan bacía es el yelmo de Malino como el jaez deste buen hombre albarda!" (539).

The owner of the basin objects to the knight's arguments and sets out to refute them with the counter argument of common opinion, asking the other lodgers present for their consensus: "–¿Qué les parece a vuestras mercedes, señores –dijo el barbero–, de lo que afirman estos gentiles hombres, pues aún porfían que ésta no es bacía, sino yelmo?" (45: 540).

The barber from the knight's village now decides to intervene, defending the knight's false premise by means of the argument of authority of the specialist of the profession, called into court to give his erudite opinion on the case:

> –Señor barbero, o quien sois, sabed que yo también soy de vuestro oficio, y tengo más ha de veinte años carta de examen, y conozco muy bien de todos los instrumentos de la barbería, sin que le falte uno; y ni más ni menos fui un tiempo en mi mocedad soldado, y sé también qué es yelmo, y qué es morrión, y celada de encaje, y otras cosas tocantes a la milicia, digo, a los géneros de armas de los soldados; y digo, salvo mejor parecer, remitiéndome siempre al mejor entendimiento, que esta pieza que está aquí delante y que este buen señor tiene en las manos no sólo no es bacía de barbero, pero está tan lejos de serlo como está lejos lo blanco de lo negro y la verdad de la mentira. . . . (540-41)

The priest from the knight's village first, and then Cardenio and Don Fernando, realize the barber's intention to have a joke, and playing along, confirm his opinion, adding the argument of the majority onto the argument of the authority of the specialist. The owner of the basin now finds his position in serious jeopardy since the majority opinion includes figures of honorable repute:

> –¡Válame Dios! –dijo a esta sazón el barbero burlado–. ¿Que es posible que tanta gente honrada diga que ésta no es bacía, sino yelmo? Cosa parece ésta que puede poner en admiración a toda una Universidad, por discreta que sea. (541)

The exclamatory remark is comic because the barber gives more credit to the opinion of these noble figures and to a figure representing the authority of the church than to what his own eyes tell him. The strength of the argument of the majority, especially a majority of high repute, is demonstrated, while at the same time its force is weakened. The humor of the episode reaches a climax when the barber attempts to explain the discrepancy between the opinion of the majority and his own. He suggests that some extrinsic influence could have affected his sense perception, the influence of alcohol. At the same time he denies the influence. The deceived barber consequently discredits himself as an eyewitness and the validity of his testimony, underscoring the limitations of the argument of the *signa*.

The final word is offered by the rural policeman, whose opinion – "–Tan albarda es como mi padre; y el que otra cosa ha dicho o dijere debe de estar hecho uva" (543) – represents the force of the letter of the law, to whose authority all who are present must submit. With the presentation of this final statement, the knight's premise crumbles and he is forced to support it by means of brute, physical force, setting off a struggle in which all of the people gathered at the inn participate. Violence supplants and denounces false reason, and the reader becomes witness to the only "logical" conclusion to a carnivalesque "juicio al revés." The verbal violence that precedes it, within the discourse of argumentation, is emblematic of the discursive violence of the text at large. It operates, as Cesáreo Bandera has shown, to disclose the interruption and ruptures of each speaker's projection of his or her individual existence by the "other," and to discover its underlying fictionality, its "arbitrariedad" (168).

Two final arguments of the authority of the law that are employed in the text are the argument of the "precedent" and the argument of "double hierarchies." The argument of the precedent departs from the principle that the rules of justice demand the application of identical treatment in similar situations. In the discourse of comic argumentation, situations are created where the rule, if applied, will disprove the truth one hopes to attain by adhering to it (Olbrechts-Tyteca194). The orator who defends his actions by means of the law of the precedent has forgotten that situations change. That which operates according to certain laws in a given situation does not in others.

The knight imagines that all the situations he encounters are patterned on the adventures narrated in chivalric romance. He accordingly follows the codes of that world. There are numerous occasions on which the knight defends his conduct by citing the codes of chivalry. A few examples will suffice to illustrate how his particular employment of such codes puts their viability into doubt.

One of the themes of Part I of *Don Quixote* is that of hunger. The knight explains to his squire that according to what he has read, the knight errant does not bring any food with him, but eats whatever he may find in the surrounding countryside, such as nuts, berries, and other foods that grow wild. The theme of abundance that forms part of the myth of the Golden Age, which is linked to the world of romance, is accepted by the knight as a reference to a real or possible world. He evokes the rules of that world only to reveal the abyss that separates that world from his own.

The theme of abundance is replaced by the theme of hunger in the text. The lack of abundance, indeed, the absence of any proper sustenance at all causes the knight to become so emaciated that he looks more like a figure of death than a great hero. On the second sally, the knight orders Sancho to put some provisions in his pack saddles. The squire pulls the contents out of the pack after the duel with the Biscayan and offers them to the knight: an onion, some cheese, and some bread crumbs. The squire tells him that the offering is too humble for such a valiant knight, but the knight refutes such assertions. He explains to his squire that at times knights errant do not eat for a month, and when they do, they eat what they find at hand. As a result, their sustenance is usually country fare, such as Sancho has offered him. He concludes by gently reproaching the squire for attempting to alter the world of chivalry and the rules that support it.

The knight and squire finish their brief meal, and the knight seems quite satisfied with the country fare, at least until they encounter the humble goatherds who invite them to eat roast goat.

The knight's satisfaction with the abundance of the fields is revealed as false when only minutes later, the knight and squire eat for a second time, and this time with great relish.

The search for food and drink lead the knight and squire to commit petty crimes and place them in dangerous situations. In the episode of the dead body, the knight allows the squire to remove the provisions from the pack saddles of the priests who have fled, even though he has already confessed that his attack was a mistake, one for which he ought to be excommunicated. Having left their own provisions at the inn by mistake, the knight and squire are ravenous and eagerly dig into their provisions. The pair journey further in hopes of finding a stream from which to drink. They finally find water, but in a dark, remote, and solitary wood. The desired sound of water is finally heard, but mixed with the thundering of clanking iron, loud enough to frighten anyone.

The incongruity of the Don Quixote's subordination to the precedent of chivalric codes is finally elicited when those codes are placed into conflict with the laws of contemporary Spain. The knight transgresses contemporary law while attempting to comply with chivalric law. His actions align him with the common and even dangerous criminal. Throughout Part I, both knight and squire are persecuted by the law. The knight attacks the Biscayan, an action carried out as the consequence of his defense of the ladies in the carriage. Although Don Quixote assures his squire at that time that knights errant are above the letter of the law, Sancho is concerned that the rural policemen will be searching for them, and suggests that they hide in a church. In his "rescue" of the galley slaves, the knight commits a serious crime and implicitly admits as much when he allows himself to be convinced by Sancho of the necessity of fleeing into the Sierra Morena. When the rural policeman finally catches up with him at the inn, Don Quixote is able to escape imprisonment himself because the priest and Don Fernando persuade the policeman that there is no sense in imprisoning a madman and because they offer to pay for the damages resulting from his criminal action.

The argument of the "double hierarchy" is closely related to the argument of the precedent (Olbrechts-Tyteca 268-71). In this argument, as the name indicates, there are two hierarchies from which to choose. One argues that if something is true in one situation, it is true in another situation. This type of logic is essential to scientific reasoning, theory and method. The logic of the argument is rendered ambiguous when the link between the two hierarchies is missing or is weak, resulting in a *non sequitur*.

The knight's pretensions to heroic conduct are unmasked by his logic of deviant figuration, reflected in his employment of the argument of double hierarchies. At the end of the episode of the fulling mills, the squire jestingly repeats his master's earlier assertion that this was the day that he would prove his glory. Having mistaken the thundering of the fulling mills for a signal of a dangerous chivalric adventure, the embarrassed knight justifies his error in judgment by affirming that his conduct was correct even if his judgment was not:

> Venid acá, señor alegre: ¿Parecéos a vos que, si como éstos fueron mazos de batán, fueran otra peligrosa aventura, no había yo mostrado el ánimo que convenía para emprendella y acaballa? (I, 20: 249)

The argument seems sound. However, we do not know how he would have behaved if a true danger would have been awaiting him. Given the knight's behavior throughout the episode, alternating between fear and foolhardiness, any deduction or anticipation of his response to a supposed danger would be difficult to make. Moreover, one cannot extrapolate or deduce what one would do in another situation, if he or she has not done anything in the given situation. The logic of the argument would have been correct, for example, if the knight would have first undertaken some dangerous adventure successfully, and then when discovering that he had erroneously mistaken an event for an adventure, justify the error by referring to the given and completed action: "given the fact that I did this then, I would have done the same now."

The knight uses the argument of double hierarchies to prove his place at the highest level of heroic perfection when he explains the reasons for his penance to Sancho. He compares his conduct to Amadís and Orlando who also carried out a penance on behalf of his lady. When his squire points out to him that his lady has given him no motive for carrying out the penance, as the ladies of those knights did, Don Quixote answers:

> –Ahí está el punto –respondió don Quijote–, y ésa es la fineza de mi negocio; que volverse loco un caballero andante con

> causa, ni grado ni gracias: el toque está desatinar sin ocasión y dar a entender a mi dama que, si en seco hago esto, ¿qué hiciera en mojado? (I, 25: 305)

Here again the knight bases his reason on false equivalences. One cannot deduce from the feigning of "locura de amor," a dry run or rehearsal, what one would do or say when experiencing the true despair of the disdained lover. Scientific hypotheses are deduced from known facts, and not from conjecture and vague abstractions.

It can be determined from the arguments analyzed thus far that in the type of argumentation that demands the linking of arguments, the truth or falsity of a thing or person is proven when the speaker establishes its logical or real relation with another thing or person. The comparison and the antithesis, thus, are important forms of linked arguments, the first establishing a positive relation between two things or persons and the second, a contradictory one. In serious argumentation the speaker must consider that the success of his or her comparison depends on certain social codes. In the deviant figuration of comic argumentation, the incompatibility between the terms of the comparison are emphasized, resulting in the inversion or destruction of the hierarchy upheld by means of the reasoning process (Olbrechts-Tyteca 214-17).

The knight supports his premise of the nobility of his lady first established in his conversation with Vivaldo, in a conversation with the duchess in Part II. He supports the premise by means of an argument of comparison, in which he tries to exalt his lady by comparing her to other great ladies in history:

> Dulcinea es principal y bien nacida, y de los hidalgos linajes que hay en el Toboso, que son muchos, antiguos y muy buenos, a buen seguro que no le cabe poca parte a la sin par Dulcinea, por quien su lugar será famoso y nombrado en los venideros siglos, como lo ha sido Troya por Elena y España por la Cava, aunque con mejor título y fama. (32: 292-93)

The exalting effect the knight wishes to achieve is mitigated by the presence of other attributes that link the two hierarchies. He cites the names of important women of history in order to exalt his lady, but as he himself confesses, the women are renowned for their infamous deeds. Although Don Quixote rectifies the terms of the comparison with the qualifying phrase, "aunque con mejor título y fama," the negative associations have already been made.

Don Quixote cites figures from history, together with chivalric heroes, as a means to exalt his own status. At the beginning of Part II, Sancho informs his master of the opinions those who have read his exploits have of him: "–En lo que toca . . . a la valentía, cortesía, hazañas y asumpto de vuestra merced, hay diferentes opiniones: unos dicen: 'Loco, pero gracioso'; otros, 'Valiente, pero desgraciado'; otros, 'Cortés, pero impertinente' . . ." (2: 56). The knight replies by comparing himself to great heroes who have suffered adversities and been subject to slander in order to exalt his own image. What he does, however, is slander the heroic figures:

> –Mira, Sancho –dijo don Quijote–: donde quiera que está la virtud en eminente grado, es perseguida. Pocos o ninguno de los famosos varones que pasaron dejó de ser calumniado de la malicia. Julio César, animosísimo, prudentísimo y valentísimo capitán, fue notado de ambicioso y algún tanto no limpio, ni en sus vestidos ni en sus costumbres. Alejandro, a quien sus hazañas le alcanzaron el renombre de Magno, dicen dél que tuvo sus ciertos puntos de borracho. De Hércules, el de los muchos trabajos, se cuenta que fue lascivo y muelle. De don Galaor, hermano de Amadís de Gaula, se murmura que fue más que demasiadamente rijoso; y de su hermano, que fue llorón. (56-57)

As the knight transforms the most exalted heroic figures into a group of misfits in his references to unseemly behavior, including, variously, dishonesty, indecency, sloth, drunkenness, lechery, and unmanly qualities, he causes the listener to perceive the ideal of heroism that they represent as somewhat less than desirable.

Comparisons are rendered comic when the terms are linked in a manner that upsets the reader's assumptions and values. This occurs, for example, when a word play is made on a comparison that has a fixed mode of expression. In the episode narrating the knight's encounter with the merchants from Toledo, one of the merchants insinuates that Don Quixote's lady is hunch-backed. The knight defends his lady by means of a popular comparison, stating that she is straighter than a spindle from Guadarrama, "es . . . más derecha que un huso de Guadarrama" (I, 4: 101). The language of the popular comparison is employed figuratively to indicate one's moral rectitude (Caballero 34). The knight employs the comparison in a literal sense, in order to prove a physical attribute, the straight posture of his lady. The image the comparison projects of his lady, however, is no less grotesque than the image of the hump-backed lady, for it transforms the lady into a gigantic, rectilinear figure, that transgresses all limits conditioning feminine beauty, and dehumanizes the lady by aligning her with inanimate objects.

When the knight describes Belerma's teeth as being as white as peeled almonds, "blancos como unas peladas almendras" (II, 23: 217), he again forgets to take certain assumptions and conventions governing comparisons into consideration. The reader accepts certain comparisons of human attributes with inanimate ones because such comparisons are consolidated by poetic tradition and tend towards the exaltation of the human attribute. For example, it is acceptable to describe the green color of the lady's eyes by comparing them to emeralds, or the whiteness of her teeth by comparing them to pearls for the attribute is exalted by its association with a precious stone.

The knight's description of the whiteness of Belerma's teeth breaks certain assumptions. While one might be able to describe the shape of the lady's eyes by comparing them to an almond placed in a horizontal position, the description of teeth as almonds is grotesque because it aligns the lady with the animal world. The pointed edge of the almond, placed perpendicularly in the mouth, projects the image of the animal, such as those belonging to the canine family, characterized by its sharp, pointed, gnawing, meat-eating teeth. Durandarte's romantic gesture of requesting that his faithful heart be delivered to his mistress is grotesquely evoked when his mistress is suddenly perceived as a potential cannibal, biologically prepared to devour the bloody organ.

After defeating him in battle, Don Quixote forces the Knight of the Mirrors to confess that the beauty of Dulcinea is superior to that of his own lady Casildea. He does so by employing a comparison of superiority in favor of Dulcinea: "—Confieso —dijo el caído caballero— que vale más el zapato descosido y sucio de la señora Dulcinea del Toboso que las barbas mal peinadas, aunque limpias, de Casildea . . ." (II, 14: 144).

The objects the fallen knight compares function as "synecdoches," that is, as parts that define the whole character of the ladies. The comparison of superiority "más" loses its function when we realize that the two objects that are compared are portrayed as possessing equivalent or near-equivalent qualities. The unsewn shoe symbolizes the fraudulent, counterfeit nature of Dulcinea. The dirtiness of the shoe symbolizes her moral impurity, debauchery, and sloth, and thus devalues the lady's physical beauty and moral virtue. Casildea's character is defined in a similar fashion. The beard is a positive attribute for a male hero, symbolizing his passion and virility. Yet for a female heroine it is a negative one, not only because it effaces the lady's femininity, but because it signals an unrestrainable sexual appetite. Although the Knight of the Mirrors jokingly affirms that his lady's beard is clean, a sign of her purity, he first states that the beard is uncombed, a fact that indicates the lady's sloth and physical neglect.

The paradox is another way of asserting the truth or falsity of something. In serious rhetoric, the paradox is employed in order to show how two thoughts, although contradictory in nature, can both be true. Although the argument of the paradox is often an intellectual one, it can also be a pathetic one. The speaker controls the listener's emotions because the paradox creates a climate of tension as it first confronts two seemingly incompatible truths, and then draws the listener out of the impasse or dilemma by showing that the contradictory ideas are reconcilable. The device is frequently employed in tragedy as well as in amatory poetry (Lausberg, 1: 334).

In comic argumentation, paradoxes are employed to draw attention to the problematical, equivocal nature of truth. The paradox is an appropriate vehicle for this purpose, since what paradox does is equivocate. It lies and tells the truth at the same time, an equivocation that is epitomized in the Liar paradox told to Sancho during his reign in Barataria (Colie 5-8). Rhetorical paradoxes lend themselves well to comic argumentation since, like all paradoxes, they criticize the limitations and rigidity of argumentation. They are self-critical and self-referential, commenting on their own method and technique. Because they call attention to the fallibility of thought, they can be called anti-rational.

One way a comic paradox is produced is when one negates something that has previously been admitted, or affirms something that has been negated. Opposing points of view are joined in a manner that neither one of them can be reduced to the other. The listener has no way out of the impasse, and therefore must perceive and treat the incompatible propositions as non-exclusive. When attempting to find a loophole, the speaker only manages to draw attention to the disparity between the opposing points of view (Olbrechts-Tyteca 159-169).

Sancho attempts to find his way out of a contradiction in a lengthy discussion with his wife about their daughter's future. Teresa vows that she would rather die before she sees her daughter become a countess, while Sancho is determined that she become one. They are unable to convince each other of their respective points of view. At the end, seeing that his wife has burst into tears, Sancho attempts to console her by credulously looking for a compromise in postponement: "Y en esto comenzó a llorar tan de veras como si ya viera muerta y enterrada a Sanchica. Sancho la consoló diciéndole que ya que la hubiese de hacer condesa, la haría todo lo más tarde que ser pudiese" (II, 5: 79).

Sancho also shows his credulousness in his confrontation with the owner of the barber's basin. Aware of the fact that the object is a basin, but determined to maintain ownership of the pack saddle, he serves his interest by calling the basin a helmet. In order to overcome the impasse between what he knows to be true and what he wishes to be true, he makes a "compromise" and calls the object "baciyelmo" (I, 44: 540), a compromise that forces the listener to realize that the object cannot be both helmet and basin; the listener must choose to believe it is one or the other.

These and other rhetorical procedures studied throughout the chapter show how the comic use of argumentation challenges the absolute truth sustained by romance. The major tenets of chivalric discourse, including moral and literary codes, are tested when the knight upholds the truth of such tenets by means of such rhetorical arguments as precedent, double hierarchies, moral authority, syllogistic reasoning, and comparisons. His speech serves to 1) reveal the limitations of such arguments in their applicability as well as in their capacity to prove the truth of a premise 2) weaken the premises he is upholding, the existence of the world of chivalry, the moral virtue of the heroes and heroines of romance and the ideal love of the knight for his lady, all of which constitute the myth of romance, and 3) reveal the other licentious self of knightly tales, condemned by the religious authority and humanist writers of the time.

Yet Cervantes is not aligned with many of the theological or humanistic thinkers of his time, who indiscriminately followed the classical model of language and literature only to become imprisoned in a discourse which limited artistic creation and prevented any true experimentation with language as a means to understand self and other. The dialogical discourse of Cervantes' text aligns him instead, as Alban Forcione has shown, with early Christian Humanism, and the figures of Erasmus and Vives. Like these great humanists, Cervantes was concerned with the varied registers of language and made wide usage of an open, expansive discourse, which is "reflective of man's variety and vitality and directly responsive to the freedom to criticize and create which was the distinctive feature of his humanity" (*Cervantes and the Mystery of Lawlessness* 16).[10]

The rhetoric of *Don Quixote* plays on the ambiguity of terms, the varying types of audience, the constant possibility of objections and the instability of premises. It is a rhetoric that demands our awareness that the language of truth can be replaced by a language of persuasion. The result or effects of difference and the logic of deviant figuration in *Don Quixote* is an "aporia" (the unpassable path). It is an ultimate impasse of thought engendered by a rhetoric that always reveals its own textual workings into the truth claims of philosophy by "boring from within," undermining philosophical categories with concepts borrowed from these philosophies themselves (Derrida, "*Ousia* and *Gramme*").[11]

Don Quixote's spiritualized, neoplatonic version of chivalry and his classical reason, the two cornerstones of logocentrism, are locked into a "reciprocal aporia" from which neither can emerge with its principles intact and on which both depend for their moments of maximum insight. And Cervantes achieves this by circumventing the conventional representation of opposition between the rational and the irrational, and joining or juxtaposing them in the mediating discourse of the comic. On the one hand the discourse of comic argumentation denounces the historical, literal "truth" of chivalry, (even a literal meaning is metaphorical) and asserts the metaphorical nature of its truth (our ways of understanding concepts such as love and heroism) while all the time reminding us of

---

[10] While Forcione's studies are helpful inasmuch as they show how dialogue functions in Cervantes' *Novelas Ejemplares* and *Don Quixote* as a sustained process of affirmation and negation, preventing any final swerve toward dogmatic assertions, his insights are obscured by his attempt to subordinate this dialogue to the ends of Christian Reform, as it was predicated by Erasmus.

[11] This process also occurs within the prologue of *Don Quixote*, Part I, and has been meticulously charted by Socrate, 71-127.

its essential metaphoricity or fictionality. On the other hand, it underscores the limitations of rational method as a means to achieve knowledge.

In consciously drawing out the inherently disruptive effects of both discourses, indeed, of all discourse, Cervantes forces the reader into a complicit relationship with the text, for upon dismantling the discourse of argumentation, the reader comes to acknowledge that the only possible way forward in the search for knowledge and truth is in the awareness of his or her own metaphysical liabilities (Forcione, *Cervantes and the Mystery of Lawlessness* 179). By escaping the impasse in this manner, and only in this manner, Cervantes is able to use the double discourse of the text to impel the reader toward an individual evaluation of ideals, values, and attitudes, and as a springboard from which to justify his own set of literary rules for his work, essential to the flourishing of the creative process. How these rules are set forth and actualized in the text will be the subject of the final chapter in this study, on the speaker-listener relationship.

CHAPTER 6

THE SPEAKER-LISTENER RELATIONSHIP

Thus far we have seen how the comic within rhetoric can be discovered in the object of discourse or *logos*, that is, in the content of the argument and the choice of theme (the use of enthymemes, maxims, *exempla* and their common *topoi*), and the style and manner in which the themes are organized and combined (*elocutio* and *dispositio*). An equally important source of the comic within rhetoric is its subjects, that is, *who* is attempting to persuade *whom*. While the *logos* belongs to the argument proper insofar as it actually or seemingly demonstrates, the speaker-listener relationship is concerned primarily with *ethos*, the speaker's moral life, attitudes and social interaction, and *pathos*, the speaker's ability to produce the "right" attitude in the hearer by means of his or her knowledge of human nature, control of the form and the timing of the discourse and the conditions under which the discourse is delivered.[1]

The major objective of Renaissance rhetorical theory is to prescribe norms for effective persuasion. According to the theory of the time, the premises of which can be found in Aristotle, Quintilian, and Cicero, the elaboration of an argument requires that two factors be considered, the theme in relation to the audience and the character or personality of the orator. In regard to the first factor, the law of decorum determines that the discourse the orator employs will have to adapt itself to the theme of the argument and to the circumstances of the audience, such as its cultural or social stan-

---

[1] Of course the content and arrangement of the argument can also embody *ethos* and *pathos*, but Aristotle distinguished *ethos* and *pathos* from *logos*. For a helpful discussion of this point and a general overview of the role of *ethos* and *pathos* in rhetoric, see Kennedy, 1-19.

dard, and the time and place in which the discourse is delivered. The vocabulary, tone, or style employed to speak before a university council must not be the same as when talking to an illiterate audience. The speaker must accept the intellectual limitations of the audience, who cannot grasp many points in a single view or follow a long chain of reasoning. In regard to the second factor, the orator will rouse the hearts of the audience to anger, hatred, indignation or some other emotion by being complete in all merits, being aware of the concerns and interests of the audience, working for what it deems as good and useful and placing in a positive light his or her identity (age, worth, authority, condition, fortune, family, upbringing).[2]

Bakhtin's notion of heteroglossia, which contains the monological/dialogical opposition, offers another context-oriented approach to language. In his work on Dostoevsky, Bakhtin is primarily concerned with "non-serious" discourse. He affirms that by providing extraordinary and daring situations and events or contexts in which an accepted truth or philosophical idea is developed and tested, carnivalesque literature engenders a "dialogizing background" that *liberates* the consciousness of the reader-listener from the consciousness and the direct word of the speaker and his or her desire to impose unilateral propositions about truth (94; Olbrechts-Tyteca 80-90).

Bakhtin's insights offer a refreshing alternative to the normative policies of traditional rhetorical theory and contribute to the understanding of comic discourse, but suffer from the same blind spots and contradictions present in classical rhetorical theory, albeit from contrary sides. His emphasis on the division between the comic and the serious causes him to maintain and even strengthen the opposi-

---

[2] Speech act theory is a modern sequel to classical rhetorical theory. In his work, *How to Do Things with Words*, J. L. Austin, founding father of speech act theory, distinguishes three types of speech acts that condition the transmittance of an idea: the locutionary act, an utterance or proposition; the illocutionary act, which can be used to "perform" certain kinds of rhetorical acts, such as advising, warning or promising; and the perlocutionary act, that is, the effect the utterance has on the listener. Austin concludes that an idea is faithfully transmitted only when certain conventions, which he specifies at length in his work, are obeyed, and which can be summed up by the formula "the utterance of certain words by certain persons in certain circumstances, and the particular persons and circumstances in a given case must be appropriate for the invocation of the particular procedure invoked" (26).

tions and hierarchies he seems to wish to overthrow. By drawing a line separating the monological and dialogical, the serious or official and the non-serious, Bakhtin is committed to decidability. An utterance either transmits its truth or intention successfully to the listener (monological speech) or it does not (dialogical). He maintains non-serious discourse on the lower rung of the hierarchy by labelling it as being framed in "daring" and "extraordinary," that is, abnormal circumstances, and thus relegates comic discourse, like carnival itself, to an outside and marginal position with respect to the "real" world and its "ordinary" circumstances.

Jacques Derrida's essay "Signature event context" is a critique of contemporary rhetorical theory, particularly, the speech act theory advanced by J. L. Austin, and by extension the classical rhetorical theory on which it is based. Derrida not only shows *before our very eyes* the flaws of Austin's idealization, but transcends and coalesces the logocentric/anti-logocentric, inside/outside, present/absent, serious/non-serious oppositions, by showing that non-serious discourse, with its situations, events, tone, and stylistic accents,— amplifies and thus makes more explicit what is always already (there) in "serious," "ordinary," and "proper" discourse.[3]

Derrida begins by denouncing as illegitimate the belief in the context-perfect situation postulated by Austin. He finds in the notion of the "speech-act" a reformulation of the philosophic stance that privileges "speech" over "writing," for the conditions of performative "felicity" demand that the speaker mean what he or she says in the sense of being presently involved with his proposition and standing up for its intention. In reply to Austin's assertion that language would have no meaning at all if its formulation were not able to repeat a coded or iterable (repeatable) utterance, Derrida argues that an utterance can be a signifying sequence only if it is iterable and only if it can be repeated in contexts where the supposed illocutionary force is no longer present.

Performatives derive their meaning from the fact that they embody conventional forms of speech already in existence before the speaker comes to use them. Therefore speech acts cannot be limited to the self-present moment of meaning. By acknowledging that

---

[3] For a discussion of this article and the extended debate betwen Derrida and Austin and Derrida and Austin's disciple, the philosopher John Searle, see Norris, *Deconstruction: Theory and Practice* 108-14 and Culler, 110-34.

the existence of a serious original utterance or entity is dependent on imitation, Derrida reverses the hierarchies established by Austin, and shows that the outside or marginal aspects of discourse are its inside, its internal norm.

Derrida supports his thesis with the example of the signature, recognized and considered as the most serious and most deliberate of acts. One intends its meaning. Signing a document is equivalent to the performative "I hereby authorize," and therefore is a speech act which seriously "performs" the signifying act it accomplishes. Derrida reproduces his signature "J. Derrida" above a printed "J. Derrida," accompanied by the following "Remark":

> (Remark: the – written – text of this – oral – communication was to have been addressed to the *Association of French Speaking Societies of Philosophy* before the meeting. Such a missive therefore had to be signed. Which I did, and counterfeit here. Where? There. J. D.) (330).

According to this formulation, the notion of signature, as all writing, is essentially and potentially paradoxical: it is and is not what it does. The notion of signature seems to reflect a moment of serious intention in the moment of writing, but that intention, now past, is always enclosed in a 'now,' "stapled to present punctuality" (328). Meaning is context-bound, but context is boundless.

Derrida does not absolutely deny the possibility of an utterance being reproduced exactly, but it would be, if such a replication could exist at all, only one aspect of iterability: "In a possible typology of iterability, the category of intention will not disappear; it will have its place, but from this place it will no longer be able to govern the entire scene and the entire system of utterances" (326). In this typology, there would no longer be an opposition between citational statements and original statement-events, with the consequence that "given this structure of iteration, the intention which animates utterance will never be completely present in itself and its content. The iteration which structures it a priori introduces an essential dehiscence and demarcation" (326).

Although I will not be analyzing speech acts in this chapter, I do feel that the debate between Derrida and Austin is pertinent to my study in that it underscores the ambiguities of all discourse, a fact that Bakhtin would have us forget. My analysis will deal with the diverse and numerous situations in which the speaker-listener relationship is framed, (which will include the recording of the intentions, attitudes and expectations of the participants, relationships existing between participants, and circumstances and conditions under which an utterance is made), and will focus on how the transformational capacity of comic, parasitic, non-serious discourse functions as a critical tool. The comic allows the reader to ponder the (im)possibility of the univocality of so-called "ordinary" language or of complete mastery of context, to treat discourse as the production of various sorts of combinations or insertions, and to perceive its ability to function in new contexts with new force.[4]

Don Quixote's arguments aim to persuade his audience of the existence of the world of chivalry, of his identity as a knight errant, of the necessity and heroic worth of his profession and of the beauty and virtue of his lady. The knight reproduces the arguments found in chivalric romance, but does not consider the conditions of his audience, such as their interest and attention. For instance, if the listener is not listening, he or she cannot be persuaded. In the episode narrating the knight's vigil of arms ceremony, the knight is incapable of capturing the attention of his audience by means of chivalric discourse. His threats to take the life of anyone who dares touch his arms are ignored by the muleteers, who go out to the well to get water for their mules. For the knight, they represent proof of his capacity for self-protection and defense against his enemies, qualities that are paramount to a knight who must defend the innocence of others. The narrator tells us that the first muleteer pays absolutely no attention to the knight's harangue and receives a beating as a result. The other muleteers are similarly unaffected by the knight's threat. Rather than being persuaded to retire, they begin to throw stones at Don Quixote and desist in their attack only when the innkeeper speaks, as the narrator ironically points out:

> "–Pero de vosotros, soez y baja canalla, no hago caso alguno; tirad, llegad, venid y ofendedme en cuanto pudiérades; que vosotros veréis el pago que lleváis de vuestra sandez y demasía."
>
> Decía esto con tanto brío y denuedo, que infundió un terrible temor en los que le acometían; y así por esto *como por las per-*

---

[4] For a general overview of Cervantes' experimentation with classical literary theory, see Forcione, *Cervantes, Aristotle and the Persiles*; and Riley, *Cervantes' Theory of the Novel*.

suasiones del ventero, le dejaron de tirar. . . . (I, 3: 92, emphasis added)

The knight is similarly unable to capture the interest or attention of his audience at the second inn, when he attempts to dissuade all of the lodgers from fighting. During the struggle caused by a verbal disagreement about the identity of the knight's helmet, the knight delivers a speech in which he soundly insists that people of such noble stature should not fight over such trivial matters. As he ends the speech, all of the participants stop fighting, but the narrator reveals that this is due not to the knight's arguments, to which no one is paying any attention, but to the persuasion of the judge and the priest and to the private interests of the audience:

> Los cuadrilleros, que no entendían el frasis de don Quijote, y se veían malparados de don Fernando, Cardenio y sus camaradas, no querían sosegarse; el barbero sí, porque en la pendencia tenía deshechas las barbas y el albarda; Sancho, a la más mínima voz de su amo, obedeció como buen criado; los cuatro criados de don Luis también estuvieron quedos, viendo cuán poco les iba en no estarlo. Sólo el ventero porfiaba que se habían de castigar las insolencias de aquel loco, que a cada paso le alborotaba la venta. . . .
>
> Puestos, pues, ya en sosiego, y hechos amigos todos a persuasión del oidor y del cura. . . . (I, 45: 545)

When the rural policemen arrive at the inn and recognize the knight known to have freed a group of dangerous galley slaves, they want to arrest him. The knight laughs and defends his action as licit behavior of a knight errant. He says his rights and privileges exempt him from the laws binding ordinary men. He states his premise of the supremacy of the knight errant as a means of exonerating himself from the accusation that he has committed a crime, one which he backs up with the argument of the precedent, the citation of rights enjoyed by knights before him. The knight constructs his speech in a perfect rhetorical style. Using the *interrogatio*, and employing the anaphora and symmetrical phrasing in order to give force to his argument, he asks:

> ¿quién fue el ignorante que firmó mandamiento de prisión contra un tal caballero como yo soy? ¿Quién el que ignoró que son

esentos de todo judicial fuero los caballeros andantes, y que su ley es su espada, sus fueros sus bríos, sus premáticas su voluntad? ¿Quién fue el. . . ? (547)

The knight's speech is ineffective, however, not only because he has not taken into consideration that chivalric law has no domain in seventeenth century La Mancha, but because no one is listening to him. While the knight is giving his speech, the priest is giving the policeman an account of the knight's madness and trying to dissuade them from arresting him:

> En tanto que don Quijote esto decía, estaba persuadiendo el Cura a los cuadrilleros como don Quijote era falto de juicio, como lo veían por sus obras y por sus palabras, y que no tenían para qué llevar aquel negocio adelante. . . . (46: 548)

Another instance occurs when Don Quixote tries to persuade Maritornes not to mistreat his hand. For a practical joke, the girl, playing the role of the daughter of the warden of the "castle," has begged the knight to give her one of his hands to touch. When he stands up on his horse to deliver his hand to her through a hole in the wall of the loft, the servant girl ties it up and runs off. Unaware that the love of the girl is only feigned, he assumes that she has acted out of vengeance. The premise of his argument is that she should not mistreat his hand. The arguments he gives to support it are logical: His hand is not at fault if he has mistreated her; if she really loved him she should not carry out such a vengeful act; and all of her vengeance should not be exercised on such a small part of his body. His arguments are not heard by the servant girl and the innkeeper's daughter, as the narrator points out:

> Pero todas estas razones de don Quijote ya no las escuchaba nadie, porque, así como Maritornes le ató, ella y la otra se fueron, muertas de risa, y le dejaron asido de manera que fue imposible soltarse (I, 43: 528).

The knight's arguments are rendered ineffective due to the absence of an audience in the knight's defense of the passage of a main road in the episode of the feigned Arcadia. He carries out the act in imitation of those described in chivalric romance and to express his gratitude for the hospitality he received from the shepherds and shepherdesses. The knight declares he will stay on the main road for two days and claim to all who might pass by that except for Dulcinea, the young maidens are unequalled in beauty. He then gives a discourse on gratitude in which he affirms the importance of returning good works, and when that is not possible, one should make public the good works received. He ends his speech by claiming that he will show his thanks in the second manner. He departs and travels to the main road, not far from the fields where he had encountered the young men and women disguised as shepherds and shepherdesses, and defends the beauty of the shepherdesses by challenging to a duel anyone who might doubt or try to refute his words. The narrator reminds us that no one is there to hear him: "Dos veces repitió estas mismas razones, y dos veces no fueron oídas de ningún aventurero . . ." (II, 58: 480).

Sometimes a person can be bodily present but unable to pay attention to the speaker. When Don Quixote delivers a discourse in which he compares and contrasts the tranquil life of the humble with the troubled and restless life of those destined to be great, the eloquence and logic of his speech cannot move Sancho, as the narrator indicates, because he is sleeping: "A todo esto no respondió Sancho, porque dormía, ni despertara tan presto si don Quijote con el cuento de la lanza no le hiciere volver en sí" (II, 20: 186).

The orator's speech cannot persuade a listener if the latter is not able to understand it. The language the speaker employs may be correct, but it causes discordance if it is inadequate. According to rhetorical theory, the public should be moved when a speech is well delivered and the logic is sound. In *Don Quixote*, the listeners are often moved by the strange discordance of the knight's speeches. His lofty, learned style and his chivalric jargon, while appropriate in narrating chivalric adventures, seem strange to those who encounter the knight on the roads of La Mancha. The narrator often describes the passers-by as "maravillados" and "extrañados" by his discourse, as well as by his physical appearance (his skinniness and knightly costume).[5]

The farm laborers carrying statues of saintly images to their village are bewildered as Don Quixote begins to explain to them the relation between the saintly images they are carrying and his knight-

---

[5] The surprise the knight's speech elicits has been linked to the concept of *admiratio*. See Eduardo Urbina.

ly profession. He identifies the saints and contrasts their good fortune with his bad one. He concludes by describing the enchantment of Dulcinea and his hopes to disenchant her. The narrator then describes the peasants' puzzled reaction: "Admiráronse los hombres así de la figura como de las razones de don Quijote, sin entender la mitad de lo que en ellas decir quería" (II, 53: 473).

The speech the knight delivers before a group of humble goatherds on the Golden Age is inappropriate, due to the cultural level of the audience. In the knight's discourse, arguments are given as a manner of describing the beauty and perfection of the ancient society and of justifying his own task of restoring it, but they cannot convince the goatherds because they cannot understand his speech:

> Toda esta larga arenga –que se pudiera muy bien escusar– dijo nuestro caballero, porque las bellotas que le dieron le trujeron a la memoria la edad dorada, y antojósele hacer aquel *inútil razonamiento* a los cabreros, que, sin respondelle palabra, embobados y suspensos le estuvieron escuchando. (I, 11: 157, emphasis added)[6]

The millers and fishermen in the enchanted boat episode are equally puzzled by the knight's chivalric jargon. After they fish the knight out of the water, he declares that he cannot save the people inside the mill (which he calls "prisión") because the adventure is reserved for another knight. The narrator then explains the surprise the humble folk felt upon hearing his speech:

> Los pescadores y molineros estaban admirados, mirando aquellas dos figuras *tan fuera del uso*, al parecer, de los otros hombres, y no acababan de entender a dó se encaminaban las razones y preguntas que don Quijote les decía. . . . (II, 29: 267, emphasis added)

The knight's exaltation of feminine beauty and virtue forms part of chivalric discourse. Such speech becomes discordant when the knight employs it to address the two prostitutes at the first inn. The narrator explains how the girls are struck by the discordance of the speech: "Mirábanle las mozas, y andaban con los ojos buscán-

---

[6] For a rhetorical analysis of this episode, and a general discussion of the discordance in the knight's speech, see Mackey.

dole el rostro, que la mala visera le encubría; mas como se oyeron llamar doncellas, cosa tan fuera de su profesión, no pudieron tener la risa ..." (I, 2: 83). The knight's love epistle to his lady is similarly inappropriate, and therefore cannot move Dulcinea/Aldonza, for as Sancho indicates, she will not be able to understand it, much less appreciate it. She is unfamiliar with chivalric jargon because she cannot read, and she would be too occupied with her farm duties to even be interested in such matters.

As interaction between Don Quixote and Sancho intensifies, the squire increasingly imitates his master's chivalric style. At the beginning of Part II, Sancho explains to Teresa that his economic need obligates him to travel once more with Don Quixote: "... y si Dios quisiera darme de comer a pie enjuto y en mi casa, sin traerme por vericuetos y encrucijadas, pues lo podía hacer a poca costa y no más de quererlo, claro está que mi alegría fuera más firme y valedera ..." (5: 73). Sancho's serious attempt to justify his actions have no effect on Teresa since, as she admits, she cannot understand a word of his speech, due to its "rodeada manera."

In the episode of the enchantment of Dulcinea, Sancho imitates the learned speech of the knight, to the detriment of the knight's desire to exalt his lady. While attempting to convince the knight that the peasant girl before them is his lady, he underscores the inappropriateness of his master's discourse. Sancho's lofty speech ("–Reina y princesa y duquesa de la hermosura, vuestra altivez y grandeza sea servida de recebir en su gracia y buen talente al cautivo caballero vuestro ..." [II, 10: 109]) does not move the country girls, because they have never heard such language before, nor read a book of chivalry.

The persuasive intention of an argument can be deflected resulting in the displacement of the listener's attention onto the ambiguity of discourse when there are simultaneous inconsistencies and discordances in the reactions of the audience, due to the varying cultural levels of the listeners and the knowledge they have of the speaker. In Don Quixote's defense of the identity of the basin as "helmet" to the barber and other guests at the inn, the narrator underscores these differences: "Para aquellos que la tenían del humor de don Quijote era todo esto materia de grandísima risa; pero para los que le ignoraban les parecía el mayor disparate del mundo ..." (I, 45: 542) (Trueblood 7).

Discordance is inadvertently produced in the knight's poetic discourse and intentionally in the discourse of other characters as well as of the narrator when other types of discourse are juxtaposed with it. The knight's contemporary speech suddenly gives way to the employment of chivalric archaisms, and his employment of a learned style gives way to legal terminology, thieves' jargon, billingsgate speech and colloquialisms. The result of these "brusque insertions" is that the change of style or tone calls attention to language itself and away from the argument being developed, weakening its effect on the listener.

The arguments Sancho develops in order to persuade his master to wait until morning to discover the origin of the terrible noise in the adventure of the fulling mills are effective in triggering an emotional response in the reader, until the end of the speech, when he inserts a chivalric archaism:

> Yo salí de mi tierra y dejé hijos y mujer por venir a servir a vuestra merced, creyendo valer más y no menos; pero como la cudicia rompe el saco, a mí me ha rasgado mis esperanzas, pues cuando más vivas las tenía de alcanzar aquella negra y malhadada ínsula que tantas veces vuestra merced me ha prometido, veo que, en pago y trueco della, me quiere ahora dejar en un lugar tan apartado del trato humano. Por un solo Dios, señor mío, que *non se me faga tal desaguisado*. . . . (I, 20: 239, emphasis added)

The narrator's description of Dorotea's staging of her role as princess in distress underscores the falsity of her identity by brusquely inserting chivalric archaisms:

> Y en llegando junto a él, el escudero se arrojó de la mula y fue a tomar en los brazos a Dorotea, la cual, apeándose con grande desenvoltura, se fue a hincar de rodillas ante las de don Quijote; y aunque él pugnaba por levantarla, ella, sin levantarse, *le fabló en esta guisa*. . . . (I, 29: 364, emphasis added)

Soon after, the priest insinuates before the "princess" that the valorous knight has committed the criminal action of liberating some dangerous galley slaves. The knight does not respond, but Sancho speaks up, asserting that his master was indeed the culprit. His use of chivalric archaism has the effect of showing how his master's heroic intention has resulted in criminal action:

> –Pues mía fe, señor licenciado, el que hizo esa *fazaña* fue mi amo, y no porque yo no no le dije antes y le avisé que mirase lo

que hacía, y que era pecado darles libertad, porque todos iban allí por grandísimos bellacos. (I, 30: 371, emphasis added)

Don Quixote often reveals the fraudulence of his knightly role as he intersperses blasphemies and vulgar expressions in his speech. Abusive words, indecent terms, and blasphemies constitute the discourse of "billingsgate," the speech of the marketplace. Bakhtin explains that such frank and open speech brings people together in the marketplace, where the rules of decorum and propriety that separate high and low classes are broken down (*Rabelais* 145-95; Cortazar). Don Quixote employs a learned and lofty tone in order to set himself apart and above others. As he inserts indecent expressions in his discourse, his pretensions to convince his audience of his superior status are weakened.

The knight inserts billingsgate expressions in one of the most crucial moments of his chivalric career, when he has begun his mission to rescue the princess Micomicona and her kingdom from a giant that has besieged them. Traveling towards the kingdom in the company of the princess, the knight engages in conversation with Sancho, informing him that he has no intention of marrying the princess. When Sancho sees his hopes of winning a countship crumble, he implores his master to marry the lady. When he openly states that she is more beautiful than Dulcinea as a means to support his viewpoint, Don Quixote gives the squire a great blow and recriminates him bitterly before the princess:

> –¿Pensáis –le dijo a cabo de rato–, villano ruin, que ha de haber lugar siempre para ponerme la mano en la horcajadura, y que todo ha de ser errar vos y perdonaros yo? Pues no lo penséis, bellaco descomulgado, que sin duda lo estás, pues has puesto lengua en la sin par Dulcinea. Y ¿no sabéis vos, gañán, faquín, belitre, que si no fuese por el valor que ella infunde en mi brazo, que no le tendría yo para matar una pulga? Decid, socarrón de lengua viperina, y ¿quién pensáis que ha ganado este reino y cortado la cabeza a este gigante, y héchoos a vos marqués, que todo esto doy ya por hecho y por cosa pasada en cosa juzgada, si no es el valor de Dulcinea, tomando a mi brazo por instrumento de sus hazañas? Ella pelea en mí, y vence en mí, y yo vivo y respiro en ella, y tengo vida y ser. ¡Oh hideputa bellaco. . . ! (I, 30: 377-78)

As the knight hurls insults at his squire, he mixes familiar speech, such as the idiom "poner mano en la horcajadura," to treat something with excessive familiarity, and the blasphemies with the lofty concepts of courtly love. The knight employs chivalric archaisms and learned concepts here and elsewhere as a manner of convincing others of his and his lady's noble identity and attempts to conform his speech patterns to those specified by the humanist language model of proper language. Yet according to the rhetorical treatises of the time, the elocution of the orator must be "elegante," and elegance consisted in the elimination of any words that could be considered obscene or unusual. The alternating of such words with the high style neutralizes the rousing effect the speech should generate. The hearer is forced to take notice more of the discordance in the form of the discourse than of the cohesiveness of the argument, the claim of the exalted status of the lady and of their ideal love.

As Sancho begins to imitate his master's speech, he commits the same type of errors as his master, alternating chivalric archaisms and a rhetorical style with popular expressions and billingsgate speech. When the priest introduces Sancho to Dorotea, he employs chivalric discourse in order to convince the squire that the lady is really a princess in distress and that she has come to ask the knight for a boon. Sancho attempts to rise to the occasion by employing the same type of discourse, but ends by mixing it with popular expressions:

> –Dichosa buscada y dichoso hallazgo –dijo a esta sazón Sancho Panza–, y más si mi amo es tan venturoso que *desfaga ese agravio y enderece ese tuerto, matando a ese hideputa dese gigante* que vuestra merced dice.... (I, 29: 363, emphasis added)

The narrator's discourse is replete with vulgar details, colloquialisms, popular sayings, and billingsgate. He inserts such expressions as a means of calling attention to some unheroic trait of the knight. For example, the narrator employs chivalric discourse in his description of the knight's penance, in imitation of chroniclers of chivalric romance who wish to poetically exalt their heroes. He then deviates from his models as he concludes his description with a radical change in discourse. The narrator explains that the knight spends his time during his penance

> ... en suspirar, y en llamar a los faunos y silvanos de aquellos bosques, a las ninfas de los ríos, a la dolorosa y húmida Eco, que le respondiese, consolasen y escuchasen ... y en buscar algunas yerbas con que sustentarse en tanto que Sancho volvía; que, si como tardó tres días, tardara tres semanas, el Caballero de la Triste Figura quedara tan desfigurado, que no le conociera la madre que lo parió. (I, 26: 321)

The narrator's ideal portrait of the valiant and virtuous hero is transformed into the grotesque portrait of a body in retreat as the narrator extrapolates and carries out the logical consequences of the fasting of the penitent hero, underscored by word play on the word "figura" and by the colloquial phrase.

The knight also inserts legal jargon in his speech, transforming his phrases into indecent expressions. He incorporates a legal phrase in defense of his liberation of the galley slaves:

> Yo topé un rosario y sarta de gente mohína y desdichada, y hice con ellos lo que mi religión me pide, y lo demás allá se avenga; y a quien mal le ha parecido, salvo la santa dignidad del señor licenciado y su honrada persona, digo que sabe poco de achaque de caballería, y que miente como un hideputa y mal nacido; y esto le haré conocer con mi espada, *donde más largamente se contiene*. (I, 30: 371-72, emphasis added)

The verbal aggression is aimed at Sancho. By excluding the priest from his threats, he maintains the possibility of not having his assertions challenged. His description of the criminals and his action to liberate them combine qualities of the saint and sinner. The knight's attempt to portray the dangerous criminals as victims or martyrs is shown in his description of them, "Yo topé un rosario. . . ." He thus exalts simultaneously his own role as liberating hero, "hice con ellos lo que mi religión me pide." His saintly image is immediately weakened, however, as he justifies his "religious" conduct by means of indecent expressions.

Don Quixote first backs up the truth of his affirmations by calling those who doubt his assertions liars, employing the popular expression "miente como un hideputa." He then threatens to attack whoever puts his virtuous action into doubt, "le haré conocer con mi espada, donde más largamente se contiene." The phrase "donde más largamente se contiene" is employed in legal terminology to signify that one is explaining in a brief manner what can be found in a more complete form in print. The knight's particular employment of the term transforms it into an indecent expression as he uses it to indicate that he will attack the "lower parts" of anyone who disputes his arguments. Such a threat serves to highlight the knight's inability to justify the legality of his actions by a sound argumentation and discredits the truth of his premise by showing that the only means he has left to prove it is that of physical force.

After reading Part I of *Don Quixote*, Sansón Carrasco imitates the knight's legal discourse in a manner that undermines the knight's attempt to exalt himself as hero. When he appears before Don Quixote, masquerading as Knight of the Mirrors, he tells the knight that he had duelled with Don Quixote and won, hoping in this way to cause Don Quixote to challenge him to a duel. The knight falls into the trap, but before the duel begins, he asks the Knight of the Mirrors if he indeed looks like the knight he had fought. Sansón responds that he cannot affirm the truth of his premise absolutely:

> –A eso vos respondemos –dijo el de los Espejos– que parecéis, como se parece un huevo a otro, al mismo caballero que yo vencí; pero según vos decís que le persiguen encantadores, no osaré afirmar si sois *el contenido* o no. (14: 141, emphasis added)

Sansón imitates the knight's speech as he mixes ancient modes of speech with modern ones and legal terminology with colloquial expressions. Sansón's opening phrase "A eso vos respondemos" is an ancient formula employed in the Court of Castile. The person who spoke in the name of the king would answer the petition of a subject with this phrase. Sansón thus begins by according himself the authority of the king. He then gives his premise, that Don Quixote looks identical to the knight he had previously duelled and employs a modern colloquialism, "parecéis, como se parece un huevo a otro," only to put his premise into doubt, "no osaré afirmar si sois el contenido o no."

Sansón employs a legal phrase similar to that of the knight's in the galley slave episode, but with a somewhat different meaning. The phrase "el contenido" refers to a purported criminal, as cited in legal documents. By means of the phrase, Sansón transforms the acclaimed hero into an alleged criminal against whom legal action is being taken. At the same time, he juxtaposes the legal phrase with the colloquial expression, giving the former yet a new meaning. What the joker ends up calling the knight's supposed impostor, and implicitly the knight himself, is an egg yolk or unhatched chicken.

Another character in Part II, Don Antonio, has also read Part I of the knight's exploits and imitates his use of legal terminology. Don Antonio welcomes the knight to his city, imitating the style in which heroes are welcomed in chivalric romance: "–Bien sea venido a nuestra ciudad el espejo, el farol, la estrella y el norte de toda la caballería andante, *donde más largamente se contiene*" (61: 507, emphasis added). Don Antonio mixes chivalric discourse with legal terminology in a manner that undermines the power of chivalric discourse to exalt the hero, for by using the legal phrase as an elliptic remark, he cuts short the praise of the magnanimous hero, which is usually never lengthy enough to describe the hero's valor.

The orator's discourse can be harmonious, and his or her logic well-constructed, and yet still not cause the listener to be persuaded if the listener does not show good will towards the speaker and a desire to be convinced. A good argument will not be persuasive if the listener is an object from the plant or animal world. In *Don Quixote*, the knight's rhetorical virtuosity and his awe-inspiring threats do not move his audience when the knight mistakes the prosaic objects and animals dwelling in the farm region of La Mancha for powerful enemies such as those described in chivalric romance.

In the knight's defense of the passage of the main road, he orders a herd of bulls to admit that the shepherdesses of the Arcadia are unsurpassed in beauty: "Confesad, malandrines, así a carga cerrada, que es verdad lo que yo aquí he publicado; si no, conmigo sois en batalla" (II, 58: 481). Heedless of the knight's threats, the bulls trample him and his squire, throwing them to the ground. Don Quixote leaps to his feet and begins to run after them, challenging them to a duel and demanding that they stop their flight and confront him. As he concludes his threats, the narrator underscores their futility: "Pero no por eso se detuvieron los apresurados corredores, ni hicieron más caso de sus amenazas que de las nubes de antaño" (481). The knight's demonstration of the ideal of gratitude he sustained earlier serves to weaken his promise. According higher priority to his humiliation than to the ideal of gratitude he supports, he breaks his word and leaves immediately, before defending the passage for two days and making public the good works of which he had been recipient.

Don Quixote's threats to the windmills he believes to be giants are equally ineffective, since the inanimate objects cannot be dissuaded from fleeing or persuaded to enter into battle. He cries similar threats to the windmills:

> –Non fuyades, cobardes y viles criaturas, que un solo caballero es el que os acomete.
> Levantóse en esto un poco de viento, y las grandes aspas comenzaron a moverse, lo cual visto por don Quijote, dijo:
> –Pues aunque mováis más brazos que los del gigante Briareo, me lo habéis de pagar. (I, 8: 129-30)

What causes surprise in both of these episodes is that the nonhuman objects, the bulls and the windmills, take on human attributes, acting as if they possessed human will. The bulls run as if they were escaping from some fearful enemy and the arms of the windmills move as if threatening to attack the knight. On both occasions, however, the knight's "opponents" are affected not by the intrinsic truth or reasoning power of his threats, which they do not have the capacity to understand, but by extrinsic elements which form part of the narrator's affirmations, and which he employs to discredit the knight's claims. The narrator explains that the bulls run at a fast pace down the main road because they are herded by the cattlemen and that a gust of wind has caused the arms of the mills to move. The knight and squire's misadventure with a herd of six hundred pigs in Chapter 63 of Part II, and Don Quixote's "cattish" and "bellish" adventure at the ducal palace in Chapter 46, function in a similar manner.

Human beings can also be unwilling to be persuaded by an argument. Although they possess will and desire, they also possess a particular predisposition or lack of disposition towards certain arguments, often irrational in nature. Surprising moments occur in *Don Quixote* when the most tender and forceful speeches have absolutely no effect on the knight, almost as if he were an object from the animal or vegetable world, deprived of human comprehension, will or, more importantly, the rational processes.

In the episode of the fulling mills, Sancho delivers a speech in which he reminds Don Quixote of the fearful conditions and the moral responsibility the knight has towards him. The knight's reply confirms that Sancho's words have no effect whatsoever:

> –Falte lo que faltare –respondió don Quijote–; que no se ha de decir por mí, ahora ni en ningún tiempo, que lágrimas y ruegos me apartaron de hacer lo que debía a estilo de caballero; y así, te ruego, Sancho, que calles.... (I, 20: 240)

At the beginning of Part II, the knight's niece similarly attempts to dissuade Don Quixote from fulfilling his knightly duties. She tells him that the chivalric tales he has read are fictitious. The knight attempts to justify his exercise of the chivalric profession by his discourse on pedigrees, in which he maintains that the profession of arms is a means by which the poor can rise to the highest level. He concludes, however, by confessing that he is determined not to listen to anyone who might try to stop him. His confession mitigates the power of the discourse on pedigrees to move us, as well as his previous assertion that his actions are governed by destiny:

> Dos caminos hay, hijas, por donde pueden ir los hombres a llegar a ser ricos y honrados: el uno es el de las letras; otro, el de las armas. Yo tengo más armas que letras, y nací, según me inclino a las armas, debajo de la influencia del planeta Marte; así, que casi me es forzoso seguir por su camino, y por él tengo de ir a pesar de todo el mundo, y será en balde cansaros en persuadirme a que no quiera yo lo que los cielos quieren, la fortuna ordena y la razón pide, y *sobre todo, mi voluntad desea*.... (6: 83-84, emphasis added)

The disjunctive "y sobretodo" serves to uncover the falsity of the supposed causes for carrying out his profession, namely, the desire to carry out virtuous action and the impulse of destiny, by placing them in opposition to his personal desires ("lo que . . . mi voluntad desea").

Complementary to the knight's indisposition to be persuaded of something that will prevent him from complying with his profession is his predisposition to be convinced by anyone who shares his beliefs, or seems to, regardless of the actual content of the argument. The innkeeper at the first inn is a character who imitates the knight's chivalric style for the purpose of having fun with Don

Quixote. In his advice to Don Quixote about how he should travel and what provisions he should carry, he continues to imitate his guest's lofty discourse, telling him:

> ... que tuviese por cierto y averiguado que todos los caballeros andantes, de que tantos libros están llenos y atestados, llevaban bien herradas las bolsas, por lo que pudiese sucederles; y que asimismo llevaban camisas y una arqueta pequeña llena de ungüentos para curar las heridas que recebían. . . . (I, 3: 89)

The knight's belief in chivalry causes him to take the innkeeper's arguments at face value. The innkeeper knows that by speaking to Don Quixote in chivalric style, he can make arguments convincing to him. Indeed, Don Quixote is so moved by the innkeeper's speech that on his second sally he follows out the innkeeper's instructions to the letter. He carries with him money, clothes and medicines, and thus makes important concessions to the prosaic reality surrounding him.

Other characters manage to control the knight's actions and conduct in a similar fashion, causing him to act against his own beliefs. The major plot sequences of the tale are devised by characters who have knowledge of the knight's predisposition towards chivalric arguments and who employ them in their discussion with him for their own purposes. The most important examples are the priest's elaboration of the chivalric pseudo-adventure, the rescue of the princess Micomicona and Sancho's enchantment of Dulcinea.

Sancho's personality acts as a complement to his master's. Many of the humorous aspects of the squire's character stem from his predisposition to believe certain hypotheses. The impetus with which his own economic interests and ambitions cause him to believe in the premises of his master lead him to give more credit to them than to what he sees before his eyes. Thus, when Don Quixote affirms that they have giants with whom to battle, the squire responds not by questioning the possibility that a giant could be found on the Manchegan plain, but by asking his master to be more specific in his reference: "¿Qué gigantes?" (I, 8: 129). Similarly, in the pseudo-adventure planned by the priest, Sancho becomes convinced that Dorotea is really the Princess Micomicona, even when he knows of the priest's plan to bring the knight back to the village. Although the squire was not present at the priest's encounter with Dorotea and at their joint decision that she substitute the priest's role as princess, the substitution is evident, and Sancho simply gives more priority to his own desires, the possibility of his master conquering the giant, winning the kingdom and giving him a countship, than to what his own logic might tell him. The duchess's skill in convincing the squire that Dulcinea is really is bewitched by some evil enchanter operates according to the same principle. Sancho at least partially suspends his belief in what he knows is true, that Dulcinea was never enchanted, in order to serve his own goal: the attainment of the governorship.

Other characters, and even the reader, are shown to be influenced by their own beliefs and desires, often irreducible and irreconcilable to the logic of any argument, and practically always bound to values so ingrained within their personalities as to be almost impossible to reject or even objectively analyze. The projection of the problem of the involvement and complicity of the listeners (other characters and the reader) in the knight's and squire's folly can best be grasped by exploring the second important factor in the speaker-listener relationship: the character of the speaker.

An argument can be rendered ineffective and its logic weakened if the reputation of the orator is put into doubt, namely, if he or she is known to be dishonest, a criminal, or a madman. In contrast to the ignorant characters in the text who know nothing about Don Quixote and have never read a book of chivalry, such as the muleteers, goatherds and farmers, and who are therefore only bewildered by the knight's arguments, are those who are "in the know." These characters have read books of chivalry or Part I of *Don Quixote*, or know the knight personally. Surprisingly, they are convinced by many of the knight's assertions, in spite of the knowledge they have of his folly, because they share with him a predisposition towards certain arguments.

The shepherds and shepherdesses reenacting Camoes' and Garcilaso's eclogues have knowledge of the folly of the knight because they have read Part I of *Don Quixote*. Yet they share his idealism and are willing to read in the narration of his exploits what their own beliefs dictate to them, rejecting or ignoring any other discourse within the tale which challenges or upsets the status quo of the hierarchies the knight wishes to embody. They have fled to the countryside to reenact the fictional pastoral scenes just as the knight has fled to the roads of La Mancha to transform his life into a work of art. For them, Don Quixote is a hero, and they receive him as such when the knight identifies himself:

> ¿ . . . qué ventura tan grande nos ha sucedido? ¿Ves este señor que tenemos delante? Pues hágote saber que es el más valiente, y el más enamorado, y el más comedido que tiene el mundo, si no es que nos miente y nos engaña una historia que de sus hazañas anda impresa, y yo he leído. (II, 58: 478)

Another young shepherdess agrees with the above-cited affirmations of her friend: ". . . dicen dél que es el más firme y más leal enamorado que se sabe, y que su dama es una tal Dulcinea del Toboso, a quien en toda España la dan la palma de la hermosura" (478).

The young men and women then proceed to treat the knight with reverence, inviting him to share their meal and placing him at the head of the table. When the meal is over, the knight gives his discourse on gratitude. Sancho intervenes as the knight concludes, putting the orator's character into doubt:

> –¿Es posible que haya en el mundo personas que se atrevan a decir y a jurar que este mi señor es loco? Digan vuestras mercedes, señores pastores: ¿hay cura de aldea, por discreto y por estudiante que sea, que pueda decir lo que mi amo ha dicho. . . ? (479)

The knight grasps his squire's intention, and the aggression against his character and furiously recriminates Sancho. Only when the shepherds and shepherdesses witness his anger do they begin to doubt the character of the knight, as the narrator indicates: "Y con gran furia y muestras de enojo, se levantó de la silla, dejando admirados a los circunstantes, haciéndoles dudar si le podían tener por loco o por cuerdo" (480).

The humor of the episode results from the reaction of the young men and women, who continue to believe that the knight is a great hero in spite of his foolish actions, and only waver in their opinion without completely rejecting it, as they witness his choleric reaction to the squire's insinuations. Finally, although they attempt to persuade the knight not to defend the passage of the road as proof of his gratitude, they do not consider the knight mad for wishing to carry out such an action. On the contrary, they consider it evidence of his valorous conduct, for the narrator explains that the reason they give to dissuade him from carrying out the defense of the road is that "no era menester nuevas demostraciones para conocer su ánimo valeroso, pues bastaban las que en la historia de sus hechos se referían . . ." (480).

The knight's discourse of the benefits of the career of arms over letters, also given over the dinner table, is delivered to a group of individuals that shares his affinity towards the profession of arms and is thus moved by the knight's arguments, in spite of the knowledge the group has of the knight's folly. The reaction of the audience, including Don Fernando, Dorotea, Cardenio, Luscinda, and the captive, tells us at least as much about their predisposition as it does about the credibility of the knight's arguments, as the narrator points out:

> De tal manera y por tan buenos términos iba prosiguiendo en su plática don Quijote, que obligó a que, por entonces, *ninguno de los que escuchándole estaban le tuviese por loco; antes, como todos los más eran caballeros, a quien son anejas las armas, le escuchaban de muy buena gana.* . . . (I, 37: 466, emphasis added)

Don Lorenzo is another character who shows a certain predisposition to the knight's arguments. The young man has been informed by his father of the folly of the knight, and engages in conversation with Don Quixote in order to find out exactly what the nature of his folly is. They begin by discussing the boy's profession, that of studying and writing poetry. Lorenzo affirms that he does not consider himself a "poet," a name reserved for the truly talented. The knight responds that his humility is rare, since most poets are proud. As the discussion develops, the knight reveals his own profession, describes its characteristics and states his own goal to rise to heroism. Lorenzo finally reports to his father that the knight is indeed mad, although at times he is lucid.

The discussion is interrupted by lunch, and immediately following, the knight begs Lorenzo to recite some of his verses. After the boy reads his gloss, the knight questions him about his poetry and discusses with him the rules of the gloss, impressing the boy with his erudition on this matter. He ends the discussion with praise for the boy's poetic talents. The result of this final part of their discussion on poetry is that the boy is more predisposed to disregard his previous opinion of the knight and to give credit to an argument which is not necessarily forceful, namely, that the gloss is good, because it coincides with his own beliefs. The narrator points out the disparity:

> ¿No es bueno que dicen que se holgó don Lorenzo de verse alabar de don Quijote, aunque le tenía por loco? !Oh fuerza de la adulación, a cuánto te estiendes, y cuán dilatados límites son los de tu juridición agradable! (II, 18: 175)

The knight's praise is sincere. Unlike his "amigo discreto" who criticizes the gloss because of the narrowness of its rules and expression, the knight is enthusiastic about any type of human endeavor that demands the execution of an action according to a rigid set of rules. The knight's praise tells us more about the character of the listener than about the quality of the orator's verses. Not only is the "truth" of the knight's praise not proven, but the young man's premise put forth in the first part of the discussion with the knight, that of his humility, is further discredited.

The son's willingness to believe certain arguments acts as a complement to his father's. The Man in Green boasts to the knight that he is a man of high morals and describes himself as a man who puts into practice in his daily life the highest Christian virtues: charity, cleanliness, humility, good works, and devotion to God. It is clear from his description that he is susceptible to moral argumentation. It is not surprising, therefore, that he should be persuaded by the moral arguments contained in Don Quixote's discourse, in which he defines the virtues of poetry as well as the proper moral attitude of the father towards his children, that of love and acceptance of their choices and preferences. Because of a certain affinity in his moral concepts, the Man in Green gives more credit to the arguments of the knight's speech than to the actual source of the arguments. The narrator indicates the effect such arguments have on the gentleman: "Admirado quedó el del verde gabán del razonamiento de don Quijote, y tanto, que fue perdiendo de la opinión que con él tenía, de ser mentecato" (16: 157).

The two themes of the knight's discourse, the relationship between father and children and the defense of poetry, are academic in nature and were popular topics in discourses of classical rhetoric.

The knight's delivery of the speech is a correct, at times even eloquent, exposition of arguments which seem sound in rhetorical abstractions. Yet the knight's academic discourse is not much different from the Man in Green's speech on his Christian conduct. The absolute values they contain are undermined by the speaker's practical display of them.

The gentleman's boastful assertion of his Christian humility is inherently discordant. His cold and calculating list of his daily duties and conduct ("Alguna vez como con mis vecinos y amigos . . . oigo misa cada día, reparto de mis bienes con los pobres, sin hacer alarde de las buenas obras . . ." [53]) offers a negative exposition of Christian life by converting a warm, spontaneous and natural Christian feeling and spirit into some magic formula which, if followed, will lead to sainthood, as Sancho's prostration before him underscores.[7]

The knight similarly puts his own ideals into doubt. He defends the purity of poetry, affirming that such purity is reflected in the poetry of a chosen few who are knowledgeable and talented enough to deserve the title of poet, and condemns the practice of poetry by those who do not have expertise. Yet when the knight enters the Man in Green's house and cites the verses of one of Garcilaso's sonnets, ("–Oh dulces prendas, por mí mal halladas . . ." [18: 168]), to refer to some water jugs made in El Toboso and which remind him thus of Dulcinea, he demonstrates how even the purest poetry can be "manoseada." Similarly, while defending the freedom of sons to choose their own destiny, he offers to take Don Lorenzo with him, advising him to give up his profession of poetry for the profession of arms. He says that he will educate him to be virtuous, according to the canons of his own profession.

The empirical reader's point of view of Don Quixote is inevitably controlled by these listeners. No matter what role the author creates for the reader, namely, that they pertain to the national, social or intellectual rank of the main speaker or to a different one, the author enjoins the reader to identify with the fictive audience

---

[7] Percas de Ponseti, in her most recent work, *Cervantes the Writer and Painter of "Don Quijote,"* 38-41, shows how superimposed visualizations of the Man in Green make explicit the duplicitous nature of the character. Weiger, *In the Margins of Cervantes*, 74-82, judges the Man in Green's narrowness of perspective on life to be the result of his failure as a reader.

(Kennedy 6). The reader begins to take on a fictive listener's or fictive reader's role. Taking his or her cues from the narrator's continuously reiterated comments about these listeners' opinions of the speaker, namely, that he is prudent in his words but mad in his actions, the fictive reader is first swayed by verbal arguments that ostensibly already coincide with his or her own beliefs and then confronted with the source they are derived from (a foolish *hidalgo*), as are these other listeners. But the fictive reader is then led one step further when situations are created that show how the listener, with whom the fictive reader has already identified, is in turn governed by irrational desires and necessities which override the strength of any logical argument or weakness of any illogical one.

Moreover, the narrator's continued assertion of the discrepancy between the knight's words and action is a parody of one of the most important *topoi* of paradox regarding human behavior, one in which the speaker attempts to control the attitudes and perceptions of the audience. Human beings are made up of both reason and volition. The speaker should appeal to the audience's ironic awareness of the disparity between human action and intention, will and ability, what one says and what one does. According to the classical canon, no other *topos* of paradox is so effective as this one.

In serious tragic or dramatic discourse the author may attempt to control the context by portraying these contrary human aspects embodied in the speaker as irreconcilable and underscoring this dilemma so as to persuade the audience of the speaker's position, however weak it might be. Or an author may attempt to control the context by creating a character who reflects a selfhood with controlled reason and volition, according to the humanist formula of *integritas*. A comic discourse is engendered when contexts framing the speaker's discourse free the listener from an emotional identification with both speaker and audience. In the rhetorical situations described above, the fictive reader is distanced when the narrator reproduces the *topos* of the discrepancy between the actions and words of a character in contexts which reveal such oppositions as false, eliminate differences and thus expose the folly or irrational forces *inherent* in the supposedly rational discourse of the speaker.

Thus, no substantial difference exists between the knight's works and his words. The knight espouses an absolute belief in the protection of the needy, regardless of whether they need help or not or are deserving of it or not, and his actions support such beliefs.

He defends the virtue, chastity and beauty of all women, whether they are faithful or unfaithful, and he acts according to such beliefs. Finally, he supports the value of knowledge, whether it be morally illuminating or not, and his actions confirm his support of his absolute ideal. The possible unwillingness of the reader to reexamine his or her beliefs reflects a predisposition to the knight's beliefs and indisposition to the implicit author's discourse, the latter of which underscores, by means of the recreation and representation of context, the limits of such beliefs. As James A. Parr has shown in his recently published work, *Don Quixote: An Anatomy of Subversive Discourse*, to identify with the character's beliefs and values is to ignore "the multitude of signals counselling distance" and such an attitude on the part of the reader "requires a leap of faith, even a certain willfullness" (119).

The implicit author plays on his knowledge of the fictive reader's beliefs by means of the speaker-listener relationship. By putting the reader's highest ideals in the mouth of a mad knight and having them exercised in a variety of situations which show them to be ineffective, inapplicable, useless, and often even the cause of conflict, aggression, and criminal conduct, and exposing the involvement of the listeners who initially criticized his conduct, Cervantes attempts to create a discourse powerful enough to alter the reader's predisposition towards certain beliefs.[8]

Thus far analysis has focused on the internal aspect of the speaker-listener relationship, that is on the dialogue between Don Quixote and other characters, as well as on the external speaker-listener relationship implicitly established between the author and the reader. Complementary to these two relationships is another external speaker-listener relationship, explicitly established between the narrator and the reader on the one hand and the narrator and the other authors of the tale on the other. An extended dialogue develops as a result of these relationships in which the truth and intention of the narrator's discourse is discussed in terms of the rules of

---

[8] The gender of the speaker can also influence the effect or lack of effect the speaker is to have on the audience. In her insightful essay, "Notorious Signs, Feminist Criticism and Literary Tradition," Munich shows how Marcela's eloquent speech at Gristóstomo's funeral, in which she defends her conduct against the conventionaled "femme fatale" image accorded to her by Ambrosio, Grisóstomo and others present, "cannot compete with the language on her flesh; women's words have no force to speak the truth or 'undeceive'."

decorum governing the form, timing, and conditions of the discourse.

Beyond the numerous devices employed By Cide Hamete that cause his discourse to be inadequate for a poetic or historical narration of a hero, such as word plays, colloquial expressions, pleonasms, comic hyperboles, prayers and entreaties, billingsgate speech, and brusque insertions of other types of jargon not pertaining to historic discourse, he employs other devices having to do with the form of his discourse which put his premise of the "truth" of his narration into doubt.

The historic truth of Cide's narration should not be conditioned only by what he narrates but by *how* he narrates. The narrator of the historic narration must have a sound knowledge of the genre and follow its rules and conventions. In this manner the narrator will make his chronicle more authentic, since the reader has certain expectations and assumptions about history. While pretending to follow the canons of serious historic discourse, Cide Hamete at once parodies the pretensions of historicity of the narrators of chivalric romance and manifests the fictional nature of his own work.[9]

The technique employed in historical discourse that Cide Hamete frequently imitates is that of precision. Cide reveals the artificiality of the device as he transcends the bounds set by the logic of serious rhetoric and employs precise details when it is not necessary to do so, either because the audience does not care about such details, or because according to codes of decorum, such details would be better left unmentioned (Olbrechts-Tyteca 145-156).

The comic use of the device of precision functions thanks to certain social assumptions. Common opinion holds that the more precise one is in the telling of some event, the "truer" it will seem. The fallibility of this assumption is shown when Cide is precise about details peripheral to the tale he is narrating and which therefore hold no interest for the reader, such as the type of tree against which the knight is leaning ("... de una haya o de un alcornoque"),

---

[9] Several important studies on the fictional author device include Riley, *Cervantes' Theory of the Novel*, 323-34, Forcione, *Cervantes, Aristotle and the Persiles*, 155-66, El Saffar, 114-39, Haley, Socrate, 33-51 and Parr. For a more detailed account of the role of Cide Hamete and the other narrative voices, I refer the reader to these works.

the type of wood in which he is hiding ("que así como don Quijote se emboscó en la floresta, encinar, o selva junto al gran Toboso ...") and the sex of the mules on which the peasant girls are riding ("pollinos, o pollinas"), and which usually appear in episodes involving the narration of fantastic events.

Cide Hamete also evokes precise details that are inappropriate to historic or poetic discourse when he reveals the knight and squire's indecorous gestures, actions and conduct. He seems to take delight in debasing his hero. Thus Cide Hamete does not remain silent about the naked knight's somersaults in the Sierra Morena, his near naked appearance in his duel with the wine bags, his dirty thighs exposed, the description of the infrahuman bed in the loft of the second inn, Sancho's blanket tossing, and his defecation from fear in the fulling mills episode. In providing these details, Cide Hamete not only transcends the accepted limits of propriety for a historic narrator, but suddenly expands the historian's partial view of the protagonist. Rising above to the aerial view of omniscience, Cide Hamete transforms himself into the "sabio encantado." He reminds the reader of the fictional nature of his tale by disclosing facts about the knight and the squire that cause Sancho to tremble with fear. Sancho tells his master of his reaction to what Sansón Carrasco had told him about the tale:

> ... dice que me mientan a mí en ella con mi mesmo nombre de Sancho Panza, y a la señora Dulcinea del Toboso, con otras cosas que pasamos nosotros a solas, que me hice cruces de espantado cómo las pudo saber el historiador que las escribió. (II, 2: 57)

The Moor challenges the rules of decorum governing official literary genres when he employs a discourse that is not in agreement with his character. He professes faith in Mahoma and yet interjects oaths in the narration such as "Juro como católico cristiano ..." (II, 27: 249). He also has other characters in his narration employ a form of discourse that is inadequate to their character, or to the time and place in which it is spoken. Don Quixote's narration of his vision in the Cave of Montesinos, in which the old is mixed with the modern, is not accepted as true by anyone. In general, the knight's action, conduct and speech is discordant: he acts as if he were young when he is old and as if he were strong when he is little more than a skeletal frame. Sancho's alternation from a low to a high style gives rise to a discordance that causes the translator, in Chapter 5 of Part II, to question whether such an ignorant character could reason with such elegance.

Parallel to but in contrast with Cide's narration are other stories that exist inside and outside of his narration. These narrators also commit breeches of decorum. A dialogue opens up and is extended throughout the narration, in which the second author and the translator participate in order to make comments on the Moorish author's infractions. The characters within the tale also participate, making comments on Cide's narration and on the other tales narrated within his narration, and on works existing outside of it.

Don Quixote reproaches Maese Pedro's assistant for having the Moors ring bells when Melisendra escapes "porque entre moros no se usan campanas, sino atabales, y un género de dulzainas que parecen nuestras chirimías; y esto de sonar companas en Sansueña sin duda que es un gran disparate" (II, 26: 244). The implicit author criticizes the dramatists of the time, specifically Lope de Vega, for lacking mastery in their art by having Maese Pedro respond that the *comedias* of the time contain such errors and yet are not held in less esteem.

The young man impersonating Dulcinea in the duke and duchess's pseudo-adventure forms part of an embedded narration within the narration of Don Quixote's imagined tale of his life as knight errant, which in turn is embedded within Cide Hamete's "historia." He must play the role of the enchanted noble lady desperately in need of a valiant hero. He commits breeches of decorum when he reproaches Sancho in a low style, employing vulgar blasphemies when Sancho refuses to whip himself on her behalf. Sancho calls attention to his flaw:

> Pero querría yo saber de la señora mi señora Dulcinea del Toboso adónde aprendió el modo de rogar que tiene: viene a pedirme que me abra las carnes a azotes, y llámame alma de cántaro y bestión indómito, con una tiramira de malos nombres, que el diablo los sufra. (II, 35: 317)

The figure of the devil that introduces the caravan of enchanters and enchanted figures in the pseudo-adventure employs a Christian oath, "—En Dios y en mi conciencia . . ." (II, 34: 309), an incongruity which Sancho points out:

> —Sin duda —dijo Sancho— que este demonio debe de ser hombre de bien y buen cristiano; porque, a no serlo, no jurara en "Dios y en mi conciencia." Ahora yo tengo para mí que aun en el mesmo infierno debe de haber buena gente. (309)

Sancho is also surprised to find that *seguidillas* are composed in Candaya, a type of poem composed in contemporary Spain, and that a marriage seal is delivered to a court bailiff there.

The translator complains that Cide has Sancho talk to his wife in a style inappropriate for a village farmer, in Chapter 5 of Part II, and the Canon from Toledo intervenes in the extended dialogue to criticize the narrators of chivalric romance for similar discordances:

> ¿Qué ingenio, si no es del todo bárbaro e inculto, podrá contentarse leyendo que una gran torre llena de caballeros va por la mar adelante, como nave con próspero viento, y hoy anochece en Lombardía, y mañana amanezca en tierras del Preste Juan de las Indias, o en otras que ni las descubrió Tolomeo, ni las vió Marco Polo? (I, 47: 565)

The priest responds by complaining of the *comedia* for similar anachronisms and ruptures in the unity of time, place and action.

As the extended dialogue develops, the narrations within Cide Hamete's narration approach those outside of it and become mirrors of them, refracting their discordances. Cide Hamete's tale stands in opposition to them. If in those "other" works rules were broken because the narrators did not possess enough art to create a consequent and convincing form of discourse, Cide's disobedience to the rules of decorum are conceived of and developed in the tale as a manner of achieving a greater sense of internal truth and logic.

In Cide Hamete's work, it is possible for Don Quixote to act as if he were young when he is old, and strong when he is sick, as his niece affirms in Chapter 6 of Part II, and for him to undertake knightly adventures in seventeenth century La Mancha. As Cide explains, the *hidalgo* has gone mad and in his fantasies believes he is a young knight. The knight can see seventeenth century peasant girls from La Mancha do somersaults in the same cave in which ancient legendary figures of romance dwell because all of these figures form part of a world of dreams where anything can happen, a world that cannot be measured by rational systems of logic. The knight's squire can speak in a rhetorical style because he is clever, has a good memory, and is quick to imitate others, such as the priest of the village and the knight with whom he keeps constant company. Finally, he can travel twenty leagues from the Sierra Morena to El Toboso in such a short period of time because, as the narrator explains, the squire never really goes at all. Sancho simply tells his master that he has gone and come back as part of a plan to take his master back to his village.

The second author and Don Quixote make comments regarding the Moor's racial heritage that defame the "author" of the tale, calling him and those of his race "mentirosos" and "quimeristas." With these comments they succeed in unmasking Cide's pretended role as chronicler or historian. Yet they cannot find fault with his narration, one that reveals itself as fiction, and yet seems plausible. What Cide discovers and shows concretely by means of his tale is that no precepts are general enough to generate the logic and truth of every text. The tale that is to be told generates its own rules, and these rules, that give a sense of truth to the tale, are conditioned by and contingent on the subject matter the author selects. Umberto Eco describes this contingency in regard to his own narrative work. *El nombre de la rosa*:

> Considero que para contarlo primero lo primero que hace falta es construirse un mundo lo más amueblado posible, hasta los últimos detalles. Si construyese un río, dos orillas, si en la orilla izquierda pusiera un pescador, si a ese pescador lo dotase de un caracter irascible y de un certificado de penales poco limpio, entonces podría empezar a escribir, traduciendo en palabras lo que no puede no suceder. ¿Qué hace un pescador? Pesca (y ya tenemos toda una secuencia más o menos inevitable de gestos). ¿Y qué sucede después? Hay peces que pican, o no los hay. Si los hay, el pescador los pesca y luego regresa contento a casa. Fin de la historia. Si no los hay, puesto que es irascible, quizá se ponga rabioso...Ya lo veis, ha bastado amueblar apenas nuestro mundo para que se perfile una historia. Y también un estilo, porque un pescador que pesca debería imponerme un ritmo narrativo lento, fluvial, acompasado a su espera, que debería ser paciente, pero también a los arrebatos de su impaciente iracundia. La cuestión es construir el mundo, las palabras vendrán casi por sí solas. *Rem tene, verba sequentur.* (27-28)

If Cervantes is to forge his own fictional world, it becomes clear that Cide Hamete, the fictional author, fulfills a necessary function for him. He is not just a second self of the chroniclers of chivalric romance, parodying their ludicrous pretensions at historic truth, and the Ironist or the Tempter of the pseudo-hero, Don Quixote. He is also the second self of Cervantes, whose secret carnivalesque desire is to break the rules and conventions fixed by rhetorical-literary precepts which influenced the prose fiction of the time. Not daring or wishing to do so himself, he puts on a mask, the mask of the rebel, the demon, the infidel. He would have the fictitious Arab narrator talk for him, and even this voice would be attenuated, buried within the translator's version, which is buried with the second author's manuscript, which is inserted within Cervantes' novel ("la historia cuenta que se contó...").

Asserting his independence, Cide Hamete selects the subject matter of his story: a Spanish *hidalgo,* obsessed with chivalric tales, goes mad and decides to become a knight errant. He contracts a clever and ambitious peasant from his village to become his squire and accompany him on his adventures. He then proceeds to design and trigger some of the possible combinations that can emerge as a result of the nature of the subject. Given that the mad knight believes that everything he sees belongs to the world of chvalry and what he sees are the objects and people belonging to the rural farmland of seventeenth century La Mancha, the knight will mistake the windmills for giants, inns for castles and prostitutes for princesses. If the characters he encounters are humble and have not read chivalric tales, they will be bewildered by his language and actions. If the knight attacks them, they may go along with his humor if they are of a peaceful nature, or become angry and return his attack if they are not. If they have knowledge of chivalric tales and understand the nature of his folly, they can try to correct Don Quixote's errors in judgment or perception or go along with his humor for their own benefit. Other options are possible.

The development of the relationship between knight and squire follows an intrinsic logic as well. Given the hedonistic and overly ambitious nature of the squire and his constant subjection to dangerous situations, he will eventually, in spite of his credulousness, come to distrust his master. He has an option to defend himself against such threats to his person by leaving his master, an option that occurs to him on more than one occasion but which he does not select because the story would then end, or he can seek self-defense and retaliation. What is true about Don Quixote and Sancho applies as well to other characters introduced in the text that interact with both knight and squire.

The action of *Don Quixote* emerges spontaneously, naturally, effortlessly, or so it seems, each link generating the next, producing its own logic and coherence as it goes along, causing the reader to perceive the action and characters as if they were "true" in spite of the extravagant nature that distinguishes them. Simultaneously, the ruptures and interjections of the various narrative voices operate to remind the reader of the tale's underlying artifice, and consequently, of its susceptibility to clefting and permutation.

Finally, the style of the work is also circumscribed by the subject matter selected. The narration of *Don Quixote* requires the mixed style that characterizes consciously parasitic, non-serious, dialogical discourse. The discordant combining and alternating of the high and the low, the familiar and the exotic, and the ancient and the modern, foreign to the conventional law of decorum, is the only possible style for a narrator telling the tale of a knight who wishes to resurrect the world of chivalry, while at the same time underscoring the illusiveness of that world and the values that sustain it.

As the narration unfolds, proving itself to be consequent with itself, the timidity of the author seems to fade and the Moorish narrator, whose voice is hidden among the babbling voices of the other authors and characters, blares forth triumphantly. Standing before the author of the apocryphal *Quixote*, the Moor's pen hails the genius of his own creation, one that cannot be imitated or expropriated:

> Para mí sola nació don Quijote, y yo para él; él supo obrar y yo escribir; solos los dos somos para en uno, a despecho y pesar del escritor fingido y tordesillesco.... (II, 79: 592)

EPILOGUE

Having analyzed the comic across the varying levels of the narrative, as well as from the vantage point of diverse theories, several critical and theoretical questions have emerged that I have not thus far directly addressed: Can the relationship between the comic and the serious, the marginal and dominant voices and ideologies be determined and defined by theory? What is the difference, if any, between comic ritual and the comic literary work? To what extent can a comic interpretation of *Don Quixote* explain the text as a whole? How do the various theories used throughout my study, not necessarily pertaining to the comic, contribute to or detract from an understanding of the comic? How can the text of *Don Quixote* foreground a theory of the comic, that is, what are the interimplications of text and theory? And finally, what is the specificity of the comic in Cervantes' work? My discussion in the pages that follow will alternate among these questions, and will move freely from text to theory and back again. I will be returning to theories presented in relation to partial aspects of the text and reading them in light of the entire text. I will also be analyzing critical issues in Cervantine scholarship as well as particular episodes of the text not discussed in the previous chapters.

The precise relationship of the comic to hegemonic structures or ideologies is difficult to determine *a priori*, due to contradictions of logic and intention in the varying theories on ritual as well as the inherent dialogical nature of the comic vision itself. For both Frazer and Girard, the scapegoat ritual is a conservative one. Frazer shows how the ritual act of violence is committed on the surrogate victim in order that the life-giving forces not be abolished but maintained in their state of transcendent purity. For Girard, the killing of the false god/rival, who blocks the fulfillment of desire, is effected in order that desire for the idol be perpetuated. In a world without God, there must be a cycle of desire and violence endlessly repeating itself. Frazer's and Girard's theories of scapegoating reflect not a comic or critical use of scapegoat rituals, but a determining structure that describes and prescribes ritual as a religion and science of human behavior.

Bakhtin's emphasis on movement and transformation within the carnival rituals and within discursive practices of the polyphonic novel seems to support and celebrate a process of alterity, substitution, change, and difference, "the birth of something new and better" (*Rabelais* 67). Yet the revolutionary implications of the carnival ritual are counteracted by the cyclical structure of carnival. Occurring on the days preceding Lent, carnival activities are eventually subsumed by the "law" of the Church. By means of the ritual killing of the king/fool, the activities of carnival insure the continuance, now in a purged and renewed form, of the ideologies of the dominant order, a process which the emerging official activities complement and complete (fasting and penitence).

The internal structure of carnival is, moreover, patterned after the structure of the dominant order. While the terms and positions of power are inverted in class, sexual or religious hierarchies, the system itself (the erection of hierarchies and values set up in binary oppositions) is conserved. In terms of ethics, this mimetic structure, even with its reversals, is undesirable because it undermines and is even incompatible with the impetus for change. Given the risks involved in ascribing a resistant function to an element or action that may function quite well within the logic of the dominant order, one is led to wonder if difference can be acknowledged and fomented within the dualism of the comic ritual. *Can* a resistant function be ascribed to the comic?[1]

As long as the relationship between the dominant and the marginal is structured as an "either/or" proposition, governed by a politics of replaceablity or substitution in space and chronology, giving itself as a double, but mutually exclusive discourse, the notion of difference cannot be acknowledged. The comic vision in a literary work can follow the alternating and cyclical rhythm of its ritual counterpart, but it can also deviate from it by dint of the

---

[1] This is the subject of Stallybrass's and White's study.

reading processes. The comic is not bound to the cyclical and thus repetitive movement of ritual, because it exerts its force in the dialogic process engaging the author and reader. The comic can be an authentic dialectical interplay, powerful enough to engender in the consciousness of the reader a "destructive genesis" of the traditional orders of knowledge and thought maintained by a particular collectivity.

The cyclical structure of comic ritual is transformed from an "either/or" to an "and/both" and an "and/but" proposition in the comic literary work, that is, it is contained by dominant discourse and resistant to it, by virtue of its parasitic form.[2] The impiety of the comic, although radical in its implications, holds no claim to independence from the values of a collectivity, but rather aims towards a "repositioning," a disrupting, resistant process, occurring from within the terms of the law and its discourse, by means of the techniques of parody, heteroglossia and polyphony. A voice and its value is heard from another space or context, but is not severed from the core values of Western tradition. The parodic spirit acts as an agency of transition which mediates differences without nullifying the differential play. The word in living conversation, retransmitted in the literary text, is always oriented toward a future answer word and toward a future reader who is enjoined, by means of the dialogic process, to acknowledge the polyphonous, unfixed nature of meaning. Thus, meaning and value within the comic vision move forward to new positions by means of the ongoing dialogue that the text reconstitutes and perpetuates (Bakhtin, *The Dialogic Imagination* 280).

The comic is destructive inasmuch as it tears asunder monologism's exclusive claim to truth. This "murderous" function of the comic, an obvious preliminary step in the transvaluation of values, was the object of study in Chapter 1, in its focus on Don Quixote as embodiment of the ideal knight, and in Chapter 2, in its scrutiny of Sancho as sacrificial double of the chivalric hero and as embodiment of the humanist's ideal of natural knowledge. Indeed, the presence of the cyclical and alternating movement endemic to comic ritual seems to prevail in the depiction of the characters and plot material, characterized respectively by the inversion of roles and hi-

---

[2] Mayne examines both the conservative and resistant functions of the comic in relation to gender.

erarchies and by a chain of episodes involving death and resurrection. This alternation remains up to the end of the manuscript, in Sancho's final plea to his master: ". . . levántese desa cama y vámonos al campo vestidos de pastores, como tenemos concertado: quizá tras de alguna mata hallaremos a la señora doña Dulcinea desencantada, que no haya más que ver" (II, 74: 589-590) and in Don Quixote's intransigent rejection of chivalric romance, one which his friends the curate, the barber and Sansón Carrasco appropriately perceive as a folly not unlike that of his blind acceptance of it:

> Ya soy enemigo de Amadís de Gaula y de toda la infinita caterva de su linaje; ya me son odiosas todas las historias profanas del andante caballería; ya conozco mi necedad y el peligro en que me pusieron haberlas leído; ya, por misericordia de Dios, escarmentando en cabeza propia, las abomino.
> Cuando esto le oyeron decir los tres, creyeron, sin duda, que alguna nueva locura le había tomado. (II, 74: 588)

An aporia of meaning and value informing the ritual of comic violence unfolds within the disguise, action, and discourse of Don Quixote and Sancho. Chapters I and II of this study showed how these central characters represent both the scene of the law and the scene of its transgression. But this paradoxical "comic" scene epitomizes the depiction of all other supporting characters as well, thus embracing and defining the entire poetic and historic world that Cervantes has recreated. The participation of the collectivity in the fool's play is one of the distinctive features of carnival, and one that Cervantes incorporates. In other comic forms, such as comedy, caricature, or the clown's performance at the circus, the "entertainer" performs alone on the stage. Carnival, in contrast,

> does not know footlights, in the sense that it does not acknowledge any distance between actors and spectators. Footlights would destroy carnival, as the absence of footlights would destroy a theatre performance. Carnival is not a spectacle seen by the people; they live in it and everyone participates, because its very idea embraces all the people. (Bakhtin, *Rabelais* 7)

The elimination of the stage implies that carnival is life itself, a space in which real people live. Don Quixote's madness is not just a means by which the reader can view the chivalric ideology in a new light, but also a means to discover the foolish participation of the entire collectivity (a microcosm of seventeenth century Spain) in the same ideological vision of the world. The implicit author fictionalizes both the historical and poetical realities, alternating, juxtaposing and finally overlapping them in the text because he wants to show their common link: a shared ideology.

As the action progresses, the knight's friends and acquaintances are all drawn to the world the knight wishes to restore. The priest and the barber condemn the bulk of the knight's chivalric tales and send them to the flames. Yet they are well versed in matters of chivalry, and prior to the knight's first sally, had the custom of discussing daily the events narrated in these books with their friend and neighbor. They too take to the road, as Sansón Carrasco will do in Part II. Indeed, the curate becomes the "hero" of Part I, subjugating the giant Pandafilando, and rescuing the "princesa." The canon criticizes the knightly tales because of the failure of the authors to adhere to the rules of unity. Yet he has written a hundred pages of his own chivalric romance.

The rationalistic and level-headed Vivaldo scoffs at the knight's fantastic beliefs. Yet as he discusses the great virtue of Don Galaor with the knight, he reveals a profound knowledge and interest in chivalric romance. His inordinate curiosity in the tale of Gristóstomo's misfortunes leads him to grab the papers out of Ambrosio's hands before he is given permission to do so, in order to read the poetic narration of the youth's mad and passionate love for Marcela.

Dorotea is also an avid reader of romance, a fact which is confirmed by the expertise with which she plays out her role as damsel in distress in Part I. Don Fernando and the captive no longer consider the knight mad as soon as they listen to his speech on arms and letters in which the knight gives preeminence to the former, because they too are soldiers and uphold the same values as the knight. The shepherds and shepherdesses of the feigned Arcadia are impressed by the knight's attempt to defend the passage of the main road, because they act in accordance with his ideology, as their theatrical performance reflects.

If the knight is attracted to the heroic myth and dreams of being hailed as a great hero at his entrance to great cities and of being received in the palaces of nobles, kings and other great personages,

Sancho is taken with the idea of rising to the level of count or king. If the knight dreams of beautiful princesses falling in love with him, Maritornes is equally attracted to the love affairs narrated in romance, and the innkeeper's daughter shows interest in the descriptions of the suffering of the enamored knights.

If the knight is intrigued by the fantastic duels the knights wage against powerful enemies, the priest is equally intrigued by the fantastic actions attributed to heroes in the so-called "histories," just as the innkeeper of the second inn is attracted to the descriptions of great battles. It is the innkeeper, indeed, who informs us that the interest in these tales is so great that at times as many as thirty people gather at his inn to listen to one of the lodgers read a knightly tale.

In sum, the popularity of chivalric romance confirms that members of the knight's collectivity, in all of its sectors, identify with the conventions and ideals transmitted by these works and of those found in similar literary genres. While all of these characters may reject Don Quixote's claim that the events narrated in these tales are historically true, they do accept as absolutely "true" the ideology they espouse.

The ritual killing of the knight and of the ideology he embodies is in large part due to the complicity of these other participants. While causing the knight to deviate from his ideals by means of their masquerades and practical jokes, they degrade and subvert their own ideals. The logical consequence of their complicity is the reversal of the action in which they engage, namely, the trickster tricked, the biter bitten, and the inversion of roles, the saint turned sinner, the noble, beautiful princess turned into courtesan or specter, the king turned fool or criminal, the friend turned foe.

Thus, the priest condemns the knight's undiscriminating adherence to the law governing the Christian mission of the knight errant in the knight's liberation of the galley slaves. He affirms that the knight has reversed the heroic action of carrying out good works, committing a crime for which "se pierda su alma y no se gane su cuerpo." Yet for the sake of charity and good works, namely, the salvation and cure of his so-called friend," the priest participates in cruel actions against the knight, creating a pseudo-adventure in which the knight is caged in and driven back to his village on an ox cart, "embaído y tonto." The barber's mocking and ridicule of his friend is no less cruel than that of the priest, as evidenced by his important participation in the reviling of the knight and of his supposed heroic feat in the winning of Mambrino's helmet in Chapter 23 of Part I.

In a conversation with the knight, the duchess discredits the knight's affirmations of the nobility of his lady, and thus her exalted status, but her own exalted status is degraded when Doña Rodríguez reveals the somewhat less than perfect beauty of the lady. Her Achilles' heel is confirmed by the presence of certain open wounds in her leg.

The duke isolates the knight from his knightly role, transferring his duties and the rewards that result from the fulfillment of them to to his rustic counterpart, Sancho. He gives advice to the governor-elect about how to prepare himself morally and physically for his new office and devises the pseudo-trials, such as the hunt, the penitence and the rescue of the bearded damsels-in-distress for this purpose. Yet the immoral conduct in the duke's own rule is underscored when Doña Rodríguez reveals to Don Quixote that the duke refuses to defend the honor of her pregnant daughter by obligating the seducer to marry her. His attitude derives from the fact that the father of the boy, a rich farmer who lives in one of the duke's many villages, lends the duke money and goes surety for him in his dirty business dealings.

It may seem an incongruity that members of a collectivity who partake, at least superficially, in the same ideology as the knight, would participate with such relish in actions that put into ridicule a shared ideology. The incongruity is only an apparent one, however. A comparison with the plot of Miguel Mihura's comedy, *La bella Dorotea*, reveals a coherence within the contradiction. In the play, the feminine protagonist is jilted and refuses to return home from the altar to face the ridicule of the other members of her community. She decides instead to walk down the "calle real" dressed in her wedding gown, until she finds a fiancé to take her back to the altar.

Just as it is acceptable, even admirable, for Don Quixote to believe in the ideologies transmitted to him in his readings, it is correct behavior for the young girl to walk down the "calle real" looking for a husband, as do all of the other girls in the provincial town. But as soon as she puts on the wedding dress and does so, she is shunned by those gentlemen who had previously been her most ardent suitors and is mocked, ridiculed, and considered mad by her entire community, as is Don Quixote by his. She is finally approached by a commission of women representing the feminine members of the community who, affronted by the girl's conduct, threaten to lock her up if she does not take off the gown.

The aggressive attitudes of the other members of the respective collectivities reflect the failure to consciously recognize the contingencies and limitations in the ideals, customs and conventions adhered to and supported by all of its members. The girl's dress and the rusty arms of Alonso Quijano are threatening to their respective neighbors because they mock their undiscriminating acceptance of pre-existing truths. Yet when the participants defend themselves against such mockery by ritually "killing" or doing away with the fool, they only succeed in ritually killing their own gods. In doing so, they enter the circle and cycle of death and resurrection that Alonso Quijano mimes with his abomination of the knightly role and with his demise.

Throughout the adventures of the knight, the actions of the other characters have created situations intended to expose Don Quixote's exaggerated imperfections. Yet they have succeeded in exposing the same imperfections in themselves as well in the process. One ultimately comes to view with distrust the knight's "prudent" rejection of his knightly role and reinsertion into the community. The cumulative result of the action of the tale is that the folly of the so-called "prudent" members of the collectivity is made equivalent to, and in some aspects, more foolish than the folly the knight has recently renounced.

These secondary characters are crucial to the comic action of the plot, because they show that the comic has critical implications for the practice of values in Cervantes' society at large, values that are transmitted and received vis-a-vis the literary production. The introduction and progressive aggressivity of these blocking characters, as well as of the Arab narrator, has led to a major critical impasse in Cervantine scholarship. Part II of *Don Quixote* has been signalled by several critics as reflecting a significant development in the moral stature of the protagonist, leading to the reader's increased identification with the character (a cyclical interpretation of the knightly character and his values) (Allen I: 83; Mancing; *The Chivalric World* 191-209; Mandel 158). According to this argument, the reduction of the knight's chivalric archaisms, his increased number of learned or moral discourses, the introduction of characters with dubious intentions towards Don Quixote and the numerous critical remarks made by the implied author attacking the Arab historian's reputation and intentions all serve to displace comic irony and parody away from the main character and towards the secondary characters and narrators.

Yet James Parr has recently argued convincingly against this thesis, in his discussion of the narrator and the supporting characters, in the chapter entitled "Affinity and Alienation" in his recent work *Don Quixote: An Anatomy of Subversive Discourse*. According to Parr, just because Don Quixote might have to share his position as the object of laughter with any other of a number of characters or narrators, one cannot necessarily infer that we are driven to a position that is close to him:

> The fact that there is distance between author and agent does not mean that there is, by default as it were, authorial affinity for the Knight. Both the Moor and the Knight are treated ironically throughout. . . . Aesthetic distance from the chronicler, the narrators, the characters and from over-involvement in the several stories is very definitely an end in itself in *Don Quixote*. (79-80)

If there are moments that we are inspired with pity for an abused Don Quixote, there are also moments of impatience and frustration with his blindness: his nocturnal meeting with Doña Rodríguez, his "amorous" exchanges with Altisidora, his destruction of Maese Pedro's puppet figures, his grotesque representation of the chivalric world in the Cave of Montesinos. As Parr states, "For every instance that might be cited of our being drawn nearer to the protagonist, at least one other could be found of our being distanced" (79).

By being maintained at a distance from the narrator and the other characters, as well as from the main character, the reader is no longer forced to choose (the either/or alternative) between reason and passion, between social mores and conventions and individual action, or between the blind idealism of chivalric ideology, embodied by Don Quixote and the secondary characters' harsh, practical criticism of such idealism, a behavior clearly identifiable with the conduct of the Cynic philosophers of the time. In his discussion of Cynic philosophy, Forcione underscores the Renaissance humanists' rejection of the inhumane practice by which the Cynics critique the illusions that enslave humanity, and such behavior as hypocrisy, cruelty, slander, and intolerance (*Cervantes and the Humanist Vision* 249-60). Such behavior is easily applicable to Don Quixote's acquaintances and so-called friends.

The reader becomes increasingly distrustful of the hypocritical cruelty of these secondary characters and narrators, and aware of his or her own implications in the errors and deceptions that are a continued source of amusement. The reader comes to view the mutually exclusive attitudes presented with a keener sense of discrimination than his or her models, moving not closer to Don Quixote and his attempt to rigorously apply an ideology or belief system, but towards a more humane position or attitude with respect to the knight's dilemma. There are difficulties inherent in applying an abstract idea, value, or belief to a"real-life" situation. Yet it is not impossible.

The dialogues examined in Chapters 4, 5 and 6 of this study underscore the re-positioning process that occurs in the comic literary work. They serve as practical educative devices or what Parr calls "transparent object lessons," whereby values accepted by most readers (human love, heroism, justice) found in romance and informed by classical rhetorical mechanisms for "revealing" the truth are produced and inserted (the 'and' part) in situations which demand a discernment and reevaluation of their usage, limitations and pertinence, (the 'but' part), and of the discursive mechanisms themselves which determine and convey them (73). While the character, in his madness, doggedly insists on the truth of his original assertions, a stance which results in a variety of mishaps, the reader can come to recognize and consciously acknowledge the role that abilities, interest, personal desires or benefit play in our understanding and exercise of values. The reader can ultimately realign these factors influencing human behavior so as to permit the practice of critical thought and the translation of one's inner self (values and beliefs) successfully into the external world.[3]

This "distant" identification with the protagonist foregrounds the ethical value of the reading processes. The more our hero fails in his attempt to perform the translation of his values to the world, the more the reader desires to stand in for him and make good his mistakes with his or her experience (prior to and by means of the

---

[3] Parr sees as a major paradox in the characterization of Don Quixote the "contrast and tension between inner and outer worlds," 118.

reading processes). The development of personality and moral stature takes place, then, not so much in the character and in the text as in the reader and the reading processes. Cervantes' work shows us that the comic educates not by moralizing but by inference, by setting up equations that cannot always be solved with one right answer, as well as by its contestatory power, that is, by its capacity to respond to values of a previous text and to generate a response in the reader. If we come to identify with the main character in the end, it is because of our change of position from passive observer to recipient of and active contestant in this evaluating and self-evaluating process.

For Bakhtin, the view of knowledge and truth as a process and an experience is best presented by means of the comic. His theory rests on techniques evinced by Erasmus and the circle of Christian Humanists that followed Erasmus' teachings, one in which Cervantes can clearly be included, as Alban Forcione's works *Cervantes and the Humanist Vision* and *Cervantes and the Mystery of Lawlessness* have shown. Erasmus illustrates in *The Praise of Folly* that the comic underscores the complexities of human thought and action and shows that the truth of a situation or the value of an action cannot be reduced to a general law, but must be individually determined by means of the experience of the concrete circumstance (*Cervantes and the Humanist Vision* 175-77). The fulfillment of the subject's destiny and identity, *sine qua non* of the chivalric ideology, is, according to a comic vision, forever deferred. The comic subject position, essentially analogous to that of all human beings, is constantly being recast in a carnivalesque body image, marked by its holes, openings and convexities.

Comic theory can thus be defined as a description of the pierced, fragmented body of the surrounding ideological world. It is a story, but also and even more importantly, a *history*, by means of which the human consciousness of our time may come into contact with the existence of the world narrated. While theory deciphers or translates the otherwise unheard or marginal voices of this history, the comic story unleashes them and lets them speak with the privileged voices of the time, displacing monologic meaning with polyphony and difference.

The ethical dimension of the comic, with its emphasis on the recuperation and production of meaning, may seem foreign to the type of deconstruction theory exemplified by Derrida's *Of Gram-*

matology, referred to in Chapter 5 of this study. The subversion of dominant values practiced by deconstructive Derridean critics is similar to the subversions the critic detects at work in the comic text (thus the utility of deconstruction as a description of the processes of deviation in rhetorical devices). But deconstruction differs from comic subversion. Derrida, in his *Of Grammatology,* deconstructs not only dominant meanings and values, but every other value as well, in order to free meaning from *any* dependency on the *logos*. Because of its negativity, deconstruction fails to or refuses to account for change in the social structure or even the human subject (Kristeva, *Revolution* 142-43).

While deconstruction remains forever enclosed in the field of the signifier alone, the comic produces meaning or meanings within a historical context, which the text recreates or constitutes and through which the reader accesses critical thought. Chapters 4 and 5 of this study, on word play and argumentation, illustrate Cervantes' ability to reflect the heterogeneity of meaning and the productivity of the comic, as a means to impel the reader towards a positive acknowledgment and recognition of at least one other meaning, sense or intention in a given situation and in a given discourse. The productive heterogeneity of the comic can be described in the same terms that Kristeva describes the heterogeneity of "semanalysis," as "a moral gesture, inspired by a concern to make intelligible, and therefore socializable, what rocks the foundation of sociality" ("The System and the Speaking Subject" 32). Derrida's article "Signature Event, Context" marks a greater approximation to the comic vision and more clearly defines the specificity of the comic in *Don Quixote* in its acknowledgment that meaning and truth indeed exist, even if they may change from minute to minute and are utterly dependent on a specific context, and that they exist somewhere at the frontier between text and context and between language and history.

The interpolation of the so-called "serious" genres, the Italian *novella*, pastoral romance and the Moorish adventure tale, are instrumental to the constitution of the productivity of the text's discourse and the polyphonous consciousness it engenders in the reader. As counterparts or "doubles" of Don Quixote's story, they function comically, as integral and integrating elements of the main plot. The outer and inner surfaces of the text play with and against each other, as sequence, but also as juxtaposition. Dorotea's tale, a fragmented but not separate part of the dominant comic narrative, illustrates the technique of polyphony or difference within the integrated text.

The suspense and wonder that the story instills in the readers of *Don Quixote* and the listeners *in* the story underscore the generalized susceptibility readers have to romance fiction. The characters in the tale, like Don Quixote himself, participate both in the historical world of seventeenth century Spain, and the world of romance. Just as Don Quixote narrates his story, sets up the romance conflicts, and asks other characters to participate in them with him, even against their will, Dorotea engages in her romance fiction, replete with the three stages of romance: the perilous journey and minor adventures, the crucial struggle or near-death conflict, the duel, and the *anagnorisis*, the marriage of the couple and the supposed emergence of a new and better world. The themes of truth and illusion and the concomitant motifs of disguise and masquerade, encountered in both romance and comedy, can be found in Don Quixote's adventures and Dorotea's tale. Beyond the parallel constructions lie the interimplications of the main story to the interpolated one. More concretely, the manner in which the reader will interpret the romance plot depends on the manner in which he or she interprets the dominant narrative.

Dorotea's romance quest to retrieve her lost honor and self-exaltation is literally the other side of the story of Don Quixote's romance quest. Don Quixote's desire to rescue the damsel in distress and acquire wealth and fame converges on Dorotea's desire to recover her honor and simultaneously raise her social rank. Both wish to make good their illusion or ideal of self-exaltation. Like Don Quixote, Dorotea reads and is seduced by chivalric romance. Her identification with the female heroines in these stories is a motivating factor in her acquiescence to Don Fernando's advances. Unlike Don Quixote, who actively initiates his transformation, Dorotea must passively wait to become engaged in conflict. She oscillates into the position of the beautiful damsel to be seduced, as she later does into the role of the Princess Micomicona only when she can see and imagine herself in a position parallel to her literary counterparts, as the object of desire in Don Fernando's fiction, his speech, songs and letters:

> ... me daba un no sé qué de contento verme tan querida y estimada de un tan principal caballero, y no me pesaba ver en sus

papeles mis alabanzas: que en esto, por feas que seamos las mujeres, me parece a mí que siempre nos da gusto el oír que nos llaman hermosas. (I, 28: 350)[4]

Like Don Quixote, Dorotea suffers the consequences of the deception of her ideal, effected by the mediation of lived experience. The fragility of her role as virtuous damsel-to-be-loved is underscored by Dorotea's elliptic description of her seduction and her wordplay on "damsel": (". . . y con volverse a salir del aposento mi doncella, yo dejé de serlo . . ." (I 28: 354).

Just as Don Quixote repeats his attempts at exaltation in his successive sallies to prove his heroism, Dorotea takes flight in pursuit of Don Fernando, in order to find a way to oblige him to marry her as he had promised the night he fulfilled his desires. Yet her continued reading of romance in the midst of her adventure, the "Tale of Foolish Curiosity," and her identification with the female heroine, lead her to a further estrangement from that imaginary figure of exaltation and desire, and cause her to complete her romance quest in a manner that makes the ideals of feminine virtue and beauty projected in romance contingent upon concrete circumstances, events, and the intentions, interests and benefits of others.

Dorotea learns from the story of Camila's seduction and adulterous affair with her husband's best friend, Lotario, of the continued threat of losing her exalted status, even after the vows of marriage have been taken (the presumed *anagnorisis*), and of the necessity of finding ways, virtuous or not, to engage her husband's desire. She observes how Camila must maintain her status as object of desire by participating, first innocently and then consciously, in the staged seduction her husband has planned.

In the final scene in which Dorotea appears, the split image of Dorotea as exalted figure is rendered. Dorotea's "success," obtained by Don Fernando's compliance with his vows, is counteracted by the reader's awareness of the heroine's continued conflict: the urgency with which she wishes to once again become an object of her husband's desire. Her identification and imitation of her literary

---

[4] I develop in greater detail the problems with which the female reader in *Don Quixote* becomes engaged in my article "The Seduction of Fiction and the Gendered Reader in *Don Quixote:* Dorotea's tale," forthcoming in *Revista Canadiense de Estudios Hispánicos*.

counterpart, Camila, is ironically underscored by Sancho's description of her as a whore. The narrator's observations follow:

> ... yo tengo por cierto y por averiguado que esta señora que se dice ser reina del gran reino Micomicón no lo es más que mi madre; porque a ser lo que ella dice, no se anduviera hocicando con alguno de los que están en la rueda, a vuelta de cabeza y a cada traspuesta.
> Paróse colorada con las razones de Sancho Dorotea, porque era verdad que su esposo don Fernando, alguna vez, a hurto de otros ojos, había cogido con los labios parte del premio que merecían sus deseos —lo cual había visto Sancho, y pareciéndole que *aquella desenvoltura más era de dama cortesana que de reina de tan gran reino* ... (I, 46: 551-52, my emphasis).

The heterogeneity of meaning and value in Cervantes' work that Dorotea's image and story so vitally dramatize is foreign to romance fiction and the types of facile identifications that that genre engenders within the reading processes. Heterogeneity is the hallmark of a comic vision and cornerstone of any theory of the comic. Paradoxically, as Joe Natoli points out in his discussion of the relationship between carnival and theory, heterogeneity is also foreign to theory, since it resists the reductive process of systematicity. Yet it is only by bringing the comic into a system or theory and defining its specificity, that it can ever hope to be apprehended (22-23).

One could try to imagine a narratable human action or discourse unconfined by one of two relationships to the dominant order: opposition, contradiction and inversion (the either/or proposition), or by a critical inclusiveness (the and/both and and/but ones), all of which can be found in Cervantes' work. One could try to imagine a text/world in which neither gods nor virgins would need to be erected or desecrated. A comic work in general, and Cervantes' in particular, certainly brings us closer to such a text, but necessarily stops short of its materialization, because the comic will always be imbricated within the systems of thought and values against which it pushes. Any attempt to depart from a position external to that logic would certainly usher us through and beyond the threshold of the comic.

WORKS CITED

Abellán, José Luis. *El erasmismo español*. Madrid: Ediciones Espejo, 1976.
Adrados, Francisco. *Fiesta, comedia y tragedia*. Barcelona: Planeta, 1972.
Allen, John Jay. *Hero or Fool? A Study in Narrative Technique*. 2 vols. University of Florida Monographs, Humanities, nos. 29 and 46. Gainesville: U of Florida P, 1969, 1979.
Alonso, Amado. "Prevaricaciones idiomáticas de Sancho." *Nueva Revista de Filología Hispánica* 2 (1948): 1-20.
Alonso, Dámaso. "Sancho-Quijote, Sancho-Sancho." *Del Siglo de Oro a este siglo de siglas*. Madrid: Gredos, 1962. 53-63.
Alter, Robert. *Partial Magic: The Novel as a Self-Conscious Genre*. Berkeley: U of California P, 1975.
Asensio, Eugenio. "Entremeses." *Suma Cervantina*. Ed. J. B. Avalle-Arce and Edward C. Riley. London: Tamesis Books, 1973. 171-97.
Auden, W. H. "The Ironic Hero: Some Reflections on Don Quixote." *Cervantes: A Collection of Critical Essays*. Ed. Lowry Nelson, Jr. Englewood Cliffs, NH: Prentice-Hall, 1969. 73-81.
Auerbach, Erich. *Mimesis: The Representation of Reality in Western Literature*. Trans. Willard Trask. Princeton: Princeton UP, 1968.
Austin, J. L. *How to Do Things With Words*. New York: Oxford UP, 1965.
Avalle-Arce, J. B. "Cervantes and the Renaissance." *Cervantes and the Renaissance: Papers of the Pomona College Cervantes Symposium. November 16-18, 1978*. Ed. Michael D. McGaha. Easton, PA: Juan de la Cuesta,1980. 1-10.
Bakhtin, Mikhail. *Problems of Dostoevsky's Poetics*. Trans. R. W. Rotsel. Ann Arbor, MI: Ardis, 1973.
———. *Rabelais and His World*. Trans. Hélène Iswolsky. Cambridge, MA: M.I.T. Press, 1968.
———. *The Dialogic Imagination*. Ed. Michael Holquist. Trans. Caryl Emerson and Michael Holquist. U of Texas P Slavic Series 1. Austin, TX: U of Texas P, 1981.
———. "The Problem of the Text (An Essay in Philosophical Analysis)." Trans. William Mandel. *Soviet Studies in Literature* 14 (1977-1978): 3-33.
Bandera, Cesáreo. *Mimesis Conflictiva*. Madrid: Gredos, 1975.
Barasch, Frances. *The Grotesque. A Study in Meanings*. The Hague-Paris: Mouton, 1971.
Barthes, Roland. *Mythologies*. Trans. Annette Lavers. New York: Hill & Wang, 1982.
———. *Writing Degree Zero*. Trans. Annette Lavers and Colin Smith. 4th ed. New York: Hill and Wang, 1979.
Bataillon, Marcel. *Erasmo y España*. Trans. A. Alatorre. 2nd ed. México: Fondo de Cultura Económica, 1966.

Bentley, Eric. "Farce." *Comedy: Meaning and Form.* Ed. Robert W. Corrigan. 2nd ed. New York: Harper & Row, 1981. 193-211.
Bergson, Henri. *Laughter.* Trans. C. Brereton. New York: Macmillan, 1914.
Bernstein, Michael André. "When the Carnival Turns Bitter: Preliminary Reflections Upon the Abject Hero." *Bakhtin. Essays and Dialogues on His Work.* Ed. Gary Saul Morson. Chicago and London: The U of Chicago P, 1986. 99-121.
Bleznick, Donald William. "Don Quijote's Advice to Governor Sancho Panza." *Hispania* 40 (1957): 62-65.
Booth, Wayne C. *A Rhetoric of Irony.* Chicago: The U of Chicago P, 1974.
Bowra, C. M. *Heroic Poetry.* London: Macmillan & Co., 1952.
Brantley, Franklin O. "Sancho's Ascent into the Spheres." *Hispania* 53 (1970): 37-45.
Brenan, Gerald. *The Literature of the Spanish People.* 2nd ed. Cleveland:World Publishing Co., 1957.
Caballero, Justo. *Guía Diccionario del "Quijote."* México: España Errante, 1970.
Campbell, Joseph. *The Hero With a Thousand Faces.* Princeton: Princeton UP, 1949.
Caro Baroja, Julio. *Carnaval.* Madrid: Taurus, 1969.
Cascardi, Anthony J. *The Bounds of Reason. Cervantes, Dostoevsky, Flaubert.* New York: Columbia UP, 1986.
Cassirer, Ernst. *The Individual and the Cosmos in Renaissance Philosophy.* Trans. M. Domandi. New York: Harper Torchbooks, 1964.
Castro, Américo. *El pensamiento de Cervantes.* New ed. Ed. Julio Rodríguez-Puértolas. Barcelona-Madrid: Noguer, 1972.
Cervantes Saavedra, Miguel de. *El ingenioso hidalgo don Quijote de la Mancha.* Ed. Luis Andrés Murillo. 5th ed. 2 vols. Madrid: Castalia, 1987.
Charney, Maurice. *Comedy High and Low: An Introduction to the Experience of Comedy.* New York: Oxford UP, 1978.
Close, Anthony J. "Don Quixote's Love for Dulcinea." *Bulletin of Hispanic Studies* 50 (1973): 237-55.
———. "Sancho Panza: Wise Fool." *Modern Language Review* 68 (1973): 344-57.
———. *The Romantic Approach to "Don Quixote": A Critical History of the Romantic Tradition in "Quixote" Criticism.* Cambridge, MA: Cambridge UP, 1978.
Colie, Rosalie L. *Paradoxia Epidemica: The Renaissance Tradition of Paradox.* Princeton: Princeton UP, 1966.
Corley, Ames Haven. "Word-play in the *Don Quixote.*" *Revista Hispánica* 40 (1917): 543-91.
Cornford, Francis. *The Origin of Attic Comedy.* Cambridge, MA: Cambridge UP, 1934.
Correas, Gonzalo. *Vocabulario de refranes y frases proverbiales.* Ed. Louis Combet. Bordeaux: Institut de'études iberiques et ibero-americaines de l'université de Bordeaux, 1967.
Cortázar, Celina S. de. "Lo cómico y lo grotesco en el *Poema de Orlando* de Quevedo." *Filología* 122 (1966-1967): 95-135.
Covarrubias, Sebastián de. *Tesoro de la lengua castellana o española.* Ed. Martín de Riquer. Barcelona; Turner, 1943.
Culler, Jonathan. *On Deconstruction: Theory and Criticism After Structuralism.* Ithaca: Cornell UP, 1982.
De la Fuente, Ann. "Mock-Heroic Narrative Techniques in Ariosto and Cervantes." Diss. U of Texas at Austin, 1976.
Derrida, Jacques. *Margins of Philosophy.* Trans. Alan Bass. Chicago: U of Chicago P, 1982.
———. *Of Grammatology.* Trans. Gayatri Chakravorty Spivak. Baltimore: Johns Hopkins UP, 1974.

Di Battista, Maria. *Homer to Brecht: The European Epic and Dramatic Traditions.* Ed. M. Seidell and E. Mendelson. New Haven: Yale UP, 1977.
Dudley, Edward. "Don Quixote as Magus: The Rhetoric of Interpolation." *Bulletin of Hispanic Studies* 49 (1972): 355-68.
Dunn, Peter N. "La cueva de Montesinos por fuera y por dentro: Estructura épica, fisonomía." *Modern Language Notes* 88 (1973): 190-202.
———. "Two Classical Myths in Don Quixote." *Renaissance and Reformation* 9 (1972): 2-10.
Durán, Manuel. "El *Quijote* a través del prisma de Mikhail Bakhtine: carnaval, disfraces, escatología y locura." *Cervantes and the Renaissance: Papers of the Pomona College Cervantes Symposium. November 16-18, 1978.* Ed. Michael D. MacGaha. Easton, PA: Juan de la Cuesta, 1980. 71-86.
Eco, Umberto. *Apostillas a "El nombre de la rosa."* Trans. Ricardo Pochter. Barcelona: Lumen, 1983.
Efron, Arthur. *"Don Quixote" and the Dulcineated World.* Austin: U of Texas P, 1971.
Eisenberg, Daniel. *A Study of "Don Quixote."* Newark, DE: Juan de la Cuesta, 1987.
———. "Cervantes 'Don Quijote' Once Again: An Answer to J. J. Allen." *Estudios literarios de hispanistas norteamericanos dedicados a Helmut Hatzfeld con motivo de su 80 aniversario.* Ed. Josep M. Sola Solé, Alessandro Crisafulli, and Bruno Damiani. Barcelona: Hispam, 1974. 103-10.
El Saffar, Ruth. *Distance and Control in "Don Quixote": A Study in Narrative Technique.* Chapel Hill: UNCSRLL P, 1975.
Entwistle, William J. *Cervantes.* Oxford: Clarendon Press, 1940.
Flores, Ralph. *The Rhetoric of Doubtful Authority: Deconstructive Readings of Self-Questioning Narratives, St. Augustine to Faulkner.* Ithaca: Cornell UP, 1984.
Flores, R. M. *Sancho Panza Through Three Hundred Seventy-Five Years of Continuations, Imitations and Criticism. 1605-1980.* Newark, DE: Juan de la Cuesta, 1982.
Forcione, Alban K. *Cervantes and the Humanist Vision: A Study of Four Exemplary Novels.* Princeton: Princeton UP, 1982.
———. *Cervantes and the Mystery of Lawlessness.* Princeton: Princeton UP, 1984.
———. *Cervantes, Aristotle and the Persiles.* Princeton: Princeton UP, 1970.
Foucault, Michel. "[Don Quixote in the Lettered World.]" *Critical Essays on Cervantes.* Ed. Ruth El Saffar. Boston, MA: G. K. Hall, 1986. 117-21. Rpt. from *The Order of Things: An Archaeology of the Human Sciences.* New York: Random House, 1973. 56-60.
Frazer, Sir James George. *The New Golden Bough.* Ed. Dr. Theodor H. Gaster. New York: S. G. Phillips, 1959.
Frye, Northrop. *Anatomy of Criticism: Four Essays.* Princeton: Princeton UP, 1957.
García de la Torre, J. M. "Aspectos de la creación lingüística en Cervantes." *Cervantes: Su obra y su mundo. Actas del 1 Congreso Internacional sobre Cervantes.* Madrid: EDI-6, 1981. 87-92.
Garin, Eugenio. *La revolución intelectual del Renacimiento.* Barcelona: Crítica, 1981.
Girard, René. *Deceit, Desire, and the Novel.* Trans. Yvonne Freccero. Baltimore, MD: Johns Hopkins UP, 1977.
———. "Myth and Ritual in Shakespeare." *Textual Strategies: Perspectives in Post-Structuralist Criticism.* Ed. Josué Harari. Ithaca: Cornell UP, 1979. 189-212.
———. *The Scapegoat.* Trans. Yvonne Freccero. Baltimore: Johns Hopkins UP, 1986.
———. *Violence and the Sacred.* Trans. Patrick Gregory. Baltimore: John Hopkins UP, 1977.

Gombrich, Ernst H. *Ideals and Idols. Essays on Values in History and in Art*. Oxford: Phaidon, 1979.
Hamerton-Kelly, ed. *Violent Origins: Walter Burkert, René Girard and Jonathan Z. Smith on Ritual Killing and Cultural Formations*. Stanford: Stanford UP, 1987.
Hacthoun, Augusto. "Los mecanismos del humor en el habla de Sancho Panza." *Actas del sexto congreso internacional de hispanistas*. Ed. Alan M. Gordon and Evelyn Rugg. Toronto: U of Toronto, 1980. 365-67.
Haley, George. "The Narrator in *Don Quixote*: Maese Pedro's Puppet Show." *Modern Language Notes* 80 (1965): 146-65.
Harari, Josue ed. Preface. *Textual Strategies. Perspectives in Post-Structuralist Criticism*. Ithaca: Cornell UP, 1979.
Hatzfeld, Helmut. *El "Quijote" como obra de arte del lenguaje*. Madrid: CSIC, 1966.
Hayman, David. "Towards a Mechanics of Mode: Beyond Bakhtin." *Novel* 16 (2) (1983): 101-20.
Hendrix, W. S. "Sancho Panza and the Comic Types of the Sixteenth Century." *Homenaje ofrecido a Ramón Menéndez Pidal*. Vol. 2. Madrid: Hernando, 1925, 2 vols. 485-94.
Herrero, Javier. "Dulcinea and Her Critics." *Cervantes* 2 (1982): 23-42.
———. "Sierra Morena as Labyrinth: From Wildness to Christian Knighthood." *Critical Essays on Cervantes*. Ed. Ruth El Saffar. Boston, MA: G. K. Hall, 1986. 67-80.
———. "The Beheading of the Giant: An Obscene Metaphor in *Don Quixote*." *Revista Hispánica Moderna* (4) (1976): 141-149.
Huizinga, J. *The Waning of the Middle Ages*. Trans. F. Hopman. Garden City, NY: Doubleday/Anchor, 1954.
Iffland, James. *Quevedo and the Grotesque*. 2 vols. London: Tamesis Books: 1978-1982.
Johnson, Caroll B. "A Second Look at Dulcinea's Ass, *Don Quixote*, II, 10." *Hispanic Review* 43 (1975): 191-98.
Joly, Monique. "Ainsi parlait Sancho Pança." *Les Langues Nèolatines* 69 (1975): 3-37.
———. *La bourle et son interpretation*. Toulouse: Ibérie Recherche, U de Toulouse, 1982.
———. "Le discours métaparémique dans *Don Quichotte*." *Richesse du proverb*. Ed. F Suard and C. Buridant. Vol. 2. Lille, 1984. 2 vols. 245-60.
Jones, Joseph R. "The Liar Paradox in *Don Quixote*." *Hispanic Review* 54 (1986): 183-93.
Kaiser, Walter. *Praisers of Folly*. Cambridge, MA: Harvard UP, 1963.
Kayser, Wolfgang. *The Grotesue in Art and Literature*. Trans. Ulrich Weisstein. Bloomington: Indiana UP, 1963.
Kennedy. William J. *Rhetorical Norms in Renaissance Literature*. New Haven: Yale UP, 1978.
Kern, Edith. *The Absolute Comic*. New York: Columbia UP, 1980.
Kris, Ernst. "The Psychology of Caricature." *Psycho-analytic Explorations in Art*. E. H. Gombrich and Ernst Kris. New York: Schocken, 1964.
Kristeller, Paul Oskar. *Renaissance Thought*. 2 vols. New York: Harper Torchbooks, 1961, 1965.
Kristeva, Julia, *The Kristeva Reader*. Ed. Toril Moi. New York: Columbia UP, 1986.
———. "Word, Dialogue and Novel." *Desire in Language: A Semiotic Approach to Literature and Art*. Ed. Leon S. Roudiez. Trans. Thomas Gora, Alice Jardine and Leon S. Roudiez. New York: Columbia UP, 1980. 64-91.
Lacoue-Labarthe, Philippe. "Mimesis and Truth." *Diacritics* 8:1 (1978): 10-23.

Lausberg, Heinrich. *Manual de retórica.* Trans. José Pérez Tiesco. Vol. 1. Madrid: Gredos, 1983. 3 vols.
Levin, Harry. *The Myth of the Golden Age in the Renaissance* (Bloomington: Indiana UP, 1969.
Mackey, Mary. "Rhetoric and Characterization in *Don Quixote.*" *Hispanic Review* 42 (1974): 51-66.
Madariaga, Salvador de. *Guía del lector del "Quijote": ensayo psicológico sobre el "Quijote."* 6th ed. Buenos Aires: Editorial Sudamericana, 1926.
Mancing, Howard. *The Chivalric World of 'Don Quijote': Style, Structure, and Narrative Technique.* Columbia: U of Missouri P, 1982.
Mandel, Oscar. "The Function of the Norm in Don Quixote." *Modern Philology* 55 (1958): 154-163.
Márquez Villanueva, Francisco. "La génesis literaria de Sancho Panza." *Fuentes literarias cervantinas.* Madrid: Gredos, 1973. 20-94.
Mayne, Judith. "Marlene Dietrich, The Blue Angel and Female Performance." *Seduction and Theory: Readings of Gender, Representation and Rhetoric.* Ed. Dianne Hunter. Urbana and Chicago: U of Illinois P, 1989. 28-46.
McFadden, George. *Discovering the Comic.* Princeton: Princeton UP, 1982.
Molho, Mauricio. "Raíces folklóricas de Sancho Panza." *Cervantes: Raíces folklóricas.* Madrid: Gredos, 1976. 217-336.
Moreno Báez, E. *Reflexiones sobre el "Quijote."* Madrid: Prensa Española, 1968.
Morón Arroyo, Ciriaco. *Nuevas meditaciones del "Quijote."* Madrid: Gredos, 1976.
Munich, Adrienne. "Notorious Signs, Feminist Criticism and Literary Tradition." *Making a Difference: Feminist Literary Criticism.* Ed. Gayle Greene and Coppélia Kahn. London and New York: Methuen, 1985. 238-59.
Murillo, Luis Andrés. *A Critical Introduction to "Don Quixote."* New York: Peter Lang, 1988.
———. *The Golden Dial: Temporal Configuration in "Don Quijote."* Oxford: The Dolphin Book Co., 1975.
Nabokov, Vladimir. *Lectures on "Don Quixote."* Ed. Fredson Bowers. New York: Harcourt Brace Jovanovich, 1983.
Natoli, Joe, "Tracing a Beginning Through Past Theories." *Tracing Literary Theory.* Ed. Joseph Natoli. Urbana and Chicago: U of Illinois P, 1987. 3-26.
Nelson, William. *Fact or Fiction: The Dilemma of the Renaissance Storyteller.* Cambridge, MA: Harvard UP, 1973.
Nicoll, Allardyce. *El mundo de Arlequin.* Barcelona: Seix Barral, 1977.
Norris, Christopher. *Deconstruction: Theory and Practice.* London and New York: Methuen, 1982.
———. *Derrida.* Cambridge, MA: Harvard UP, 1987.
Oëlschlager, Victor R. B. "Sancho's Zest for Quest." *Hispania* 35 (1952): 18-24.
Olbrechts-Tyteca, Lucie. *Le comique du discours.* Bruxelles: Institut de Sociologie, 1974.
Panofsky, Erwin. "Renaissance and Renascences." *Kenyon Review* 6 (1944): 201-236.
Parr, James A. *Don Quixote: An Anatomy of Subversive Discourse.* Newark, DE: Juan de la Cuesta, 1988.
Percas de Ponseti, Helena. *Cervantes the Writer and Painter of "Don Quijote."* Columbia: U of Missouri P, 1988.
———. *Cervantes y su concepto del arte.* 2 vols. Madrid: Gredos, 1975.
Potter, Murray A. "The Horse as Epic Character." *Four Essays.* London: Oxford UP, 1971.
Predmore, Richard L. *The World of "Don Quixote."* Cambridge, MA: Harvard UP, 1967.

Read, Malcolm K. "Language Adrift: A Re-Appraisal of the Theme of Linguistic Perspectivism in *Don Quixote.*" *Forum for Modern Language Studies* 17 (1981): 271-85.
Redondo, Agustín. "De Don Clavijo a Clavileño: Algunos aspectos de la tradición carnavalesca y cazurra en el *Quijote* (II, 38-41)." *Edad de Oro* III (1984): 181-99.
———. "El personaje de Don Quijote: tradiciones folklórico-literarias, contexto histórico y elaboración cervantina." *Nueva Revista de Filología Hispánica* 29 (1) (1980): 36-59.
———. "El proceso iniciático en el episodio de la Cueva de Montesinos del Quijote." *Cervantes: Su obra y su Mundo. Actas del I Congreso Internacional sobre Cervantes.* Ed. Manuel Criado de Val. Madrid: EDI-6, 1981. 749-60.
———. Tradición carnavalesca y creación literaria." *BH* 80 (1978): 39-70.
Rico Verdú, José. *La retórica de los siglos XVI y XVII.* Madrid: CSIC, 1973.
Riley, Edward C. *Cervantes' Theory of the Novel.* Oxford: Clarendon Press, 1962.
———. "Don Quixote and the Imitation of Models." *Bulletin of Hispanic Studies* 31 (1954): 3-16.
———. "Metamorphosis, Myth, and Dream in the Cave of Montesinos." *Essays on Narrative Fiction in the Iberian Peninsula in Honour of Frank Pierce.* Ed. R. B. Tate. Oxford: The Dolphin Book Co., 1982. 105-19.
Riquer, Martín de. "Cervantes and the Romances of Chivalry." *Don Quixote.* Ed. Joseph R. Jones and Kenneth Douglas. Trans. Joseph R. Jones. New York: W. W. Norton, 1980. 895-913.
———. "Cervantes y la caballeresca." *Suma Cervantina.* Ed. J. B. Avalle-Arce and Edward C. Riley. London: Tamesis Books, 1973.
Rivers, Elias. "El gran acierto del Quijote" *Insula* 42, No. 488-489 (Julio-Agosto, 1987): 1, 4.
Robert, Marthe. *The Old and the New: From 'Don Quixote' to Kafka.* Trans. Carol Cosman. Berkeley and Los Angeles: U of California P, 1977.
Roberts, Gema. "Ausencia y presencia de Dulcinea en El Quijote." *Revista de Archivos, Bibliotecas y Museos* 82 (1979): 809-26.
Rogers, Edith. "Don Quixote and the Peaceable Lion." *Hispania* 68 (1985): 9-14.
Romero Flores, Hipólito R. *Biografía de Sancho Panza: Filósofo de la sensatez.* Barcelona: Aedos, 1952.
Rosenblat, Angel. *La lengua del "Quijote."* Madrid: Gredos, 1971.
Russell, P. E. *Cervantes.* New York: Oxford UP, 1985.
———. "*Don Quixote* as a Funny Book." *Modern Language Review* 64 (1969): 312-26.
Saldívar, Ramón. *Figural Language in the Novel: The Flowers of Speech from Cervantes to Joyce.* Princeton: Princeton UP, 1984.
Serrano-Plaja, Arturo. *Realismo Mágico en Cervantes.* Madrid: Gredos, 1967.
Sieber, Harry. "Literary Time in the 'Cueva de Montesinos.'" *Modern Language Notes* 86 (1971): 268-73.
Socrate, Mario. *Prologhi al "Don Chisciotte."* Venezia: Marsilio Editori, 1974.
Spitzer, Leo. "Perspectivismo lingüístico en el 'Quijote'." *Lingüística e historia literaria.* Madrid: Gredos, 1955. 135-87.
Stallybrass, Peter and Allon White. *The Politics and Poetics of Transgression.* Ithaca: Cornell UP, 1986.
Steig, Michael. "Defining the Grotesque: An Attempt at Synthesis." *Journal of Aesthetics and Art Criticism* 29 (1970-1971): 253-60.
Stewart, Marilyn Gump. "The Festive Irony of Carnival: Comic Affirmation in *Don Quixote, The Brothers Karamazov,* and *The Reivers.*" Diss. Dallas,1980.

Sullivan, Constance. "Gender Markers in Traditional Spanish Proverbs." *Literature Among Discourses: The Spanish Golden Age*. Ed. Wlad Godzich and Nicholas Spadaccini. Minneapolis: U of Minnesota P, 1986. 82-102.
Swain, Barbara. *Fools and Folly During the Middle Ages and the Renaissance*. New York: Columbia UP, 1932.
Sypher, Wylie. "The Meanings of Comedy" in Comedy: *Meaning and Form*. Ed. Robert W. Corrigan. 2nd ed. New York: Harper & Row, 1981. 36-44.
Thomson, Philip. *The Grotesque in German Poetry*. Melbourne: The Hawthorn Press, 1975.
Todorov, Tzvetan. *Mikhail Bakhtin: The Dialogical Principle*. Trans. Wlad Godzich. Theory and History of Literature 13. Minneapolis: U of Minnesota P, 1984.
Togeby, Knud. *La estructura del "Quijote."* Ed. and trans. Antonio Rodríguez Almodóvar. Sevilla: Universidad de Sevilla, 1977.
Torrente Ballester, Gonzalo. *El "Quijote" como juego*. Madrid: Punto Omega, Guadarrama, 1975.
Trueblood, Alan S. "La risa en el *Quijote*." *Cervantes* 4 (1984): 3-23.
Unamuno, Miguel de. *Our Lord Don Quixote: The Life of Don Quixote and Sancho with Related Essays*. 1905. Trans. Anthony Kerrigan. Bollingen Series no. 85.3. Princeton: Princeton UP, 1967.
Urbina, Eduardo. "El concepto de *admiratio* y lo grotesco en el *Quijote*." *Cervantes* 9 (Spring 1989): 17-33.
Vilanova, Antonio. "La *Moria* de Erasmo y el prólogo del *Quijote*." *Collected Studies in Honor of Américo Castro's Eightieth Year*. Oxford: Lincoln Lodge Research Library, 1965. 423-433.
Weiger, John G. *In the Margins of Cervantes*. Hanover: UP of New England, 1988.
Welsford, Enid. *The Fool: His Social and Literary History*. Gloucester, MA: Peter Smith, 1966.
Welsh, Alexander. *Reflections on the Hero as Quixote*. Princeton: Princeton UP, 1981.
Williamson, Edwin. *The Half-Way House of Fiction: "Don Quixote" and Arthurian Romance*. Oxford: Clarendon Press, 1984.
Wind, Edgar. "Orpheus in Praise of Blind Love." *Pagan Mysteries of the Renaissance*. New York: W. W. Norton & Co. 1958. 53-80.
Wright, Thomas. *A History of Caricature and the Grotesque in Literature and Art*. 1865. New York: Frederick Ungar, 1968.
Ziomek, Henryk. *Lo grotesco en la literatura española del Siglo de Oro*. Madrid: Alcalá, 1983.

INDEX

Abellán, José Luis, 65
Adrados, Francisco, 56, 68, 92
Alcibiades, 64
Allen, John Jay, 209
Alonso, Amado, 102, 119
Alonso, Dámaso, 90
Alter, Robert, 123
Antisthenes, 101
Arias Montano, Benito, 127-128
Aristotle, 25-27, 29, 61, 169
Asensio, Eugenio, 43
Auden, W. H., 32
Auerbach, Erich, 31
Austin, J. L., 170-173
Avalle-Arce, J. B., 65
Avellaneda, Alonso Fernández de, 58

Bakhtin, Mikhail, 11-13, 16, 18-25, 29-30, 32-33, 35-38, 45-46, 55, 68, 71, 76, 85-86, 96-97, 100-102, 170-172, 203-204, 212
Bandera, Cesáreo, 158
Barasch, Frances, 18
Barthes, Roland, 15, 24
Bataillon, Marcel, 65, 122
Bembo, Pietro, 122
Bentley, Eric, 43
Bergson, Henri, 29
Bernstein, Michael André, 30
Bleznick, Donald W., 95
Booth, Wayne C., 32
Bosch, Hieronymus, 21
Bowra, C. M., 35
Brantley Franklin, O., 91, 97
Brenan, Gerald, 83
Brueghel, Pietro (Elder), 21, 62
Bruni, Giordano, 64

Caballero, Justo, 150, 152-153, 164
Campbell, Joseph, 32
Camoens, Luis de, 188
Caro Baroja, Julio, 44-46, 54, 68, 72, 92, 96-97
Cascardi, Antonio, 33
Cassirer, Ernst, 63
Castro, Américo, 38, 65, 99
Charney, Maurice, 29, 43, 66-67, 75, 100, 135
Cicero, 169
Close, Anthony, J., 9, 76, 83, 99
Colie, Rosalie, L., 165
Corley, Ames Haven, 102
Cornford, Francis, 12, 25, 60
Correas, Gonzalo, 152
Cortázar, Celina S. de, 180
Covarrubias, Sebastián de, 150
Culler, Jonathan, 33, 171
Cusanus, Nicholas, 63

Derrida, Jacques, 13, 126, 128-130, 167-168, 171-172, 212-213
Di Battista, Maria, 31
Dostoevsky, Fyodor, 100, 102, 170
Du Bellay, Joaquin, 122
Dudley, Edward, 42
Dunn, Peter N., 68, 87-88
Durán, Manuel, 33

Eckhart, Johann (Meister), 63
Eco, Umberto, 199
Efron, Arthur, 43
Eisenberg, Daniel, 31, 50
El Saffar, Ruth, 195
Entwistle, William J., 83
Erasmus, Desiderius, 63-65, 98, 167, 212

Fernández de Córdoba, Gonzalo, 133
Ficino, Marsilio, 64
Flores, Ralph, 131
Flores, R. M., 99
Forcione, Alban K., 65, 98-99, 167, 173, 195, 210-212
Foucault, Michel, 123
Frazer, Sir James George, 12, 16-18, 25, 60, 202-203
Frye, Northrop, 24-26, 28, 32, 72, 85, 101

García de Paredes, Diego, 133
García de la Torre, J. M., 105
Garcilaso de la Vega, 188, 192
Garin, Eugenio, 127
Girard, René, 12, 27-28, 30, 33-34, 202-203
Gombrich, Ernst H., 10
Groot, Hogues de, 63

Hacthoun, Augusto, 119
Haley, George, 195
Harari, Josué, 15
Hatzfeld, Helmut, 102
Hayman, David, 29-30
Hendrix, W. S., 90
Herrero, Javier, 42, 78, 83
Huizinga, Johann, 33

Iffland, James, 56

Joly, Monique, 70, 95, 149
Johnson, Caroll B., 81
Jones, Joseph R., 97

Kaiser, Walter, 61-62, 64
Kayser, Wolfgang, 30
Kempis, Thomas, 63
Kennedy, William J., 169, 193
Kern, Edith, 84
Kris, Ernst, 28-29
Kristeller, Paul Oskar, 127
Kristeva, Julia, 21, 30, 101, 213

Lacoue-Labarthe, Philippe, 33
Landino, Cristóforo, 64
Lausberg, Heinrich, 119, 129, 137, 140, 146, 156, 165
Levin, Harry, 68
Lucian, 101
Lukács, Georg, 33-34

Mackey, Mary, 177
Madariaga, Salvador de, 83
Mancing, Howard, 32, 72-73, 209
Mandel, Oscar, 209
Márquez Villanueva, Francisco, 90
Mayne, Judith, 204
McFadden, George, 90
Menippus, 101
Mihura, Miguel, 208-209
Molho, Mauricio, 74, 90
Moreno Báez, E., 43
Morón Arroyo, Ciríaco, 95
Munich, Adrienne, 194
Murillo, Luis Andrés, 39, 87

Nabokov, Vladimir, 9
Natoli, Joe, 216
Nebrija, Elio Antonio de, 122
Nelson, William, 130
Nicoll, Allardyce, 98
Norris, Christopher, 130, 171

Oëlschlager, Victor R. B., 97
Olbrechts-Tyteca, Lucie, 103, 118, 131, 134, 147, 159-160, 162, 166, 170, 195

Palmieri, Nicoló, 64
Panofsky, Erwin, 63
Parr, James A., 101, 194-195, 210-211
Percas de Ponseti, Helena, 40, 87-88, 192
Petrarch, 64
Petronius, 101
Phaedo, 101
Philip II, 95
Plato, 13, 64, 101, 128-129
Plautus, 25
Poliziano, 64
Potter, Murray A., 48
Predmore, Richard L., 50

Quevedo, Francisco de, 122
Quintilian, 169

Rabelais, François, 63-64
Read, Malcolm K., 102
Redondo, Agustín, 56, 86, 91, 95
Rico Verdú, José, 119, 127
Riley, Edward C., 33, 86, 173, 195
Riquer, Martín de, 31
Robert, Marthe, 33, 71, 123

Roberts, Gema, 76
Rogers, Edith, 114
Romero Flores, Hipólito R., 97
Rosenblat, Angel, 32, 102, 118
Russell, Peter E., 9, 31, 43
Ruysbroek, Jan Van, 63

St. Paul, 62
Saldívar, Ramón, 123, 131
Sánchez de las Brozas, Francisco, 127
Saussure, Ferdinand de, 128
Searle, John, 171
Seneca, 64
Serrano-Plaja, Arturo, 33
Shakespeare, William, 27, 63
Sieber, Harry, 87
Socrate, Mario, 101, 167, 195
Socrates, 61, 64, 129
Spitzer, Leo, 38, 102, 117, 121
Stallybrass, Peter, 203
Steig, Michael, 29
Stewart, Marilyn Gump, 30, 59
Sullivan, Constance, 146
Swain, Barbara, 62
Sypher, Wylie, 17, 60, 84

Terence, 25
Thomson, Philip, 100

Tirso de Molina, 122
Titus, 17
Todorov, Tzvetan, 22
Togeby, Knud, 49
Torrente Ballester, Gonzalo, 33, 82
Trueblood, Alan S., 178

Unamuno, Miguel de, 9
Urbina, Eduardo, 176

Valdés, Juan de, 122
Varro, 101
Vega Carpio, Lope de, 197
Vilanova, Antonio, 65
Vives, Luis, 167

Weiger, John C., 192
Welsford, Enid, 62
Welsh, Alexander, 33
White, Allon, 203
Williamson, Edwin, 123
Wind, Edgar, 63-64
Wright, Thomas, 28, 39

Xenophon, 101

Ziomek, Henryk, 72

NORTH CAROLINA STUDIES IN THE ROMANCE LANGUAGES AND LITERATURES

I.S.B.N. Prefix 0-8078-

Recent Titles

BAROQUE FICTION-MAKING. A STUDY OF GOMBERVILLE'S "POLEXANDRE", by Edward Baron Turk. 1978. (No. 196). *-9196-7.*

THE TRAGIC FALL: DON ÁLVARO DE LUNA AND OTHER FAVORITES IN SPANISH GOLDEN AGE DRAMA, by Raymond R. MacCurdy. 1978. (No. 197). *-9197-5.*

A BAHIAN HERITAGE. An Ethnolinguistic Study of African Influences on Bahian Portuguese, by William W. Megenney. 1978. (No. 198). *-9198-3.*

"LA QUERELLE DE LA ROSE": Letters and Documents, by Joseph L. Baird and John R. Kane. 1978. (No. 199). *-9199-1.*

TWO AGAINST TIME. *A Study of the Very Present Worlds of Paul Claudel and Charles Péguy,* by Joy Nachod Humes. 1978. (No. 200). *-9200-9.*

TECHNIQUES OF IRONY IN ANATOLE FRANCE. Essay on *Les Sept Femmes de la Barbe-Bleue,* by Diane Wolfe Levy. 1978. (No. 201). *-9201-7.*

THE PERIPHRASTIC FUTURES FORMED BY THE ROMANCE REFLEXES OF "VADO (AD)" PLUS INFINITIVE, by James Joseph Champion. 1978. (No. 202). *-9202-5.*

THE EVOLUTION OF THE LATIN /b/-/u̯/ MERGER: A Quantitative and Comparative Analysis of the *B-V* Alternation in Latin Inscriptions, by Joseph Louis Barbarino. 1978. (No. 203). *-9203-3.*

METAPHORIC NARRATION: THE STRUCTURE AND FUNCTION OF METAPHORS IN "A LA RECHERCHE DU TEMPS PERDU", by Inge Karalus Crosman. 1978. (No. 204). *-9204-1.*

LE VAIN SIECLE GUERPIR. A Literary Approach to Sainthood through Old French Hagiography of the Twelfth Century, by Phyllis Johnson and Brigitte Cazelles. 1979. (No. 205). *-9205-X.*

THE POETRY OF CHANGE: A STUDY OF THE SURREALIST WORKS OF BENJAMIN PÉRET, by Julia Field Costich. 1979. (No. 206). *-9206-8.*

NARRATIVE PERSPECTIVE IN THE POST-CIVIL WAR NOVELS OF FRANCISCO AYALA "MUERTES DE PERRO" AND "EL FONDO DEL VASO", by Maryellen Bieder. 1979. (No. 207). *-9207-6.*

RABELAIS: HOMO LOGOS, by Alice Fiola Berry. 1979. (No. 208). *-9208-4.*

"DUEÑAS" AND "DONCELLAS": A STUDY OF THE "DOÑA RODRÍGUEZ" EPISODE IN "DON QUIJOTE", by Conchita Herdman Marianella. 1979. (No. 209). *-9209-2.*

PIERRE BOAISTUAU'S "HISTOIRES TRAGIQUES": A STUDY OF NARRATIVE FORM AND TRAGIC VISION, by Richard A. Carr. 1979. (No. 210). *-9210-6.*

REALITY AND EXPRESSION IN THE POETRY OF CARLOS PELLICER, by George Melnykovich. 1979. (No. 211). *-9211-4.*

MEDIEVAL MAN, HIS UNDERSTANDING OF HIMSELF, HIS SOCIETY, AND THE WORLD, by Urban T. Holmes, Jr. 1980. (No. 212). *-9212-2.*

MÉMOIRES SUR LA LIBRAIRIE ET SUR LA LIBERTÉ DE LA PRESSE, introduction and notes by Graham E. Rodmell. 1979. (No. 213). *-9213-0.*

THE FICTIONS OF THE SELF. THE EARLY WORKS OF MAURICE BARRES, by Gordon Shenton. 1979. (No. 214). *-9214-9.*

CECCO ANGIOLIERI. A STUDY, by Gifford P. Orwen. 1979. (No. 215). *-9215-7.*

THE INSTRUCTIONS OF SAINT LOUIS: A CRITICAL TEXT, by David O'Connell. 1979. (No. 216). *-9216-5.*

ARTFUL ELOQUENCE, JEAN LEMAIRE DE BELGES AND THE RHETORICAL TRADITION, by Michael F. O. Jenkins. 1980. (No. 217). *-9217-3.*

A CONCORDANCE TO MARIVAUX'S COMEDIES IN PROSE, edited by Donald C. Spinelli. 1979. (No. 218). 4 volumes, *-9218-1* (set); *-9219-X* (v. 1); *-9220-3* (v. 2); *-9221-1* (v. 3); *-9222-X* (v. 4).

When ordering please cite the *ISBN Prefix* plus the last four digits for each title.

Send orders to: University of North Carolina Press
P.O. Box 2288
CB# 6215
Chapel Hill, NC 27515-2288
U.S.A.

NORTH CAROLINA STUDIES IN THE ROMANCE LANGUAGES AND LITERATURES

I.S.B.N. Prefix 0-8078-

Recent Titles

ABYSMAL GAMES IN THE NOVELS OF SAMUEL BECKETT, by Angela B. Moorjani. 1982. (No. 219). *-9223-8.*

GERMAIN NOUVEAU DIT HUMILIS: ÉTUDE BIOGRAPHIQUE, par Alexandre L. Amprimoz. 1983. (No. 220). *-9224-6.*

THE "VIE DE SAINT ALEXIS" IN THE TWELFTH AND THIRTEENTH CENTURIES: AN EDITION AND COMMENTARY, by Alison Goddard Elliot. 1983. (No. 221). *-9225-4.*

THE BROKEN ANGEL: MYTH AND METHOD IN VALÉRY, by Ursula Franklin. 1984. (No. 222). *-9226-2.*

READING VOLTAIRE'S "CONTES": A SEMIOTICS OF PHILOSOPHICAL NARRATION, by Carol Sherman. 1985. (No. 223). *-9227-0.*

THE STATUS OF THE READING SUBJECT IN THE "LIBRO DE BUEN AMOR", by Marina Scordilis Brownlee. 1985. (No. 224). *-9228-9.*

MARTORELL'S "TIRANT LO BLANCH": A PROGRAM FOR MILITARY AND SOCIAL REFORM IN FIFTEENTH-CENTURY CHRISTENDOM, by Edward T. Aylward. 1985. (No. 225). *-9229-7.*

NOVEL LIVES: THE FICTIONAL AUTOBIOGRAPHIES OF GUILLERMO CABRERA INFANTE AND MARIO VARGAS LLOSA, by Rosemary Geisdorfer Feal. 1986. (No. 226). *-9230-0.*

SOCIAL REALISM IN THE ARGENTINE NARRATIVE, by David William Foster. 1986. (No. 227). *-9231-9.*

HALF-TOLD TALES: DILEMMAS OF MEANING IN THREE FRENCH NOVELS, by Philip Stewart. 1987. (No. 228). *-9232-7.*

POLITIQUES DE L'ECRITURE BATAILLE/DERRIDA: le sens du sacré dans la pensée française du surréalisme à nos jours, par Jean-Michel Heimonet. 1987. (No. 229). *-9233-5.*

GOD, THE QUEST, THE HERO: THEMATIC STRUCTURES IN BECKETT'S FICTION, by Laura Barge. 1988. (No. 230). *-9235-1.*

THE NAME GAME. WRITING/FADING WRITER IN "DE DONDE SON LOS CANTANTES", by Oscar Montero. 1988. (No. 231). *-9236-X.*

GIL VICENTE AND THE DEVELOPMENT OF THE COMEDIA, by René Pedro Garay. 1988. (No. 232). *-9234-3.*

HACIA UNA POÉTICA DEL RELATO DIDÁCTICO: OCHO ESTUDIOS SOBRE "EL CONDE LUCANOR", por Aníbal A. Biglieri. 1989. (No. 233). *-9237-8.*

A POETICS OF ART CRITICISM: THE CASE OF BAUDELAIRE, by Timothy Raser. 1989. (No. 234). *-9238-6.*

UMA CONCORDÂNCIA DO ROMANCE "GRANDE SERTÃO: VEREDAS" DE JOÃO GUIMARÃES ROSA, by Myriam Ramsey and Paul Dixon. 1989. (No. 235). Microfiche, *-9239-4.*

CYCLOPEAN SONG: MELANCHOLY AND AESTHETICISM IN GÓNGORA'S "FÁBULA DE POLIFEMO Y GALATEA", by Kathleen Hunt Dolan. 1990. (No. 236). *-9240-8.*

THE "SYNTHESIS" NOVEL IN LATIN AMERICA. A STUDY ON JOÃO GUIMARÃES ROSA'S "GRANDE SERTÃO: VEREDAS", by Eduardo de Faria Coutinho. 1991. (No. 237). *-9241-6.*

IMPERMANENT STRUCTURES. SEMIOTIC READINGS OF NELSON RODRIGUES' "VESTIDO DE NOIVA", "ÁLBUM DE FAMÍLIA", AND "ANJO NEGRO", by Fred M. Clark. 1991. (No. 238). *-9242-4.*

"EL ÁNGEL DEL HOGAR". GALDÓS AND THE IDEOLOGY OF DOMESTICITY IN SPAIN, by Bridget A. Aldaraca. 1991. (No. 239). *-9243-2.*

IN THE PRESENCE OF MYSTERY: MODERNIST FICTION AND THE OCCULT, by Howard M. Fraser. 1992. (No. 240). *-9244-0.*

When ordering please cite the *ISBN Prefix* plus the last four digits for each title.

Send orders to: University of North Carolina Press
P.O. Box 2288
CB# 6215
Chapel Hill, NC 27515-2288
U.S.A.

The Department of Romance Studies Digital Arts and Collaboration Lab at the University of North Carolina at Chapel Hill is proud to support the digitization of the North Carolina Studies in the Romance Languages and Literatures series.

www.ingramcontent.com/pod-product-compliance
Lightning Source LLC
Chambersburg PA
CBHW030649230426
43665CB00011B/1018